ONE TIME AROUND THE WHEEL

ONE TIME AROUND THE WHEEL

by
Sean Croke

Hawthorn School of Plant Medicine

Revelore Press
Olympia WA
2023

Book design by Jenn Zahrt.
Illustrations by Morgan Singer.
Cover art by Dagny Salazar *&* Jenn Zahrt.

Publisher's Cataloging-in-Publication
(Provided by Cassidy Cataloguing Services, Inc.).
Names: Croke, Sean, author. | Hawthorn School of Plant Medicine, sponsor-
           ing body.
Title: One time around the wheel / by Sean Croke.
Description: First edition. | Olympia WA : Revelore Press, 2023. | Includes
           bibliographical references.
Identifiers: ISBN: 978-1-947544-41-3 (paperback)
Subjects: LCSH: Herbs--Therapeutic use--Northwest, Pacific. | Medicinal
           plants--Northwest, Pacific. | Herbs--Seasonal variations--North-
           west, Pacific. | Medicinal plants--Seasonal variations-- Northwest,
           Pacific. | Herbals--Northwest, Pacific. | Bioregionalism--Northwest,
           Pacific. | Climatic changes--Northwest, Pacific. | BISAC: HEALTH
           & FITNESS / Herbal Medications. | NATURE / Ecosystems &
           Habitats / General. | NATURE / Plants / General.
Classification: LCC: RS172.A19 C76 2023 | DDC: 615.3/210979--dc23

Printed worldwide through Ingram.

Revelore Press
1910 4th AVE E PMB141
Olympia WA 98506
United States
www.revelore.press

First printed in 2023.

DEDICATION

This work is dedicated to my partner, Thea, for all the love, support, and inspiration over the years;

To my daughter, Juniper, for being such a powerful person and for always being eager to go out harvesting plants with me;

To my just born daughter, Willow, for coming into this world to live with us;

And to my many teachers, both plant and human, who have guided my learning and transformation for my entire life.

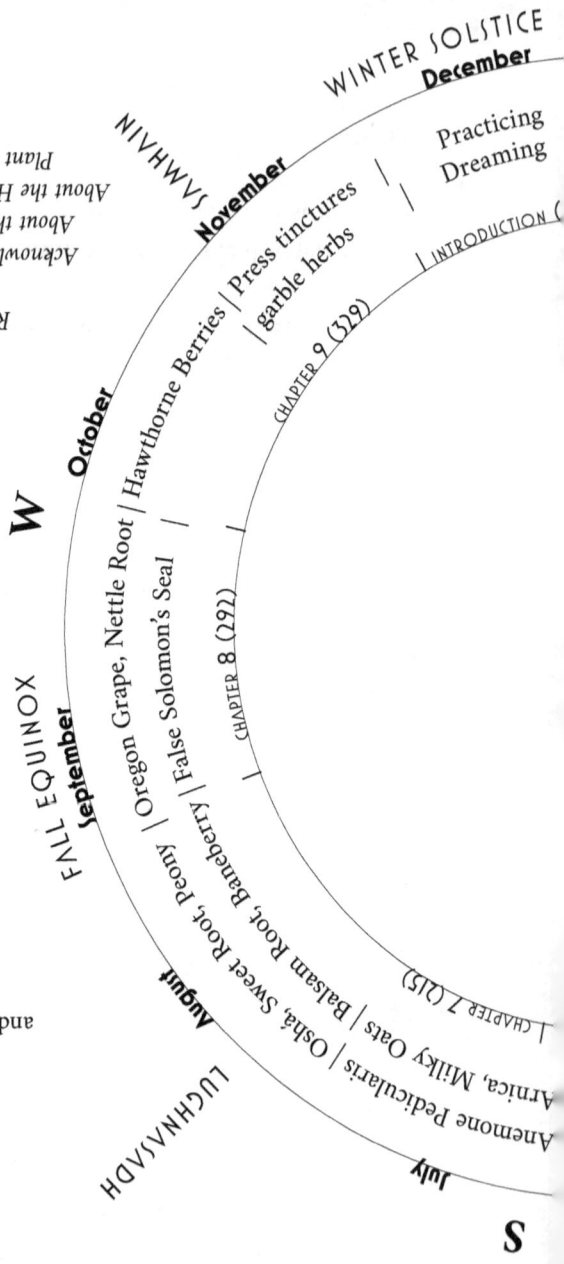

CONTENTS

INTRODUCTION / AFTERWORD

I STARTED WRITING THIS BOOK in February of 2020 as a series of essays to go along with the nine-month herb school that I run, the Hawthorn School of Plant Medicine. I wanted my students to have my lectures in written form so that they did not have to worry about taking notes while we were out in the field, where it is often raining or otherwise difficult to do so comfortably. When I wrote the first essay about Black Cottonwood, Red Alder, the lichens and the Nisqually delta and Tribe, we were at the very beginning of the COVID-19 pandemic, and it was not clear that it was going to be a very big deal. By the second class in March it was clear that big things were happening, and we could not meet for the next several months due to government-imposed lock downs, and also to keep everybody safe even without state intervention. This left me with extra free time and the need to do something to occupy my mind, as well as feeling like I wanted to make sure that my students got all the information that I could supply them with since we were not able to meet in person, so I started putting a lot of details into the essays, and then realized that I would have a book's worth of material once all nine of them were done. This year has been a truly weird and hard one, and as I sit and write this introduction at my desk in the old farmhouse just a few hundred yards away from the Black River, the numbers of infections and deaths from this virus are increasing exponentially everyday. We are just at the beginning of the Winter which I think is going to be a hard one for a lot of people, and the future beyond that time feels really unsure and unclear, I can't even tell if I am going to be able to run the school next year in the format that I am used to, or if enough people will have enough extra income to afford to take it.

NOW IT IS SEVERAL WEEKS LATER, just after Winter Solstice. The Black River, my primary teacher these days, is running so strongly and has overflowed her banks. She is about ten yards into the back fields of our farm and still rising. The Winter Solstice is a great turning point in the year. In this place where I live, which is currently called Little Rock, Washington, in the Northwest corner of the "United States" but is actually occupied Chehalis territory in Turtle Island, the Winter Solstice is a time of water, so much water. The Winter Solstice is the longest day and the shortest night of the year which occurs right around December 21st in the Northern hemisphere. At this time we like to burn large fires and light beeswax candles during the long nights to implore the Sun to come back, the Spring to return. In this specific place the Winter Solstice is prior to the true cold time of the season, and usually it is a time of lots of rain in which the rivers become their mightiest and the land gets nicely saturated with water which feeds and maintains the rain forests that are so important to this place. The Black Hills which are to the West of me are often covered by the cloud layer, and pretty soon they will start getting snow on their upper slopes, which then serves as a source of water into the Spring time, although of course the amount of snow that they are getting seems to get lighter every year as things warm up and the weather changes. The Solstice is a time of wrapping things up and a time of planning for the next year. It is a time of deep dreaming and sleeping late. It is an unfortunate and perhaps intentional aspect of "American" culture that the holiday of Christmas occurs at this same time. As much as "America" likes to pretend to not be a religious country, we all know that it is a Christian entity and so the Christian holidays dominate the lives of most of us who exist within this occupying culture who has invaded the land, so most people are kept very busy rushing all around to do all the special Christmas things and spending lots of money to buy lots of Christmas gifts. This often necessitates working overtime to be able to afford all of these things, at a time of year when the natural thing to do is to lay low, not work too much, live off the resources that you gathered during the warm months, and dream.

I have been focusing on my dreams, writing them down, making plans for the next year, and, yes, buying some presents and doing some Christmas stuff. We had our Solstice bonfire and lit our candles. The days are getting longer already and it is time to start thinking about what will happen next year. It looks like my school will take place afterall, and there is a vaccine starting to come out for COVID-19, thank the gods. I am going to use this space to introduce myself and some of my philosophy and practices around herbalism, which is what this work is primarily about.

PHILOSOPHY

This book is primarily about herbalism, which is the practice of working with medicinal plants to help humans and other people improve their health. Herbalism is an ancient practice, and is the original form of medicine I would argue. For me, as much as herbalism is about helping humans to improve their health it is also a process of enmeshment between the practicing herbalist and the plants that they work with, and above and beyond that the land upon which they live and make their being. I have been studying medicinal plants ever since I was a child growing up in the suburbs of so-called Boston, Massachusetts which is the occupied territory of the Massachusett, Wampanoag, and Nipmuc tribes. At that time there were very few wild places around me but I would spend most of my happiest times in the tiny slivers of woods that existed between the heavily populated neighborhoods which were often on land that was too sloped to build on. I convinced my Mama to buy me a copy of *Culpeper's Complete Herbal* when I was ten or eleven years old, and read the whole thing cover to cover over time even though I had no access to any of the plants nor anyone in my life who was interested in herbalism. It was not until I moved across the country to "Washington State" where I attended The Evergreen State College in so-called Olympia, Washington which is on Squaxin land that I really started to learn about working with the plants as this area is very rich in forests and other wild places in which a variety of medicinal plants grow. It is upon this landscape that I learned the plants, often while living in a series of tiny shacks made of recycled materials that did not have electricity, were wood heated, and were located in the middle of the woods. I started making medicines, and then started practicing with humans naturally over time as I was needed. I often lived in communal settings in which most people were broke and did not have much access to healthcare, so I ended up taking care of people's health concerns with the herbal medicines that I was making and learning how to work with through books, teachers, the plants themselves, and in my own body.

My herbal practice is very much tied up with my spiritual practice, and also with my politics. In terms of politics I identify as an anarchist, more in the vein of anarcho-communism than the thinly veiled libertarianism that I often see called anarchism around me, and in terms of spirituality I identify as an animist, specifically I was taught a spiritual philosophy called Bio-Regional Animism which is still my deepest practice. I have lately come to think that these two things could potentially be combined into surrealism, which is kind of anarchism that has been imbued with the sacred or the marvelous, but that is a lot to explain so I will have to settle with giving my herbalism the title of *anarcho-animist herbalism*, if that is not too pretentious.

Anarchism has a lot of baggage as a philosophy, and especially within the dominant culture has a pretty negative connotation, being linked to bomb throwing fanatics and dangerous people, but the more that I have studied the history and the lived experiences of anarchists the more that I have come to embrace this philosophy as the most life affirming that I have been able to find so far in the political arena. When I say anarchism I mostly mean a politics that is focused on mutual aid and solidarity among all peoples, especially those who are of the working classes or the 99%. My ideal anarchistic society would be decentralized, deindustrialized, and non-hierarchical. This is the dream that anarchists are working towards, a more just and equitable world. I consider myself a "big tent" anarchist, meaning that I do not have too ridgid of an idea of the type of anarchist or post revolution society that I would like to see, as long as the above ideals are at the forefront. I also prefer to live as an anarchist in an anarchist society right here and now, as opposed to waiting for the revolution, by finding the Temporary Autonomous Zones that already exist and aligning myself with them. I don't actually want everyone else to be an anarchist along with me, just allow me to be one without repression.

Mostly anarchists are defined by the things that they stand against, especially by the dominant culture that paints them as childish rebels or dangerous terrorists, and it is true that is order to bring about a just world it is important to stand in opposition to many of the structures and philosophies that are in power currently through so much of the world including patriarchy, white supremacy, capitalism, Neo-liberalism, industrialism, imperialism, militarism, the prison system, bosses in general, etc. Around me today I am inspired by movements such as Black Lives Matter and the indigenous led movements to defend sacred sites such as Standing Rock as prime examples of this philosophy in action. I am inspired by thinkers in this area such as Huey Newton of the Black Panther Party (although he identified more as a communist), Octavia Butler, Angela Davis (who identifies as a Marxist), Emma Goldman, Peter Lamborn Wilson aka Hakim Bey, Peter Kropotkin, and some of my friends and contemporaries including Margaret Killjoy, Christopher Scott Thompson, and Rhyd Wildermuth (also an autonomous) Marxist). I am a feminist, as I hope all people are. I think it is important to be clear about my politics because in many ways I see many contemporary herbalists around me perpetuating many of the problematic behaviors and philosophies of the dominant culture in their working with the plants and I think it is a disservice to the plants and the land to work with them in exploitative and destructive ways, even if that is prettied up by New Age platitudes. Herbalism is a great anarchist praxis because it has the potential to be easily accessible, does not have many professional barriers for anyone to get involved with learning it, and in many ways is already "the people's medicine." I would encourage anyone working with the plants to strive towards aligning this work with the liberation of all people, human and greater-than-human alike.

These networks of solidarity and mutual aid, for me, extend beyond the human populations and into the plant communities around me and the landscape as a whole. This is where animism comes in, which is a philosophy that is often defined as the belief that all things in the material world are alive and animated, that everything has a soul and is a person.

Many Western scholars define animism as kind of the proto-religion from which the more modern religions evolved, therefore defining animism as a kind of primitive or superstitious belief system, but I have found this concept to be much more elegant and true than any of the religious philosophies that I have been taught or indoctrinated with. To keep the philosophy within a more Western or Eurocentric lineage of thought you could replace "animism" with "panpsychism" which is the view that the mind is a fundamental and ubiquitous aspect of reality, which was a belief of Plato's among others, and the metaphor is about the same. Many Indigenous cultures around the world have a belief system that is fundamentally animist, and this shows in the ways that many of these cultures interact with the landscape upon which they live which is often much less exploitative and destructive than the religious, imperialist, colonialist cultures that have come to have such power over so much of the world. I was taught about a specific philosophy that a dear friend and teacher of mine named Marcus McCoy called Bio-Regional Animism which is essentially the belief that all things are animate, have their own wants and desires and are people, and that this extends to the land upon which we live. This personhood has a kind of "the macrocosm is the microcosm" aspect to it in that the planet as a whole can be considered a person, and a continent can be considered a person, and a bioregion can be considered a person, and a river system can be considered a person, all the way down to your house, or a rock sitting in the front yard, or a medicinal plant growing in the woods. All these people have their own unique personhood while also being enmeshed in a larger organism that is a person as well. The idea is to first acknowledge the personhood of all these being all around and within you, and then attempt to learn how to talk with them so that you can learn from them, be in alliance and solidarity with them, and become their friend. This philosophy has become my foundational spiritual belief and practice, and has informed and enriched my herbal practice in so many ways. Once you can extend the concept of personhood to the rivers, plants, mountains, cities, and prairies around you, it is easy to extend the anarchistic concept of mutual aid and solidarity to these people in the same way that you would to the human people that you live around, and this seems to me to be the way to go in this path of healing with the plants. Working with the plants and the landscape in a way that is non-exploitative and mutual beneficial is the foundation from which I try to base my practice.

I am a descendant of colonizers to this land, with Irish, English, and Jamaican ancestry. I have the benefits and privileges of being a white male in this white supremacist and patriarchal culture (whiteness and gender are both social constructs, of course, but that is a little bit off topic), and it has been a long process that I am still engaged in to figure out how to live in this place and to honor the plants, people, and landscape that I live among while being an uninvited guest in this way. Anti-colonialism or decolonialism is a crucial aspect to the liberation of the peoples of this world, and this process is being led by the Indigenous peoples of the world, although everyone has to do their part to keep the project going. I am really lucky that, even after all the horrors of genocide and forced indoctrination that took place to the Indigenous peoples of this region, there is still a strong tribal culture in this part of the world that is only getting stronger. Here in the Pacific Northwestern part of Turtle Island we are in Coastal Salish territory, which is a broad category of tribal peoples who are affiliated with one another and have lived upon and with this land for many thousands of years. I live at the base of the Salish Sea, often called the Puget Sound, which is the home of many tribes. Right around the inlets at the bottom of the Salish Sea lived the Noo-Seh-Chatl, Steh-Chass, Squi-Aitl, Sawamish, Sa-Heh-Wa-Mish, Squawksin, and S'Hotle-Ma-Mish tribes who were forced to give up their ancestral lands and become joined into one group, which is currently known as the Squaxin Island Tribe, by the deceitful Medicine Creek Treaty which was signed on Christmas day of 1854. This treaty was negotiated in Chinook Jargon, a trade language that was not complex enough for the Indigenous peoples present to negotiate the complexities of a treaty, and resulted in the ceding of some 2,500,000 acres of land to the "United States" government, one of the Eastern border of which was the Black Hills under whom I now sit. Also in this area live the Chehalis, Nisqually, Puyallup, S'Klallam, Skokomish, Quinault, Hoh, Cowlitz, Quileute, Lummi, and Makah tribes. Many tribal people today live in reservations that are a tiny fraction of the land upon which they were accustomed to moving, and many tribal ways and practices have been lost due to their violent suppression by the occupying invaders that are the citizens and agents of the "United States."

Today we are seeing a beautiful and inspiring resurgence of Tribal identities and Tribal life ways, and due to such fortunate legal decisions as the Boldt Decision in the 1970s Tribal peoples have come to have some say in the governance of the people and the lands which has been and is a boon to the environment of this area. It is complicated to be a white descendant of colonizers who loves the wild plants and places of this land and is trying to learn to be in right relationship with them due to the historical and current violence that has been and is perpetuated upon these people and this land by the occupying forces of the "United States," which I was born into. I have worked hard and been lucky to make friends and relationships within various Tribal communities in this area, and I am always trying to bear in mind that I am an uninvited guest in this place which is stolen land and to act with the respect and humility that a guest should show. In these writings I have tried to include Tribal histories, stories, and beliefs about these lands and these plants whenever I have that information available to me, and without appropriating the teachings of these cultures (I hope). I wish that I had more of this information, and acknowledge that just because I want it does not mean that it is mine or that I get it. I always welcome contact by Tribal peoples to either teach me/share their histories and beliefs, or to critique me for overstepping my bounds, or both. One project that I do provide support to that I am proud for what little involvement I do have is the Canoe

Journey Herbalists which is an Indigenous led project that provides first aid and herbal support to the Tribal members involved in the Intertribal Canoe Journey. Canoe Journey is a thirty-year-old tradition in which Tribal peoples from all up and down the West coast travel by canoe, which is the traditional manner of this landscape, along the Salish Sea and even the open ocean in a weeks-long journey to a specific Tribe's reservation where they are hosted in a great celebration. The Intertribal Canoe Journey is one of the largest gatherings of Tribal peoples in the Salish Sea and is a beautiful example of Native Pride and cultural resurgence, especially considering that most of the activities that make up the Journey would have been illegal one hundred years ago. Working with and around Indigenous communities has helped me to see some of the ways that the exploitative and extractive beliefs and actions of the culture in which I was raised have influenced my interactions with the plants so that I can always work on making them more healthy.

I also am trying to research and embrace the various herbal traditions of my own ancestral lines, both in the British Isles and Jamaica/Africa. My family also has a number of Doctors and healers in its history, and I call upon them to help me in the work that I am doing today. Many of the plants that I work with that live upon this landscape are introduced from Europe just like I partially am, and working with these weedy and "invasive" plants has proven really beneficial and foundational. My herb school is named after the Hawthorn tree who is of great importance historically and contemporarily to the peoples of the British Isles both as an herbal medicine and as a spiritual entity and gateway. They are also considered weedy and invasive by the powers that be in this area, and create an abundance of medicine that is so helpful. I also work quite a lot with the "wild" plants that grow in the bioregion in which I live, that I do not have an ancestral relationship to, and I have focused on learning how to help those plants to thrive and proliferate in the landscapes where they live by learning and applying various plant propagation techniques, many of which are inspired by Indigenous techniques for working with these same medicinal and food providing plants. I grow quite a lot of medicinal herbs on the farm upon which I live here in Chehalis territory along the Black River, helping them to make babies and sending their babies out to live in new places all the time while they help me to make medicines for myself and my community, and also of course to make some money sometimes.

So, my philosophy is important to the ways and the reasons why I do this work with the plants. The personal is political of course, and vice versa, so I want to define my own feelings and ideas during this dreaming time around the Solstice to try and explain the reasoning behind the contents of the rest of this book. Some of the basics include that the plants are people too. They are in many ways greater than humans, and they are our ancestors and elders. They were here first, and they basically created animals and humans to help to move them around in the world since they move very slowly. This is a good attitude to take when learning to interact with plants; that they actually domesticated humans not the other way around. The wildly speculative Exorphin Theory posits that the exorphins (exogenous opioid peptides, as opposed to endorphins which are endogenous) that are produced by the digestion of gluten, which is found in Wheat, essentially drugged humans, getting them addicted and domesticating them so that they would dedicate their whole lives to working the soil and making the world a better place for Wheat to live in, so that they could keep getting their exorphin fix, thus explaining why humans show all the traits of a domesticated species. While I do not 100% buy this theory, I find it interesting, and I think it points towards the true nature of the plant/human relationship than the more human centric and human dominant one that we are taught to believe. If you look at the ways in which humans all across the world have dedicated their lives and their societies to growing and caring for the plants that they love, in healthful and harmful ways both, it helps to treat them with the respect that they deserve. Without the plants all other life on the planet dies, save maybe the microorganisms but that is hard to say. Humans are so full of hubris and pride, it is helpful—to anyone, but especially a human who wants to learn to be a healer—to embrace a more humble role for humanity in the story of the world. We are the children and younger siblings, and we need the guidance and care of our elders and parents, who are the plants.

I strongly encourage anyone who is engaging in herbalism to develop a strong personal relationship with any plant that you plan to work with in your practice. Pick them from the forests yourself, or grow them in your garden yourself. In the same way that we are seeing the importance of eating locally to increase the sustainability of our food systems, the same holds true for herbal medicines. Global capitalism destroys all things beautiful, and the more that we can be in direct relationship with the medicines that we work with, and put work into getting to know them is inherently more sustainable and beautiful, than simply ordering herbs via Amazon, based upon whatever is currently popular in the marketplace on Instagram. It is also important to resist the tendency of Neo-liberalism to commercialize and monetize everything that you love, including herbalism. I see people get into herbs and promptly decide that they want to "do herbs" for a living. While it is important to try and do what you love for work, it is really easy to put your values aside in order to make money when working with the plants. Especially when it comes to wildcrafting plants, it is important to not let the need for money overwhelm the desire to not be exploitative in your wildcrafting practices. I deeply encourage looking at herbalism as a life-long learning process, and to not brand yourself as a "professional herbalist" too quickly. Take the time to get to know the plants on a personal level. Visit them in the wild and grow them in your garden. Sit with them and dream with them. Talk and sing to them. These should be the first steps, and should take years ideally.

It is also important to resist the need to become a professional and well-paid practitioner once, or if, you decide to practice as a healer for humans. Remember that there is a long tradition of working with herbs for yourself, your family, and your immediate community as an act of service more so than as a person of the "professional class" who is above and gets paid much more than the working classes of humans. The plants give to us so freely in so many ways, and embracing that generosity in your own practice is an important aspect of mutual aid and solidarity. I was trained in the clinical side of herbalism during my involvement with an anarchic and mutual aid oriented project known as the Olympia Free Herbal Clinic. This project, which is now defunct, lasted for about a decade and provided herbs and herbal consultations for free or by donation to anyone who needed or wanted them. Many people would come to the clinic to get some help and support, from college students to people who lived outside, to older people who had not had very good experiences getting healthcare. This project had a lot of ups and downs as an organization and was both beautiful and really challenging to work within, but it taught me so much about mutual aid in action and has influenced the way that I practice to this day. In my own current practice everything that I do is sliding scale down to $0, although that does not apply to my school other than for BIPOC people in the spirit of reparations. It is inspiring and uplifting how often people will pay the upper ends of the sliding scale, or if they accept the gift of free services how often they will become a long-term ally and later on come back with some money, or send other clients or students, or just come help me work in the garden. Since there is no such thing as a legally licensed herbalist here in the "United States," it is possible to work with very little overhead since there are no dues to pay or overpriced continuing education courses to take annually. It is also really important within this framework to acknowledge what your scope of practice is, and if you don't know how to help someone with their health problems tell them that and suggest that they find someone who does. I also suggest resisting the elitism of rejecting the use of pharmaceutical drugs or other Western medicines, but rather take a harm-reductive approach and meet people where they are. In many cases, what will actually work best for someone is a pharmaceutical, especially if they do not have the time or money or space to do the more elaborate and often costly process of working with herbs, supplements, meditation, and other "alternative" therapies. There are many paths to health and healing, and it is important to honor them all.

This book is a product of one time around the wheel of the year for me in my life as an herbalist and a student of this place where I live and the many people, whether they be plants, humans, hills, or rivers who have guided and influenced me during this time. I hope that it provides some inspiration and can teach you some things about the practicalities of working with the plants in a healing context as well as learning how to become enmeshed with the place where you live in a good and beautiful way. I acknowledge that I am still just learning about so many of these things and I am sure that there are a lot of things in this book that may later prove to not be true or that I will change my mind about. I would also like to emphasize that a lot of the material in this book is derived from my personal beliefs and learnings and opinions, and these should not be taken as scientific facts, although they are interspersed with more rigorously studied hypotheses and ideas. I hope that I have made it clear when I am reporting on generally accepted ideas within herbalism and when I am expressing my own personal views and philosophies. Either way I strongly encourage anyone who is learning about herbalism to always do their own research and learn from a variety of teachers and resources, there is quite a lot of bad information and myths that get promulgated by people in their push to become experts in the field so discernment is really important.

Generally, I would recommend starting from right where you are sitting right now in your studies. Go outside and take a walk around the building and see what plants are growing there. Research them and see if they have been worked with as medicines. Keep a journal or notebook of what you learn. Start picking herbs and drying them or tincturing them. Sit with the plants and ask them to tell you about themselves; this can be a surprisingly effective technique. Find the herbal elders in your community, ask the grandmas that you may know if they have any herbal tips and tricks that they want to share with you. Figure out the ways that your own body needs some support or tends to get sick and research herbs that will be helpful in those specific ways and begin to treat yourself. Start a little container garden on your patio of some easy to grow herbs such as Motherwort (*Leonorus cardiaca*) or Dandelion (*Taraxacum officinale*). The plants are really eager to help and to be in relationship in my experience, and once you start to put in the effort and open yourself up to them things just start to happen which can end up being profoundly transformative over time. Please feel free to drop me a line sometime if you want to, I love to talk about plants.

<3

~sean

December 23rd, 2020

The Farmhouse Office

"Littlerock, Washington," Chehalis Territory,

at the base of the Black Hills

1

IN THE BELLY
/ LATE WINTER PLANTS /
WE OWE IT ALL TO THE RIVERS

HERE IN THE PNW CORNER of Turtle Island, which we often refer to as "Washington State," the main element that dominates the lives of all of the people whether they are plants or animals (including human animals) is Water. This is appropriate if you choose to look at the progression of the seasons from the point of view of one of the systems utilized by the peoples of China to interpret the world around them, which is often called the Five Elements system. This is part of both Classical and Traditional Chinese Medicine (CCM/TCM) and it correlates the various seasons with one of five elements. Within this system Winter corresponds to Water. In many ways the humans especially that live in this area love to complain about all the water, the rain and the mud, and how it starts to make your house leak and mold, and how the rain clouds block out the Sun so everyone starts to get gloomy type feelings (unless they can embrace this time of year, which is a really beautiful one in many ways). It is important to remember that part of the magic of this place is that it is a temperate rain forest. Without the constant rain all Winter we would not have the lush forests full of vegetation and bryophytes that we love so much, the mountains would not be covered with snow and the rivers would run dry. The specific part of the Winter that I am talking about in this essay is late Winter, which could be called very early Spring depending on who you are and how you think about the seasons. It is at this time that the frozen stillness of the deep Winter has passed and the big storms and rains come, sometimes the snow comes at this time too. This time of year, which by the Julian calendar is the very beginning of February, is a sacred time and is one of the cross quarters in the wheel of the year, in the middle of the Winter Solstice and the Spring Equinox, known as Imbolc in the Celtic pagan traditions.

Imbolc means "in the belly" since this is the time of year when new life is just beginning to turn over and think about waking up for the warmer parts of the year, but is still dreaming. This is the time of year when the sheep are pregnant, with the lambs in their bellies, and that may be where the name Imbolc originally came from. Here on the farm where I live currently all of the sheep have bellies full of babies, who will probably come out around the Spring Equinox. This time of year is considered a sacred and powerful one in many traditions and there are several Goddesses who are celebrated around this time of year who are in many ways different reflections of one entity although they come from traditions that are in very different parts of the world from one another. The most familiar of these deities to me is Brigid who is a Goddess from the Celtic traditions of Ireland. Brigid is celebrated on February first, which is often when Imbolc is celebrated. She is the associated with the arts of medicine, poetry, and smithing as well as with serpents, sacred wells and early Spring. It is traditional to leave her food and a bed on Imbolc, and also to work on weather divination with her aid at this time. Brigid is said to be the originator of the practice known as *keening*, which is a combination of wailing, crying, and singing. She developed this practice after the death of her son.

Directly descended or inspired by the Celtic Brigid is the Haitian loa called Maman Brigitte. She is the only of the loa who is not from Africa, but from Ireland. She is the Goddess of death and cares for the dead more than they were ever cared for by the living. She is foul mouthed, likes to drink rum infused with hot peppers, and desires the living to remember and honor the dead. Maman Brigitte is closely related to and associated with Oya-Iyansan who is one of the Orisha of Candomblé, a syncretic African diasporic religion that developed in Brazil in the early 19th century and is derived from traditional Yoruba practices from West Africa. Oya-Iyansan is the patron of Odo-Oya (the Niger River) and is the Orisha of lightning and violent storms, winds, death and rebirth. She gave birth to nine still-borns and knows about suffering and death. She is associated with intense feelings and sensations, the ability to charm, and control over Death. All these entities are really tangible within the landscape at this time of year, with the howling of the winds keening away while the Rivers flood and often kill or destroy which opens up space for the new life that is just starting to emerge and stir. These mighty storms and winds also knock down a lot of tree limbs and the organisms which live upon them, which is part of the message that it is time to get out into the woods and begin the gathering season.

As an herbalist, I spend a lot of my time thinking about plants, and the main thing that I am thinking about at any one time of year is what the plants are doing, who is ready to be harvested for medicine. The Winter is a time when most of the plants are sleeping, dormant, and dreaming. It is also a nice time for us humans to slow down, sleep, and dream. There are a few groups of organisms, however, that only really come alive to their full potential during these wet winters, and that is the bryophytes and lichens. Bryophytes are an informal grouping of small, non-vascular plants that are very much dependent on the presence of water in the air in order to live their lives. There are three main types of bryophytes which are the mosses, liverworts, and hornworts. Since they do not have vascular structures (which are the structures that move water throughout a plant body) they are dependent upon the presence of water in the air or falling from the sky in order for their metabolisms to function. These organisms dry up and go into a dormant state in the hot and dry times of year, which is basically all of Summer around here. They only wake up and do all of their living, breathing, and reproducing in the cold and wet months of Winter. Lichens are a bit more complex than the bryophytes in that they are not considered plants, but are rather composite organisms that are made up of fungi, algae, and cyanobacteria that all live together in mutual

aid, often called a *mutualistic* relationship in Biology. Lichens
and bryophytes often live in the trees or in other places up in
the air where they can catch water and also sunlight. During
the warmer months they are pretty inconspicuous due to both
the fact that they dry up and go dormant, and also because the
deciduous trees all leaf out during these months and take up a
lot of the visual space in the forests. In the Winter, when all of
the deciduous trees have dropped their leaves, the bryophytes
and lichens swell up with water and begin to almost glow as
they reproduce and go about their lives; they are very easy to
spot when out in the woods.

While I do not work with many bryophytes as herbal medicines (there are some traditions of working with some species,
such as *Polytricum juniperinum*), I love to work with two species of lichen, namely *Usnea spp.* and *Lobaria pulmonaria*. Both
species are pretty abundant in the woods around me, and they
are often blown down along with the branches of trees during
the big Winter storms. Both species, like all lichens, absorb
their nutrients directly from the moisture that they get from
the air, so they will also absorb pollution such as heavy metals,
hydrocarbons, and even radioactive isotopes. In this way they
function to clean the air, and people have called them the lungs
of the forest, or put forth the idea that they keep the lungs of
the forest in good health. This also means that these lichens
may be full of toxic materials. Some have said that in this age
of industrial pollution no one should use lichens for medicine
because they are all poisoned. I still do, but do not necessarily
recommend it for everyone. From a Doctrine of Signatures

point of view, the visual appearance of both species could be said to resemble some of the anatomy of the lungs such as the alveoli. ***Lobaria pulmonaria*** has large lobes that resemble the shape of the lungs, and one side of the thallus of this species is speckled with creamy colored spots which is sometimes compared to spit up mucus! When I was studying botany *Lobaria pulmonaria* was presented to me as an example of how the Doctrine of Signatures is nonsense since the common name of this lichen is Lungwort, which my botany teacher explained was derived from the physical appearance of the lichen, which made superstitious people way back in the day think they would be good for the lungs, which we modern people now know is nonsense. Unfortunately for my botany teacher (but good for us herbalists), both *Lobaria pulmonaria* and *Usnea spp* are wonderful medicines for the lungs.

Usnea was one of the first herbal medicines that I collected and extracted into a tincture when I was first learning about herbs, up on Rock Candy Mountain in the Black Hills. They were taught to me at that time as being, very simply, an "herbal antibiotic." While today I cringe at that term, as it reduces the complexities of plant/human relations down to a biomedical, reductionist one, it served me well enough at the time. I would reach for this tincture or give it to my friends when we were sick, often in the Winter when everybody would get cruddy lungs, colds and coughs, and it would very often do the trick and either end the sickness pretty quickly or keep it from getting bad if I gave the medicine early enough. The main "active constituent" in *Usnea* is thought to be usnic acid, a benzofuran derivative that has been shown to be antibacterial.* Usnic acid has also been used in weight loss supplements, for reasons that are unclear to me, which have in turn lead to liver failure in a few individuals.† Working with isolated usnic acid can clearly lead to some unpleasant effects, and the effects of the whole herb in a human body are more complex. Usnea does indeed seem to kill off bacteria living in or on the body, but they also have a very nice expectorant effect, meaning that they promote the loosening of mucus that is stuck in the lungs and helps to move it up and out. There have been many studies on usnic acid as being helpful to break up biofilms,* which are gooey blankets that bacteria form around themselves when they are living in human bodies. Many hard-to-treat conditions have a biofilm component which makes the bacteria difficult to reach by traditional antibiotics. Many lung infections also have a biofilm component to them and for this reason I like to reach for *Usnea,* often in formulation with other herbs, in cases of lung infection and illness, but only in acute situations and not for a prolonged period.

Lobaria pulmonaria, or Lungwort, has a similar effect in the human body to *Usnea*. I find it to be a little gentler, and it

* See Francolini *et al.*
† See Ingolfsdottir.

feels more moistening and tonic than *Usnea*. It is still an herb that I only use in formulas with other herbs, and I only give it for brief periods of time. It is a great herb to work with for all sorts of lung infections and can be helpful in hard-to-treat conditions such as "walking pneumonia." *Lobaria* is tradition-ally prepared as a decoction, especially in milk, by the Indige-nous peoples of both Turtle Island and various parts of Europe. They are considered nourishing, blood building, and moisten-ing. There have been some controlled studies showing that some of the species may be helpful to heal and soothe ulcers of the gastrointestinal tract and this would presumably extend to the lungs as well, much like other moistening herbs. Indeed, the various tannins and mucilages, along with the presence of querecetin which is a potent antioxidant would point towards the reduction of inflammation on all mucosal membranes. *Lobaria* calms the cough reflex, some have hypothesized through interaction with the vagus nerve,* and while they do seem to help with breaking up biofilms and curtailing infec-tions, they do not contain usnic acid although they do contain a number of other acids such as stictic acid and norstictic acid, which may have antimicrobial abilities. They are rich in various carotenoids including the well-known (from car-rots) beta-carotene, as well as a variety of steroids including lichesterol and ergosterol, and several sugar alcohols. All the species of *Lobaria* also contain various essential oils, and the smell of the fresh thalli is so beautiful and hard to describe. It is deeply earthy and sweet, much like the forest floor upon which you find them.

* See R. Rogers.

I have heard that they can be distilled to produce an essential oil for use in perfumery, but I have never tried this since it would take quite a lot of these precious organisms to produce a very little bit of essential oil. It is possible to make a very nice perfume ingredient from these lichens by making what is called a many times folded tincture of them, meaning that you take the fresh thallus and macerate them in strong ethanol for a week or two, until the ethanol has taken on the color and fragrance of the lichen. This tincture is then pressed, and the thallus discarded. This finished tincture is then used as the menstruum for a freshly harvested batch of the lichen, making the tincture more concentrated with each repetition of the process. Each time you add a fresh batch of lichen to the same tincture is called a fold, and after folding the tincture three or four (or many more) times it starts to really take on the smell of the lichen, which again is very earthy and sweet. This many folded tincture serves as a very nice base note and also as a fixative for perfumes. The various acids in the lichens also function as fixatives for dying wool or fabric, and the various species of *Lobaria* will produce a nice orange-brown dye that will remain fixed to wool without needing to add any other ingredients to the dye bath. When I make medicinal extracts of *Lobaria* to work with I like to make a double extraction, much like I do with the various medicinal shelf mushrooms. I will usually tincture the fresh thallus in ninety-five percent (190 Proof) ethanol, let that macerate for a moon cycle, and then press the tincture and decoct either the marc or ideally an equal weight of freshly harvested *Lobaria* to what I used in making the initial tincture, then strain the decoction and reduce it in volume to be equal to the volume of the tincture and combine them in equal parts to make the finished double extraction. The final product is complex and sweet tasting and smelling, almost black in color, and seems to hold all the medicinal actions of the plant both soothing/moistening/tonic and antimicrobial. In many ways it would be nice to just work with a decoction of the fresh thallus as needed, but preserving the decoction with an ethanolic tincture means that I can just pull out the stock bottle to serve a client which is much more convenient in this busy life and world.

Several species grow in this area, all of which can be found in great abundance under the correct trees (maples usually) after the winds of Winter. *Lobaria pulmonaria* is the species that I know of as being worked with as a medicine the most. This species can be identified by the bright green color of the upper part of the thallus when it is wet. This bright almost neon green is very easy to spot and is a good indicator of species. *Lobaria pulmonaria* can also be identified by the presence of reproductive structures known as *soredia* and *isidia* on the surface of the thallus. These are visible with a strong hand lens or under a microscope. This species also has smooth lobe margins. The other most common species to run into is *Lobaria oregana* which often has a more blue-green color to the upper part of the thallus (both species have a tan underside with white spots on it which is the aforementioned spit-up-mucus signature), has frilly lobe margins, and does not have *isidia* or *soredia* present.

All species of *Lobaria* live in older and less disturbed forests, and are very sensitive to air pollution and acid rain. *Lobaria pulmonaria* grows circumglobally in the Northern forests of the globe, and while widespread they are considered endangered in some parts of the world due to industrial pollution and habitat loss. *Lobaria oregana* only grows in the forests of the Pacifc Northwest portion of Turtle Island as far as I can tell. They are all slow growing organisms, often not reaching sexual maturity until they are twenty five years old. The various *Lobarias* are a huge presence in the forests of Northwestern Turtle Island, making up some thirty-five to sixty percent of all epiphytes found in these forests, and five percent of the total foliar biomass.* They all serve the forests in a variety of ways, but especially via nitrogen fixation. The lichens absorb atmospheric nitrogen which the blue-green cyanobacteria photobionts can fix into nitrates and nitrites that serve as a food for the lichen. The trees upon which the lichens live, especially the Big Leaf Maples (*Acer macrophyllum*), will actually send out adventitious roots from the branches of the trees into clusters of *Pulmonaria* to absorb some of these forms of nitrogen as food. These fixed forms of nitrogen are also washed off of the lichens during rainfall to become food for the rest of the plants living in the forest, especially when the lichens themselves are blown off of the trees during the big wind storms and die on the ground below, they feed the trees that they have lived upon and the rest of the forest with this precious nitrogen. One study estimates that *Lobaria oregana* fixes three to four kilograms of nitrogen per year per hectare that they live upon.*

* See, eol.org/pages/2860165/

Due to the slow growing nature of the various *Lobarias*, and also their crucial ecological function within the forest of fixing nitrogen, it is important to not harvest the lichens directly from the trees upon which they live. This is also true of the various *Usneas*. During the middle to late parts of Winter the mighty storms and winds will do the harvesting for you by knocking down whole branches off of the trees that are covered in lichens, as well as blowing the lichens right off the trees. Since this time of year is so wet and cold, the wind thrown lichens will stay alive and healthy on the ground until the Summer droughts come, so you can just wander the forests and gather the lichens from the earth where they have landed. I have found that especially with *Lobaria* you can find trees in the forest that have a strong relationship with them, usually Big Leaf Maples (**Acer macrophyllum**), that will just be covered in lichens. These are often large and older trees with a huge diameter to their canopy, and after the strong storms of late Winter if you just go to these trees there will be plenty of downed lichens to provide you and your family/clients/etc. with medicine for the whole year or much more. It is important to leave most of the lichens on the ground

even though they have been blown off of the trees since they are providing food to that tree and to the forest by decomposing in place.

Even more important to learning how to harvest in a sustainable way is to take the next step and work on actively propagating these species. Both *Usnea* and *Lobaria* can easily propagate via vegetative propagules, indeed that is mostly how they propagate themselves out in the forests, clonally. I have had some luck with utilizing a method that I learned to propagate mosses to grow the lichens. This process involves gathering some fresh lichens, putting them in a blender with yogurt (or even just water, although yogurt is sticky and theoretically provides some food for the baby lichens), blending this up into a slurry and depositing the slurry in a tree where you want the lichens to live. You will have to figure out a way to protect the slurry from getting washed away by the rains of the Winter, like putting a bit of canvas over them, while still making sure that they will stay moist enough and out of too much direct Sun. These tiny lichen fragments each have the ability to become a whole new thallus, but the process is slow.

During the Winter the rivers swell and flood and really make their presence known. The landscape upon which I live is filled with various rivers and river systems which move from the hills and mountains towards the Salish Sea, also called the "Puget Sound," and thence to the ocean. If you spend much time traveling along the rivers, you will see that several species of tree really like to grow along them. The two that I would like to talk about because I love to work with them as medicines are **Alnus rubra** (Red Alder) and *Populus trichocarpa* (Black Cottonwood). Red Alder is by far one of the most common and abundant trees in this bio region. They serve an important ecological purpose (as all beings do) in the places where they live. Red Alder thrive in places where disturbances have taken place and help to heal and repair these disturbed areas in order to help turn them back into forest, or simply to help the land stay in place. This is especially noticeable along the rivers, where the alders drop their seed laden cones into the waters in the Winter when the floods are happening. During these floods the rivers often jump their banks and cause erosion, knocking over trees and other vegetation that line the rivers and exposing open ground. The alder seeds float along with the rivers and settle down on these exposed soils where they germinate in the spring. Alders grow very quickly, stabilizing these exposed soils with their root structures and providing shade to the rivers and the creatures that live in them, especially the Salmon which I will come back to. Alders are often some of the first trees to

populate areas of the landscape that have been disturbed by humans, such as clear cuts. They quickly spread their seeds over these areas and help to stabilize the soil while also creating a shady and moist environment where the evergreen trees can germinate and begin to grow.

Alders are nitrogen fixing plants. Nitrogen fixation is a very important activity that some plants do, that provides food for the entire forest. All plants require nitrogen for their growth, but they cannot eat elemental nitrogen which is unfortunate since the majority of the planet's atmosphere is made up of elemental nitrogen. In order for this very abundant nitrogen to be eaten by plants, however, it must be converted or "fixed" into nitrites and nitrates. A goodly amount of this fixation is done by lighting strikes, but the majority of it is done by bacteria. Alders live in a mutualistic (mutual aid) relationship with several species of nitrogen fixing bacteria. The alders provide the bacteria with a place to live in the form of nodes on their roots, and they also provide the bacteria with carbohydrates to eat. The bacteria, in turn, fix nitrogen from the atmosphere into ammonia and other usable forms. This nitrogen fixation feeds the alders, but it also feeds the other plants who are living around them. In this way Alders can grow in very nutrient poor and damaged soils and turn them into more nutrient rich soils upon which other species may thrive.

Another major player in the nitrogen cycle in this specific part of the world are the Salmon (*Onchorhyncus spp*). These sacred and mysterious fish have lived in the rivers since time immemorial. They are born in the rivers, and then travel out to the ocean for several years where they eat and get fat. Then, following some mysterious call, they travel for hundreds or thousands of miles back to the precise river in which they were born, often to the very same spot. Once they reach this spot they mate, lay eggs, and die. When the Salmon reach the fresh waters of the rivers they turn a deep red color, which is similar to the red color that is visible in the catkins of the Alders, or if you cut into their bark. The Salmon are made up of quite a lot of protein, which is very rich in forms of nitrogen that both plants and animals can eat. Bears and humans especially love to eat the Salmon, and will catch them at the rivers and take them up on land, eat them and poop them out into the soil, which feeds the plants. Tons of the **Salmon** also rot in and along the banks of the rivers, providing nutrients for the forests. The Salmon need shady rivers for them to be comfortable, and the Alders give them that shade.

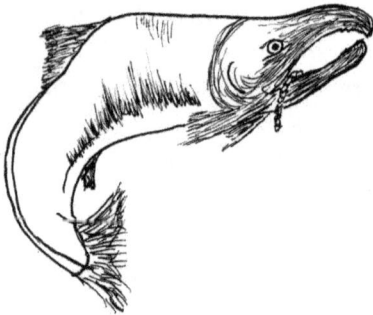

While I am talking about the Salmon and the rivers, it is very important to also talk about the Indigenous peoples who live on this land and have for millennia. The main place that I like to take students to learn about the Alders, Cottonwoods, and rivers is the Billy Frank Jr. Wildlife Refuge. This place is on the Nisqually Delta, which is named after the tribe of people called the Nisqually.

The Salish Sea has seven inlets, and each of them has a tribe associated with it. These tribes were all lumped into one tribe by the occupying federal government of the "United States of America" during a process of forced assimilation and genocide which is called the Squaxin Island tribe. We are all very lucky in this region that the tribes are composed of such strong and resilient people, and that to a certain extent the genocidal war that the occupying forces had been undertaking on the Indigenous people of this continent was starting to slow or become less necessary by the time the border of the "United States" had been extended all the way to the west coast. The Indigenous peoples of this area have and still do live upon this landscape, tending the bounty of the natural world and working hard to ensure that the land and all the people on it stay healthy, for millennia. European invasion brought with it a horrible period of genocide of the tribal members, and the destruction of much of the landscape including the logging of the great forests, the damming of the mighty rivers, and the over harvest of the salmon, to the point where many of the once abundant fish, plants, and animals are now facing extinction.

There is also a strong history of resistance by the Tribal peoples against the invaders, and Billy Frank Jr. is a good example of this. Billy Frank Jr. was a member of the Nisqually tribe who was born in 1931. He was a fisherperson his whole life, and when he was a teenager he started to have run ins with the game wardens over his right to fish. At this time the fish numbers were plummeting due to commercial overfishing by white fisherpeople, and tensions over the fish were high.

It essentially became illegal for Tribal members to harvest fish in their traditional fishing grounds using their traditional and sustainable techniques. This was especially upsetting to the Tribal members because they had been promised their right to fish in the Treaties that the Tribes made with the federal government in the 1800s when they gave up most of their lands (at gunpoint) in exchange for the right to continue to fish and gather food as they were accustomed to doing. The Treaty of Point No Point was the one made with the Tribes of the Olympic Peninsula, which was basically never honored by the government. The Treaty of Medicine Creek was the one in which the various tribes in the southern Salish Sea, including the Nisqually, Puyallup, Steilacoom, and various Squaxin Island tribes, were swindled into giving up their lands by the governor of "Washington State" at the time, Isaac Stevens. Chief Leschi of the Nisqually tribe led his people to the state capital of "Olympia" to protest this theft of their land via deception, and they refused to leave even after being ordered to do so by Stevens. This resulted in Stevens declaring martial law which was a part of what came to be called the Puget Sound War in which several tribes engaged in armed resistance to the occupying forces of "Washington State" which included both the official army and several volunteer militias. Chief Leschi was eventually captured and hanged for his role in these battles under dubious legal reasons, for which he was officially exonerated by the courts in 2004. Too little and too late.

Although the various Tribes were supposedly granted or promised access to their traditional hunting, fishing, and gathering grounds by these various treaties in exchange for their ancestral lands, in practice this was not the case at all. Indigenous life ways were generally attacked as part of the genocidal program undertaken by the colonizers to attempt to "civilize" the "savage" Indigenous peoples. They would be violently attacked and arrested for trying to fish. I honestly do not remember where I heard this story originally but at some point an Indigenous person was speaking to a class that I was a part of about their ancestor's experiences living in occupied "America," and they told us about a technique that Indigenous fisherpeople would use in order to be able to fish at their "usual and accustomed" fishing grounds which was the estuary where the capitol of the state was built, at the bottom of the inlet where the Steh-Chass people lived (now called Budd Inlet by most humans). There is a run of Chum or Dog Salmon (*Onchorhyncus keta*) that ran through there at that time, and still does today, and the Indigenous people who wanted to fish it would have to put their canoes in under cover of darkness during rain storms so that they were not very visible or audible, and they would time the strokes of their paddles with periods or heavy rain or thunder to cover the noise because there would be white people sitting up on the bridge or on the shore who would shoot at them if they saw or heard them.

All this reached a critical point during the Fish Wars of the 1960s and 1970s which were a series of "fish-ins" in which Tribal members would fish in their usual grounds and the police would violently assault and arrest them. Inspired by the Civil Rights Movement, these fish-ins were mostly non-violent direct actions though there were some instances of Tribal members bringing guns in order to protect themselves due to the intense violence that they would be forced to endure at the hands of the local police as well as white fisherpeople. Due to these protests, in 1974 the Boldt Decision was reached, which said that treaty fisherpeople must be given 50% of the total allowable catch, and led to Tribal members becoming a part of the boards that were in charge of overseeing the fisheries at large. This has lead to a much more sustainable way of fishing for all people involved, although Salmon numbers are declining at a heartbreaking rate all over the world for a variety of reasons. This is a great example of Indigenous acts of resistance that have had a big impact on curtailing the rapacious and destructive appetites of the occupying culture on the landscape and the beings that live there.

Anyway, back to Alder. Alder is a very useful medicine, and is a very abundant tree, so it is a medicine that can be harvested without damaging the overall population of the species. In the Winter I like to harvest the Alders' **catkins**, which are the male flowers. These beautiful red catkins are very abundant in the Winter and can be gathered without doing harm to the tree by picking a handful from a tree, then another handful from another, and never stripping all of them off of any one tree. An even better practice is to wander around in Alder groves after the big winds and storms of late Winter and gather the catkins that have been blown off the trees. These are usually still attached to small twigs and

branches, and these whole twigs can be processed as medicine. The bark can also be harvested in the Spring, which is best gathered from fallen trees in the rivers.

Alder functions as a very nice lymphatic, meaning that it promotes the flow of lymph in the body. The lymphatic system is a series of vessels that in many ways is the lunar mirror to the more solar cardiovascular system. The immune cells of our bodies are born in our lymph nodes and travel throughout the lymphatic system in order to reach areas of infection. The lymph system also serves to remove waste products from the body. The parallels between the lymphatic system of the body and the river systems of the landscape are very intriguing to me. The lymphatic system does not a have an organ to help it move, like the heart pumps blood. Rather, it circulates through movement of the body, alternating hot and cold, and by lymphatic herbs. Alder is very useful in any conditions where there are swollen, red, and inflamed tissues. They help to get the fluids moving and reduce swelling. There is also a cooling and pain reducing quality to Alder that is nice in infections. They are somewhat antimicrobial. Alder is very astringent, and can help to get the digestive tract tonified and reduce inflammation there, which also is a parallel to the way that the Alders keep the rivers in good health. Too much Alder can irritate the gut and lead to vomiting, so look out for that! I have found Alder to be deeply restorative to those parts of us that have been injured by the stresses of the modern world, and they can help to repopulate our clear cuts with life again, inviting the Salmon back to the rivers.

All along the banks of the rivers in the Winter, and especially in the very early Spring, there is a sweet honey like smell that is so hard to describe but is calming and heartening. It is the smell of the Black Cottonwood leaf buds as they swell with their sticky resins. *Populus trichocarpa* is the Latin name for the Black Cottonwood. These are very tall and stately trees that grow very quickly and in great abundance along the rivers. They too help to hold the rivers in place and provide shade. The leaf buds of this tree are full of a lovely, sticky, and fragrant resin that is like no other. The Cottonwoods are related to Quaking Aspens (*Populus tremuloides*), and like the Aspens they are very sensitive to the winds. During the wind storms of the Winter, the Cottonwoods shake off many of their upper branches, which fall to the ground and often root there. In this way they can clone themselves, and in this way they provide us with so much medicine. The leaf buds are the part of this tree that are most often used for medicine. They are best gathered in the late Winter or early Spring, when they are swollen with resins but before they have started to open up to let the leaves out.

Picking Cottonwood buds is a fun and lovely experience. It is a sign that the Winter is nearing its end and you end up with sticky fragrant fingers. I often begin picking Cottonwood buds right around Valentine's Day, which is associated with love and romance within the culture that I live in, and it is a lovely date to go out picking Cottonwood buds with your sweetie, including if that sweetie is yourself. A warmth and an embodied sensuality just naturally comes out when wandering along the rivers, searching for these sweet, gooey buds that the trees have simply dropped on the ground for you. Learning how to identify *Populus trichocarpa* at a distance is a pretty important part of learning how to harvest their buds, since you basically have to visit as many Cottonwood trees or groves as you possibly can in the course of a day in order to get a good harvest, since some trees do not drop any branches at all some years. Once you can learn to spot them from a distance, the Cottonwoods can also show you where the rivers are, or even where they used to be.

It can actually be really good picking in urban areas, and since Cottonwoods grow in disturbed places, traditionally along the sides of Rivers where the ground is washed away, they do very well in the disturbed areas that are cities and suburbs. They need a lot of water to be able to grow well and so the Cottonwoods can show you where the Rivers used to be in the cities, or even where they still are but now live underground since the streets and buildings have been built on top of them. The water is still there, and the trees can still drink it, and this is a good way to get in touch with the living landscape that is still present and conscious even though they have been changed so intensely by human activity.

The Cottonwoods hold some of the Sun in them, they bring a feeling of sunshine and warmth on their smell, and they are also rich in anti-inflammatory compounds such as salicylates. You can see the heat that the plant provides by looking at the catkins when they form later on in the Spring, they are bright hot red. Cottonwood buds can be infused into oil which makes a great salve that can be rubbed on sore muscles to ease the pain, or just slathered on for the smell. Honestly the smell is a huge part of the medicine of this plant, and it carries with it the Rivers and the sunshine. It is a nice practice to carry around some form of Cottonwood extract, an infused oil, essential oil, hydrosol, or even tincture when you are going to some kind of stressful or alienating event, since smelling that sweet smell can bring the joys of wandering the Rivers in the very early Spring to any environment or situation. Cottonwood oil is also really nice for burns, both sunburns and more serious ones. It helps to speed healing time. The resins are antimicrobial and encourage skin granulation so they can be applied to any numbers of scrapes, scratches, and infections to speed healing and reduce infection. The buds and twigs can also be tinctured, and in this form the medicine is very bitter, so it helps to move digestion. The salicylates can be helpful internally for general aches and pains, and the tincture serves as a nice mucolytic, meaning that it breaks up stuck mucus in the body and gets it moving. Cottonwoods can be very easily propagated from cuttings by cutting sticks off the tree in the winter and planting them in the ground in a wet area, they will root and form new trees. The best cuttings are about six feet long and have had all of the side twigs and buds removed from them. If you plant these about three feet into the ground along a river you will get pretty good strike rate. This is a good practice if you are trying to learn how to be an accomplice to the Rivers, especially those that have had all of their vegetation removed due to agriculture or development, as the Cottonwoods will root easily and grow very fast so they will quickly start to help a hurt River to rebuild, and encourage the Salmon to come back for the shade. Willows *(Salix spp.)* are also a really good species to work with in this way, but we will talk more about them later.

I hope this chapter has introduced some of the gifts of late Winter, and some plant allies that work with you during this time of year. Without the Water we would be nothing, Water is Life after all.

2

PLANT SITS/DIRECT LEARNING

ONE OF THE VERY BEST WAYS to learn about the plants and how they like to work in the human body is through direct and personal interaction between the herbalist and the herb. There are a lot of ways to go about doing this work, but I would say that the least effective way would be to learn about an herb through a book or the internet, order prefilled capsules of that herb, and start taking them. Not that this won't teach you something about how that herb works within the human organism, if the herb is of good quality and works well with your body, then you should notice some changes or feelings upon ingesting those capsules. There is so much more to working with the plants, however, and the more that you can incorporate all of your senses in a state in which you can be very open, receptive, and paying attention to subtle fluctuations in your body and emotions, the more that you can learn through this process. There is a whole spectrum of ways that people will do this kind of work but it basically comes down to spending time with the plant in question and noticing how that time spent changes you or brings about physiological activity in you. This is a form of communication, and this process in general is one of learning how to communicate with plants.

The most direct and perhaps respectful way to go about this process is to go out to the woods, or someplace where not too many humans live, with a journal, pen, and some water and find a specific plant that interests you. This can be determined either by doing research beforehand and seeking out a specific species of plant that you are interested in working with as an herb, or it can also take the form of a sort of directionless drifting through the forest, similar to the *dérive* of the Situationists in which you stroll aimlessly until someone draws you to them without too much conscious thought on your part. Sometimes a specific plant will look really nice in the sunlight, or maybe you realize that you are breathing deeper or are feeling nostalgic or something like this, so you stop walking and focus on whatever plant you have come across. Chances are they are interested in talking, or at least your body is interested in talking with them. Once you have chosen the plant, find a comfortable position and just sit with them for awhile.

It is good to do a thorough body scan practice when you first get settled down; take some time and check in with your body about where you are feeling good, where you are feeling tense, if you have any pain, if you are hungry, what your breathing is like, and so on. This is not an attempt to change anything, just a gentle check-in to get a baseline of where you are at in that specific moment. After checking in with your body, check in with your mental and emotional state (not that those things are separate). This is also not a process of trying to change things but just a scan of your self at that specific moment. So are you in a good mood? High anxiety? Sleepy? Also notice the general content and characteristics of your thought patterns at the time. Are they fast and chattery or slow and quiet? Try to note the specific things that you have been thinking about consciously and also where your mind has been going during times of wandering. This can take as long as you like, and while I have said several times that it is not about trying to force any changes, this can be a good time to focus on taking a few deep breaths and loosening up a bit, maybe unclench your jaw.

Once you have checked in with your own ground state, bring your attention to the plant that is in front of you. For a first meeting it can be nice to not even touch them, just look with your eyes and heart. The idea is to really focus on them and see what they are like. This can be intellectual in that you can really look at what kind of light they like to live in, if they are growing on a slope or a flat spot, if they seem to need a lot of water or are happy in arid conditions, basically trying to figure out their ecological niche within the larger community, which is also trying to figure out their needs and desires as a living organism. Next you can focus on how they grow as an organism, what is the shape of this plant? Does it have spines or thorns? Soft downy fir? Are they tall or do they creep upon the ground? Do they live as single individuals or are they a part of a large stand of the same kind of plant, and if so are all those plants connected to one another by underground rhizomes? What are the colors of the various parts of the plant? It is nice if they are in flower or in fruit since these are such distinctive parts of a plant's anatomy and can tell you a lot. If you are trained in botany this would be a great time to key the plant out, which certainly involves paying attention to them deeply.

Now see how this period of focusing closely on this plant and this place has changed or influenced how you are feeling in your body, mind, and emotions. There can be a really wide gradient of how this practice works with humans, and it is a lifelong practice so don't feel discouraged if the initial answer is "I feel the same." Often just the act of sitting still and carefully observing a being out in nature will be calming and settling, and can often bring up emotions that have been suppressed or ignored by the busyness of everyday life. Having a journal is nice, and you can just sit and freewrite for some time about the plant, the place, yourself, and how you all feel together. If you are so inclined, make a drawing of the plant as they are at this specific time. It is also nice to note the weather conditions, time, and date.

The plant knows that you are there. They are a living, sentient, breathing entity that are aware of the goings on in their surroundings. More and more scientific research reveals the many ways that plants are sentient and interact with the world around them in intelligent ways, and I would encourage you to do some reading in this area. After you have sat with the plant for long enough, thank them for their time and tell them you will be coming back again. Tell them your name and why you are interested in getting to know them. This might feel silly but just do it, it is good praxis. Come back to this same plant a number of times over the course of the seasons and repeat this practice.

Once you have figured out the identification of this plant to species and know that they are safe to ingest, ask them if you can pick a leaf or a bit or bark or a berry to taste. Getting consent from a plant is a tricky thing, but try to listen really deeply, look out for weather patterns shifting, and try hard to accept a "no" if that is what you get. I encourage people to assume that they have a "no" if they don't get a strong sense otherwise. Once you feel that you have gotten an enthusiastic "yes," pick a bit of the plant and taste it, chew it up very well, slowly, and pay close attention to what the plant tastes like. Some flavors to think about include bitter, astringent, sweet, salty, pungent, or spicy. As long as you are sure that the plant is safe to ingest, swallow. Now just sit and feel carefully how your body responds to the presence of this plant. Often you'll start producing saliva, and your digestive juices will get moving, but not always. Sit for a good five minutes or more just paying attention to any changes that occur, either in terms of the physiological working of your body or your thoughts or emotions. This is a very direct form of communication between the plant and you. They have produced specific chemicals in their body which you have ingested, and these chemicals are now serving as messenger molecules between the two of you. This practice can teach you quite a lot about the obvious and also subtle medicinal actions of the plant upon a human body, and can often tell you something about the personality and character of the plant and how they might like to interact with you and other humans as a teacher, accomplice, or friend.

If your plant is a medicinal plant, and you have decided that the two of you get along, this is a good time to learn about techniques to propagate this plant and do so. Maybe take some cuttings and plant them out or gather seeds to germinate at home, or even just gather seeds and plant them in the ground around the mother plant, helping them to get into the soil well. Once you have done this simple act of service then you are good to harvest I think. It is nice to also give a gift, such as tobacco or something like this, but I think the direct service of propagation is the best type of offering to give. Now harvest, very judiciously and respectfully, some of the plant and make some kind of medicine from them. I usually tincture everything as fresh as possible to get the full vital presence of the living plant. If you can, harvesting and tincturing the plant right there in the field really helps the medicine to absorb the intricacies of that plant in that specific place.

Take your medicine home and do a bunch of research on this plant, if you haven't already. There are so many good *materia medica* books about how humans like to work with various herbs as medicines, and it is best to read about the plant from diverse sources, ideally looking for how that specific plant or their counterparts are worked with by practitioners of other herbal traditions than your own, such as looking into Chinese Medicine materia medicas. It is also important to look at both modern and older sources of information to get a full picture of how this plant might be worked with.

Once the tincture is all done, take it frequently and in a variety of dosages. Drop doses are good for doing plant meditations, but it is also nice to take large doses that you still know to be safe in order to really get a sense for what the plant is capable of in a physiological sense. In a lot of "American" herbalism there is a tendency for people to like to take lower doses of plants, but many cultures work with much higher doses, and you can learn a lot by seeing what the plant can really do. While I like tinctures, there is nothing like a strong decoction of either the fresh or dried plant material to really feel what this plant does in concentration. These can taste quite intense and sometimes lead to nausea but often a nice decoction really gets to the deeper levels of the medicine, including pulling out the minerals and mucilage that a tincture does not get to as well.

It is a nice practice to take the plant everyday for a moon cycle or so to really immerse yourself with them, keeping notes as you go and visiting the plant in the woods as often as possible. This is a good time to pay attention to your dreams, and if the plant starts to show up in them that is an auspicious sign, and you should be sure to record those in your journal. I have been impressed and influenced by what I have been taught about Amazonian herbalism, and while I acknowledge that there is a lot of problematic aspects of current New Age Ayahuasca culture which is bound up in learning about this system, the technique of *dieta*, which is a big part of learning about working with plants in the Amazon, is an inspiration for these long term immersions in working with a specific plant. The *vegetalistas* who undergo this process embrace a number of disciplines in order to be more open to the plants, such as restricting their diets and avoiding other humans as much as possible while they are learning the plants. While it is nice to keep things simple, many of the people I assume will be reading this live in a very different world than the deep jungle.

Once you have really immersed yourself in a specific plant and showed up for them as an accomplice, it becomes much easier to know when they would be helpful for other humans that you may see as clients. Getting a client to learn this process can be helpful when the two of you are in discussion about what plants might aid them in their healing process. Many plants have similar medicinal qualities but certain plants will work better than others for specific people. There are many systems for trying to determine which plants or formulas would be the best fit, but a very simple and direct method is to have your client taste and sit with the various plants and see which ones taste best to them, or relieve their symptoms that they are trying to work on. Even a drop of a tincture can give a sense as to whether the plant will work for the person's symptoms by causing a subtle but noticeable shift.

Plant meditations are a great thing to do in groups. It is really interesting how often different people in the group will have very similar experiences with the plants. One really fun activity is called a *blind tasting* which involves passing an unlabeled tincture or tea around in a circle of people who are familiar with this process, having everyone take a taste and sit in silence for awhile, then share their various experiences. This will give a nice and at least somewhat objective sense of how that plant works for people, since if you have a bunch of people all having the same experience with a plant without any of them being primed by the knowledge of the plant or what sorts of medicinal effects it is supposed to have then that points towards a non-placebo type effect.

Taking the time to go through this plant meditation process with many different plants, both out in the forest and those that you grow in your garden or on your patio, is a solid way to learn about the plants and their medicinal qualities. It is important to ground this learning in the body and in direct experience. My friend, mentor, and teacher Paul Bergner once gave a talk entitled "How to Become a Master Herbalist in 25 Years or More" that I appreciated for so many reasons, but especially for this tip that he gave for becoming a really good herbalist: everyday read an entry about a plant from some materia medica, and then taste that plant in an intentional way. This is a very simple and quick exercise that really gives an embodied, felt sense to what is learned in an intellectual way through the book. I especially think that it is by long term processes such as these, and especially going out to the plants where they live, actively helping them to be more abundant via propagation and wild gardening techniques, and sitting with them again and again over time that you can get to a place of accompliceship or alliance with those plants. Once they know that you care about them and will actively tend for them and take care of them, then the plants will really work with you as healers in your practice. It is crucial to gain relationships with the plants in order to do your best work as an herbalist since that caring and solidarity will come through in the work that you do together in trying to heal other humans.

MEDICINE MAKING

Learning how to prepare the plants into potent and effective medicines is an important aspect of being an herbalist. It is possible these days to become a practicing herbalist without ever learning how to make the medicines since so many of them are easily purchased from so many different places. I would strongly suggest making your own herbal medicines for a variety of reasons, the main one being that you really know the quality of the medicine if you make it yourself. While there are many good herbal medicine companies that produce excellent products, plenty of companies or individuals make subpar products, and it can be difficult to tell which is which. Capitalism also alienates people, separated them from what they work with in their day to day lives, forcing them to be consumers of products created by others in order to do their work in the world. Making your own medicines is the opposite of alienation. When you take great care to make medicine yourself, it creates a profound sense of connection between you. I am a bioregional herbalist, and I strongly believe that the best herbs to work with are the ones that grow in the same place that you do. They breathe the same air, feel the same weather patterns, and are exposed to the same environmental stressors that the humans living in that area, so they can best help those humans to get some balance in that environment. Growing or wildcrafting the plants allows you to process them when they are fresh and full of vitality and to be sure to harvest them at the correct time for medicinal potency. It is so much cheaper to make your own medicines than to buy them, which enables you to be more generous with them both with yourself and with your clients. The price of many herbal preparations on the market makes it prohibitively expensive for a person to do a thorough round of taking herbs for a specific health condition. Finally, medicine making is really fun! As someone who has been immersed in D.I.Y. culture for a long time now, I get a special satisfaction from the long and elaborate process of making something myself instead of just buying it premade. There is even an aesthetic beauty to having herbs drying in racks in the rafters, macerating in jars of ethanol or vinegar on the shelves, or infusing into oils in the warm spot above the fridge or in the greenhouse.

INTERNAL PREPARATIONS
TEAS AND DECOCTIONS

The simplest way to prepare herbs for ingestion is also probably the oldest, which is the creation of teas and decoctions from fresh or dried herbs. In both preparations the only solvent involved is water, which is cheap and abundant (at least at this point in history). To make a tea or tisane, steep or infuse the herb in hot, or sometimes cold, water until it takes on the color and taste of the herb, at which point you drink it.

Teas are often pleasant beverages, and you can consume them casually and frequently, depending on the herbs in them, of course. Usually, dried herbs are used to make teas, but freshly harvested plant material works, too. Teas do not store very well, although they can last several days to a week if kept cool, so usually they are prepared right before they are going to be ingested. Since a tea is made by a simple infusion, not by cooking, the best types of herbs to prepare in this manner are delicate plant parts, such as leaves and flowers.

If the plant part in question is tougher or woodier, or if you are trying to extract chemicals that do not easily come out into solution, the best preparation method is known as decoction. This is like a tea, in that hot water is the solvent, but rather than steeping or infusing the herbs in hot or cold water, a decoction involves cooking the herbs and the water together. I like to chop up the plant material, place it in a cooking pot, cover the plant material with enough water so that the plant material is submerged by a couple inches, put a cover on the pot, and bring it to a rolling boil. Then lower the heat and simmer the plant material for at least twenty minutes, or so. This will make a nice decoction. If you are trying to make a strong decoction, continue to simmer until about half the water has boiled away, then strain out the plant material, and drink.

Decoctions taste strong and rich, and some of them can be pretty intense and unpleasant to drink for some people. Decoctions will often keep for a good while if they stay cold, so it is nice to make a bunch at a time and store it in the fridge to dispense as needed. Barks, roots, and woody medicinal shelf mushrooms all need a good decoction to get their medicines out. A decoction is a good preparation method if you are trying to stimulate a strong physiological reaction, since they are so concentrated and you can drink a bunch at once with relative ease. Decoctions can also be cooked all the way down to a paste which can be eaten as is or mixed with a binder like corn starch and taken as pills. The tea pills dispensed by Chinese Medicine practitioners are decoctions that have been dehydrated. Decoctions work well with both fresh and dried herbs.

DRYING HERBS

Many of the medicine making techniques can be utilized with either fresh or dried herbs. I really like to work with herbs when they are still fresh, but it is very simple and satisfying to dry herbs for later use. The main thing with drying herbs is having enough space to do it well, and also enough space to store them. To get the best quality dried herbs, gather them when they are in prime condition and hang them up to dry as soon as possible without bruising or damaging them too much. The aerial parts of plants can be bundled with string and hung up to dry that way. Be careful not to make the bundles too big, or moisture can get trapped in the center, leading to rot. Roots, barks, and mushroom slices are best dried by laying them out on a screen of some sort. Direct sunlight will bleach most herbs and lower their potency and flavor, so it is best to dry them in a warm, dry place in the shade and that has good air flow. Commercial dehydrators can work, but they are often too small to dry very much of anything unless you spend a lot of money on a big one. I have seen very nice solar powered dehydrators that produce beautiful dried herbs but I have not actually worked with one myself to understand how they work. The easiest thing is to hang the herbs up in a shady part of the house until they are dry. You want them to be cracker dry. A stem or fragment of bark should snap cleanly and crisply, and leaves or flowers should easily crumble into a powder by hand.

Once the herbs are dry, store them in an airtight container and keep them away from moisture, sunlight, and extreme heat. Glass is really nice but can take up a lot of space, so plastic bags inside of totes have worked very well for me. Dried herbs can be stored for a year or so for most plants, although some will stay good for years while others will lose some of their charm in only a few months.

Dried herbs can be prepared for consumption by powdering them using a coffee grinder, blender, or heavy-duty commercial grinder. Once powdered, they can be put into capsules for ease of dosing, mixed in with smoothies or yogurt, or mixed with honey to form an electuary, which is like a kind of chewable candy. Dried herbs can also be used to make tinctures, fluid extracts, vinegars, and infused oils. Powdered herbs are excellent for making tinctures through the method of percolation, which is a very quick way to make a strong tincture that I will not get into here.

TINCTURES

A tincture is an extraction of a medicinal herb using ethanol as the solvent. Almost all the medicine I make is in the form of tinctures. You can work with fresh or dried herbs. I prefer to use fresh plant materia, except when the final product would benefit from drying the plant first. Tinctures are nice because they are simple to make, stay good for many years, and are easy to carry around and dispense in their finished form. This also makes them do well inside the pressures of capitalism; they work especially well for people who are too busy to sit down for a cup of tea or to make a decoction. In my experience, a tincture made with freshly harvested plant material gets a certain vitality or spirit that other methods of preparation do not. Overall, there are two basic methods of making a tincture, a "folk" way and a "scientific" way, although I will point out that folk methods are also scientific.

To make a tincture, chop up the herb in question, put it in a jar, cover the plant material with ethanol (or a mixture of ethanol and water), and allow this mixture to macerate for a time. I like to let them macerate for at least one moon cycle (28 days), although in reality, most of mine macerate for much longer. Some people think two weeks is enough. Once your mixture is done macerating, strain out the plant matter (ideally use mechanical force to squeeze all the liquid out, such as a tincture press). Allow it to sit overnight, so that any fine particulates settle to the bottom of the jar. Then decant the tincture off the settled particulate, maybe through a filter, into a brown glass bottle, where you store it until needed.

3

EARLY SPRING MEDICINES OF THE BLACK HILLS

R IGHT AROUND THE EQUINOX, usually a little bit before, as the yang is just starting to rise and the yin is just starting to descend, the landscape is still mostly quiet and still in terms of plant life, although the weather is reflective of the big shift that is happening; there is usually lots and lots of rain, also often rapid fluctuations between rain/Sun/rain, and usually a little bit of snow and hail mixed in. This is the very beginning of the Greening, when the buds start to swell and the perennial herbs barely start to poke their little furled leaves up through the wet soil to begin getting some of what little sunlight is available. At this time of year, when the Sun moves from Pisces into Aries, I like to gather three herbs. These are: Devil's Club (*Oplopanax horridus* or *horridum* depending on who you ask), Western Skunk Cabbage (*Lysichiton americanus*), and Stinging Nettles (*Urtica dioica*). Another herb that I do not find in the woods, but that grows in abundance in the fields on my farm, and is very helpful for this time of year is Dandelion (*Taraxacum officinale*).

BLACK HILLS HISTORY

The main place that I like to go looking for these early Spring herbs is called the Black Hills, a name that has apparently been applied to them since before Europeans lived in this area. The only indigenous name that I have managed to find for these hills comes from a European historian writing in the 1970s who gives the traditional name of the hills as the *Klahle* hills, which means Black hills. These hills are within Chehalis tribal territory, although they have traditionally been worked with by members of the Chehalis, Nisqually, Skookumchuck, Cowlitz, and Quinault tribes. These people have and still do travel into the hills to hunt game such as deer and elk, gather berries and medicinal herbs, and gather materials for the creation of baskets, clothing, and other devices. Since travel was primarily by canoe for these people before the change of the world brought on by the European invasion and the rivers of the Black Hills are very rocky and shallow, they were not a place where there were large gatherings and settlements, although the valleys below were thickly settled especially along the rivers. I am currently waiting to hear from a Chehalis tribal historian so that I can get some more of that history of the area, but I have found some information about the "American" history of these hills.

In terms of geology, the Black Hills are a small range that are a part of a coastal range of hills that include the Willapa hills to the South, which are named after the Willapa tribe who, as far as I can tell, are no longer in existence. This range of hills, which some have called mountains but they are not very tall, the tallest of the peaks in the Black hills being Capitol Peak which is some 2,664 feet, are thought to have been created during the same seismic events that also created the Olympic mountains to the North, and are thus some fifty million years old. Micro fossils of sea life have been found at the top of Capitol Peak, thus showing that this land was under the sea perhaps several times over the course of history.

The prevailing westerly winds that come in from the Pacific Ocean hit the Black hills and rise over them, resulting in lots of precipitation (some forty to sixty inches of rain per year, at least in the early '70s, and often two to four feet of snow in the upper reaches, although warming weather has caused there to be less snow for the past several years as of this writing in March of 2020). This weather pattern causes there to be almost constant shifting cloud patterns above and around the hills, which combined with the dark forests upon their slopes gives them a darkened appearance, hence the name. The waters from the Black hills end up primarily in the Chehalis river, named for the Chehalis tribe who still live and work upon with that river to this day.

One tributary of the Chehalis river is the Black river, which runs right behind my house and this river is indeed very dark in color all year long, for reasons that I have not yet worked out. The well on the farm upon which I live is basically full of water that comes from the Black Hills, and I will be forever grateful to them for that. East of the Black Hills, there are many prairie ecosystems, which are slightly drier than much of the surrounding rain forest and are home to many unique and precious species of plant. The coastal range composed of the Black and Willapa hills plays a role in the creation of a slight rain shadow which enables these ecosystems to thrive, and of course the hills also push out a lot of the moisture in the air that comes in from the Pacific Ocean in the form of precipitation on their Western side, which results in the lush coastal forests that live all along the coasts in these areas.

The history of "American" involvement with the Black Hills begins in the late 1800s, around 1870, when the first timber claims were made by European immigrants as part of a massive land grab that was taking place all over what was then called "Oregon Territory." The federal government of the United States was essentially giving away the land that truly belonged to no one but itself, and if anything belonged and belongs to the Indigenous peoples of the area who have lived upon it for so long, in a series of Acts including the Donation Land Claim Act of 1850, which allowed any white, male US citizen to claim 350 acres of land and later on the Homestead Act of 1863 which allowed any white male citizen to claim 160 acres. The farm where I currently live was claimed by the Rutledge family under the Donation Land Claim Act, and the farmhouse in which I am writing this was built in 1862 by the Rutledge family. Like the Rutledge's, mostly people claimed the rich lands in the valleys and eschewed the lands in the hills as too hard to work with, as the idea was that people were creating farms and homesteads, but some people began to claim the land upon the hills simply to harvest the standing timber, which was beautiful old growth, and sell it. In 1880, and

I really wish I could find more information about this, there was apparently a Utopian society who came from Brooklyn, New York, who took up residence in the Black Hills, who did not last much more than one winter.

Intensive logging of the forests began in the 1880s and 1890s and really ramped up right around the turn of the century when three brothers, Tom, Joe, and Leo Bordeaux, bought up quite a lot of the land in and around the Black Hills and began a large logging operation called the Mason County Logging Company. They built a series of railroads snaking throughout the hills, and also built the logging town of Bordeaux, which still exists as a ghost town on Bordeaux Road, a bit South of the Black Hills. I like to pick Nettles there. At its peak in the 1920s and 1930s, Bordeaux was home to some 300–400 people, mostly male loggers but also many families. There was a main house where the Bordeaux family lived, a company hotel for single men, a series of houses for families, a central sawmill with a dry kiln, and massive log yards for storing the fallen timber. The railroads ran from Bordeaux to the town of Malone, which was also a logging town. The Bordeaux operation logged some fifty thousand acres of old growth forest, a great loss to the land. Luckily they left one small area of standing old growth, these days called "Old Fuzzy Top," which was too steep and difficult to log. This area later provided the seed for the replanting of the forests. All the logging resulted in huge piles of slash everywhere, which then dried out and essentially became huge piles of tinder. This coupled with the sparks generated by the railroad and the many camp fires that the workers used to keep warm while they were out in the fields as well as the tendency for farmers to just burn the huge trees in "their" fields since it was too hard to cut them down, resulted in many massive and devastating forest fires. There was a huge one in 1902 and another in 1941 that swept all up and down the West Coast. The smoke was thick from Northern California to British Columbia, and apparently it was gloomy and almost as dark as night in Seattle during the daytime during these fires.

Following this period of intense logging and uncontrolled fires (very different from the controlled burns that the tribes had done in the area to keep the underbrush clear for millennia, which was a benefit to the landscape) the town of Bordeaux was abandoned, finally becoming a ghost town by the early 1940s. During the 1930s, following the Great Depression, there was a move all across the country to "reforest" areas that had been essentially destroyed by exploitative logging practices, and the Black Hills were a part of that effort. "Washington State" bought over 33,000 acres of logged and burned-over land in the early 1930s. This would later expand to over 70,000 acres over the years. The land was paid for largely through government bonds. In 1933 Mike Webster and O.B. Wedekind found an old farmstead while searching through the area for places where roads could be built, and decided that this would be an excellent place to begin a nursery to grow out tree seedlings, to regrow the forest. The farm was built by the Civilian Conservation Corps in 1934 and the first crop of 1,250,000 Doug firs were planted by CCC members in 1936. Another nursery was later developed, and over ten million seedlings have been produced in these nurseries since that time, many of which were planted in the Black Hills. Once the CCC was disbanded in the 1940s, soldiers who were training in the forests and also volunteer high school boys took over the plantings. In 1956 the Cedar Creek Corrections Camp was first established, which was a juvenile detention center. From then until today the majority of the planting, thinning, and fire fighting within Capitol Forest, which is basically synonymous with the Black Hills, has been done by prison labor. These people work mostly for no pay, or for extremely little pay. You could call this slave labor. Today the Cedar Creek Corrections Center is a minimum security prison which houses 480 males at any one time. A friend of mine was incarcerated there, which is how I originally learned that the majority of the plantings done in the forest these days are done by prison labor.

EARLY SPRING PLANTS

Wandering through some of the woods in the Black Hills, you would not think that less than one hundred years ago the entire area was a logged out and burned-over landscape. The Black Hills in general, and especially the parts of the hills that have been designated Capitol Forest and are allowed to remain standing forests (much of Capitol Forest is being logged or is in a state of clear cut at any one time, but they hide the clear cuts from where most people hike), are beautiful lush forest full of a variety of plant species. Indeed, the Black Hills are the place where I have seen the most Devil's Club (*Oplopanax horridum*) out of all the places that I have traveled. I actually think that the disturbed and often cut nature of the Black Hills has led to Devil's Club really moving in for a variety of reasons.

Oplopanax is one of my favorite medicine plants, and they are one of the first ones that I ever worked with that led to big changes in my body and in my life. Once you have met *Oplopanax* it is hard to forget them; they really take up space and have a strong presence in the forest. This plant most often likes to grow on steep slopes above rivers or streams or otherwise wet places. The plant is hard to miss because they are basically huge spindly branches that are entirely covered in sharp spines. Often the first way that a person meets this plant is by accidentally reaching out to grab one of the branches while falling down on a slope, and the tremendous pain really makes the plant stick in your memory! *Oplopanax* is in the Araliaceae family of plants, along with Asian and American Ginseng (*Panax ginseng, P. quinquefolius*), Eleuthero, i.e., Siberian Ginseng (*Eleutherococcus senticosus*), Spikenard (*Aralia californica, A. racemosa*), and Ivy (*Hedera helix*). Like many of these plants, *Oplopanax* is a nice tonic remedy with an affinity for the lungs, which is how I first became interested in them as a medicine.

I was born prematurely to the point that I was still at the very end of my second trimester when I came out of my Mama. At the time in history in which I was born (1984), being this premature had just stopped being an almost guaranteed death sentence, but many people who were born this early still died or ended up with lifelong complications. One of the issues with being born so prematurely is that the lungs are not very well developed yet, especially that they have not yet developed a liquid called surfactant that lubricates the inner surfaces of the lungs and keeps them from sticking to one another upon exhalation. When I was born I did not have adequate surfactant, and so my lungs did not work properly, and as a result of this, I was put on a ventilator, which is a machine that essentially pushes air into and out of the lungs for the first several weeks of my life. I am told that I would fight the machine, so they had to sedate me with morphine and atropine so that my lungs would not be further damaged (which I think ties in to my deep love of drugs and altered states later in life, that some might have called drug addiction, but that is a separate story). Bless these machines and the health workers who ran them, since I would have died without them, but as a result of working with this ventilator, my little lungs were damaged which led to scarring, which led to me being pretty severely asthmatic during my childhood and into adulthood. Asthma attacks are very scary and anxiety inducing, and there is a strong connection between asthmatic symptoms and fear/ anxiety, at least for me. I was pretty heavily medicated with albuterol which is a beta2-adrenergic agonist that relaxes the smooth muscles of the lungs thus reducing the severity of or stopping entirely an asthma attack. Perhaps you have seen or used an albuterol inhaler, which also has the brand name Ventolin. Albuterol is a wonderful medicine, and I am so grateful for it, but it also has a bunch of short term side effects such as racing heart, sweating, heart palpitations, anxiety, insomnia, tremors, occasional worsening of asthma symptoms, and very rarely heart attack. Albuterol shares some molecular similarities with amphetamine and adrenaline, and I think that long term use of albuterol can be exhausting to the human animal much in the same way that using other stimulants very frequently over the long term can lead to general exhaustion. This exhaustion could also be looked at from a Chinese medicine standpoint as kidney yin deficiency, or from a Western kinda New Age health view point as adrenal fatigue. Some of the signs and symptoms of kidney yin deficiency include many of the short term side effects of albuterol such as excessive sweating (especially at night), a racing heart, palpitations, anxiety, and insomnia. So it is my belief that my lifelong dependence on albuterol, while it saved my life in many ways, led to a gradual weakening of my kidneys (in a TCM sense) that actually made my asthma symptoms worse, and also contributed to some mental health issues that I dealt with. I wonder if the inhalation of the molecule also has a negative effect on the fluids in the lungs.

When I was in my early twenties I still had pretty bad asthma. I was a tobacco smoker at this time which did not help. This was before we had anything like the Affordable Care Act (Obamacare) in the "United States of America," and I was broke and no longer covered by my parent's health insurance, so I ran out of albuterol and could not get it regularly, although my Mama (bless her) would mail me some when she could. Uncontrolled asthma is very unpleasant and led to me not getting much sleep since I often got attacks at night and would drink black coffee to stop the attack, which works very well but does not help one to get back to sleep afterwards. My partner at the time read in some book, and I have never found this book again, that Devil's Club was good for asthma. We were living in a little shack in the woods next to a ravine that was filled with *Oplopanax*. We picked some, which was my first time wild crafting a plant medicine, and made a tincture. The tincture worked very well for me. It did not stop an asthma attack quite as quickly as albuterol, which is almost instant, but it would reliably stop the attack, often after ten or fifteen minutes, often accompanied by me coughing up a bunch of phlegm. This was my first experience of having an herbal medicine really work as well as a western medicine, and I took *Oplopanax* all the time. Unlike albuterol, however, *Oplopanax* is a building tonic which helped me to regain some of the life force that I had lost during my years with albuterol and other stimulants, bringing in some of the moisture that was lost, and reducing my general inflammation levels. Part of the medicine of *Oplopanax* is very protective. In many Coast Salish cultures *Oplopanax* is thought of as a very sacred plant and as a protective plant. It is clear that this plant is a guardian of the forests and the rivers, as an *Oplopanax* patch is difficult to walk into unless you are careful around all the spines.

I mentioned earlier how my asthma had a strong emotional component, one that traces, I imagine, all the way back to my tiny baby self, who was very scared while being trapped in a plastic box with a tube in his mouth forcing air in and out of his lungs and being mostly kept away from his Mama. I carried that fear and that anxiety, which came out also as depression and feeling as if I was not really worthy of being alive, all throughout my life. Working with *Oplopanax* helped me to feel safe and to feel worthy, to feel protected even in my most vulnerable parts. Anyway, as a result of all this I slowly stopped having asthmatic symptoms, to the point that I did not need to take *Oplopanax* or albuterol anymore for many years. These days I still have occasional asthmatic symptoms around the Equinoxes, which I deal with sometimes with herbs and sometimes with albuterol. I will be forever grateful to this plant, they really started me on the path of becoming an herbalist. I still work with *Oplopanax*, mostly in formulation but also sometimes just in drop doses. They told me a while ago that they were no longer my protector and that I had grown enough to be able to protect myself and others, but it feels good to invite them in to catch up anyways. I hope this personal story gives you an idea of how the plants can change us, and an idea of the medicine of *Oplopanax*.

There is more about this plant than this, of course. *Oplopanax* is most often worked with as a lung tonic and expectorant, meaning that they help to loosen up stuck mucus in the lungs and move it up and out. They can be helpful in treating asthma, as well as for chronic smokers and people with impaired lung function of all sorts. This plant also has a tonic aspect, much like the other members of the Araliaceae family. Working with them over time is building, and seems to have a beneficial influence on the immune system and inflammation in the body. This can be seen in the reduction of my own asthmatic symptoms and also in the traditional use of this plant for arthritic pains, such as rheumatoid arthritis. This plant is worked with, especially in indigenous communities around me, to treat diabetes. They can be helpful to lower blood sugar levels and generally to balance a person's blood sugar. I generally find *Oplopanax* to be warming and stimulating, kind of yang-y, which is in balance to the often cold, damp, and dark places where they like to live, but some authors and herbalists classify this herb as cooling and moistening, and in many ways I can see the moistening aspect because of how the herb works in the body. I like to balance out *Oplopanax*, who can sometimes be pushy or harsh in their workings with humans, with something like Hawthorn (*Crataegus monogyna*) or Rose (*Rosa spp.*). I also like a simple pairing of Devil's Club and Licorice, which to me feels a lot like an analog for the heavily over harvested American Ginseng (*Panax quinquefolius*).

I used to think that *Oplopanax* only grew in the deep and primeval forests before I realized that most of the forests that I move around in are second or third growth forests, meaning that they have been cut down several times. I am starting to see that in many ways *Oplopanax* actually likes to live in somewhat disturbed areas such as the sides of rivers where trees fall over all the time, so that they can get some sunlight. The Black Hills, which as I have described have been heavily disturbed over the years, are amazingly abundant in this plant. They grow along the creek and often right along the roads. I think that the *Oplopanax* is working hard to try and protect these brutalized forests who are working so hard and bravely to grow back into themselves again. *Oplopanax* is a pretty slow growing plant. An individual stalk will grow maybe three to six inches per year, sometimes a foot. The plant spreads by seeds, often after the birds have eaten the berries and pooped out the seeds in a new place, but the most common way that this plants spreads is by layering, which is a method of vegetative propagation in which the stems will grow up towards the sky, then fall over into the wet soil and leaf litter, often on top of logs or under fallen logs that have landed on them. The stem that is lying on the ground will lose all the spines that had been on their bark, and root out from the nodes. We call these rooted stems *recumbent stems*. New upright stems will then arise from these recumbent stems, only to fall over and root themselves, and etc. until the *Oplopanax* plant comes to sometimes fill an entire ravine or creek side. We can help the plant to propagate themselves by leaning over upright stems and placing something heavy things on them so they can root, or I have also had some success planting out hardwood cuttings from the upright stems at the time of harvest.

There is some valid concern about *Oplopanx* being over harvested. While they are abundant where I live, and also in the northern part of their range (extending from Northern California to Alaska), to the point that I know that many landscapers in Alaska hate *Oplopanax* because they always have to deal with their spiny selves in the gardens that the landscapers are trying to work, *Oplopanax* only lives in a small region when you consider the whole world, and has not really taken to being grown in gardens or commercially. For a while *Oplopanax* was marketed as "Alaskan Ginseng" which broadened the herb's appeal to a mass market, and within my own herbalism community *Oplopanax* is generally considered a cool or interesting plant. Many of my teachers have really loved this plant, which is part of what drew my teachers and I towards one another. If *Oplopanax* was to become a hot herb on a global level, I would really worry about them, like if they ended up being featured on Gwenyth Paltrow's "The Goop Lab," or something like this, it could be a disaster. I acknowledge that I have spread my love for this plant far and wide, and I hope itwill not lead to the damage of the populations of *Oplopanax*. I try really hard to teach people how to propagate this plant, and I make sure to propagate this plant every year, ideally with several students or friends in tow. The best method I have found with cuttings is this: in the Fall, around the Equinox, go out to the *Oplopanax* patches and cut a few nice healthy upright stems off of a larger plant. Shoot for six feet tall. Make sure that you are cutting above a node and that you have a good knowledge of how to safely prune plants before you do this, or ideally do it with someone who knows what they are doing. Use a digging bar to make a very deep and narrow hole in the muddy earth next to a river. Cut the bottom of the cutting at an angle for maximum surface exposure and also so it is sharp and will penetrate the earth, and push it halfway into the hole, so three feet deep at least. I suggest doing this near the original stand of *Oplopanax* so that the stand can help the new cutting to survive. I have had cuttings planted in this method that have survived for three years so far and are doing well. Planting in the Spring has not been as successful for me because they fry in the Summertime drought. If you plant in the Fall then they get watered all Winter while they root and then can grow well when it warms up. To put my money where my mouth is, I am not going to say how to harvest this plant in this piece of writing. Some things are better transmitted directly from person to person and I would encourage you to seek out someone who knows how to do this in a good way (or honestly there are many other books that will tell you how). Sometimes it is best to remain silent about some things!

Another plant that grows in great abundance in many parts of the Black Hills are the Stinging Nettles *(Urtica dioica)*. They grow all throughout the old Bordeaux ghost town, in some cases growing through the cracks of the old fallen down buildings. I wonder if the people who were living there transplanted the Nettles to the site as an easy to access source of food, or if the Nettles came in later, after the soil was all churned up and presumably fertilized by the presence of humans and other animals who were pooping there. I pick the Nettles at this site, although I have thought about the fact that there were a series of railroads coming and going from this site, and railroads are notoriously toxic sites, often having had lots of petrochemicals and heavy metals dropped on them over the years. I mostly try to stay away from the places where the railroad clearly was, and also I think that picking at a site were there was a railroad some eighty years ago that has not been in operation since then, and only moved logs around for one logging operation, is a very different thing than picking Nettles alongside a currently operating railroad, which is really asking for trouble since Nettles bio accumulate metals within their beings. I have also been interacting with Nettles for many years, they grew right outside of the front door of the aforementioned shack that I was living in when I first started working with *Oplopanax*. Nettles are nice like that, in that they are somewhat camp followers who often show up in and around the places where humans live. They like edges where there is some shade and also some sunlight, and they like the extra nutrients (whether these are nitrogen from poo or other various chemicals) that humans often end up putting into the soil around where they live. You can often find Nettles growing at the edges of old farm fields, especially along the sides of old barns, which provide shade from the Sun in the otherwise open agricultural fields and collect rainwater on their sides and roofs which get funneled down to the Nettle patches on the side of the barn. If there are (or ever were) animals kept in the barn, then this provides the extra fertilizer that really helps the Nettles to thrive.

Nettles are first and foremost a wonderfully nutritious food. They come up pretty early in the Spring and are one of the first wild foods that you can gather in large amounts. They are rich in protein, iron, potassium, a great many other minerals, and vitamins A and D. While I mildly despise this term, you could certainly consider Nettles to be a "super food." They wake the body up when eaten or drank as a Spring tonic, and are always valuable for people low in iron. They provide a deep nutrition, and a special type of energy that is quite different from the feeling provided by a stimulant such as caffeine.

Nettles are a perennial plant that spread by rhizome throughout loose and fertile soil where they can get good amounts of water. They stand about three feet tall although in late Summer they can get to be up to six feet tall or more when they go to seed. The young plants are a beautiful purple color when they just start coming up out of the soil in the very early Spring, often around Imbolc. The purple color gradually fades and the entire plant becomes a vibrant green color. The leaves are oppositely carried upon the tough stems, have serrated margins, and can get as large as a small child's hand. The entire plant is covered with bristly hairs, and among these hairs are a number of silica structures that are the stingers, which are botanically known as spicules, which are a type of trichrome. Most of the stingers are on the underside of the leaves, at least that is my experience of them. These stingers will sting you! They function somewhat like tiny hypodermic syringes, and upon making contact with the skin they both cause mechanical irritation since the tips break off and become lodged in the flesh, and also they inject a very interesting chemical cocktail into it which causes a further chemical irritation. Among the many compounds that are found in the stings of Nettles are several chemicals that I know best as neurotransmitters and hormones within the human body, including serotonin, histamine, choline, and acetylcholine. You may be familiar with histamine as a compound that is involved in many allergic reactions within the body, hence the use of antihistamines such as Benadryl (diphenhydramine hcl) for seasonal allergies. Serotonin is a major human neurotransmitter that is often though of in a very simplified way as the "happiness neurotransmitter" ever since the creation of SSRIs (Selective Serotonin Reuptake Inhibitors) as a class of antidepressant drugs (Prozac is an example of these), however it plays a variety of roles within the human organism, including being involved in some forms of inflammation. The sting also contains formic acid, a compound which is found in the stings of many species of biting ants and also our local stinging jellyfish, the Lion's Mane (*Cyanea capillata*).

The combination of the mechanical and chemical irritants on the human body is often to create a painful burning/stinging sensation, often accompanied by reddening of the skin and a rash of small bumps. This is technically called *urtication* and is actually utilized in a medicinal context traditionally and contemporarily all over the world. Many people have found that intentionally stinging themselves with Nettles can help with underlying chronic pains in the body such as arthritic pain, or the pain from old or current injuries. This is known as *counterirritation*, and it works by bringing blood flow to the area in question (this is what causes the reddening of the skin) which helps to move things around and clear out debris from the area since lymph and immune cells are also brought to the area. Intentional urtication can be helpful for various chronic pains, in some cases bringing long lasting relief. It is also just a nice springtime wake up ritual to sting yourself with Nettles, or to have a friends sting you with Nettles in the form of a "nettle flogging" or something like this.

The irritation gets the blood moving and really wakes you up. I like to allow the Nettles to sting me every time I pick, and I have at various stages of my life rolled in a Nettle patch and had a friend flog me with Nettles. This practice is remarkably helpful for depression, or feelings of being stagnant or stuck, the pain really takes your mind off of your troubles and brings you into the moment.

In terms of internal medicinal use, Nettles are a nice and reliable diuretic, meaning that they encourage the release of urine from the body. This action by itself can be helpful in conditions where there is swelling and edema present in the body, and also helps to flush out built up uric acid, which is helpful in general inflammation and especially conditions such as gout, a painful buildup of uric acid crystals in the feet. Other nitrogenous waste products are also flushed out, which can benefit conditions like arthritis or eczema. Nettles shares this property, which can also be called *blood cleansing*, with several other herbs such as burdock, yellow dock, and Oregon grape. All these herbs are considered *alteratives*. An alterative basically helps to treat these types of conditions such as arthritis, eczema, liver stagnation, and other skin disorders. Nettles are also a nice astringent and inflammation reliever for the whole body, especially for the urinary tract where it can help alleviate painful urination, whether due to an infections or simply inflamed tissues. Nettles are not themselves antimicrobial, so if the painful urination is caused by an infection you would need to work with an antimicrobial herb to deal with that. Oregon Grape comes to mind. One of the more common modern reasons to work with Nettles is for seasonal allergies. I have found that the best method for doing this work is to use a tincture of the fresh plant, to start taking it *before* one's seasonal allergies start, and to take large doses frequently throughout the allergy season. Nettle seeds are largely thought of as a kidney and adrenal tonic, and the root can be worked with to lessen inflammation of the prostate in people who are living with that condition, often helping to allow the urine to flow and to lessen the constant feeling that you really need to pee, but nothing will come out.

Nettles are a great example of a martial plant, meaning a plant that is ruled by or under the influence of the planet Mars. I will not get deep into astrology or correspondences, but a big part of alchemical workings with the plants involves these correspondences between the plants and the planets. The planet Mars is thought of as a warlike, forceful planet whose traditional metal is iron. Nettles are very pushy in the way that they grow throughout an area, have the stings, and are very rich in iron.

While it is easy to gather Nettles in abundance without harming the patch by simply gathering the aerial parts early in the season, being sure to snip off the tip right above a node so that the plant can push out new growing tips as the season progresses. It is a nice practice to transplant a bit from a Nettle patch into your garden if you can. It is easy: just go to a Nettle patch while the plant is dormant (Fall through early Spring) and dig up some of the roots. They are long threadlike or rope-like rhizomes. Snip these at nodes, and plant them in your garden in an area with some Sun, some shade. They will flourish with almost no care at all and the patch will happily expand to the point where you will probably need to thin it, then you can start a patch at a friend's house or in a public area so that people can gather the plant for food.

Another plant that I would like to talk about that lives up in the Black Hills, but actually more like in the lowlands in the muddy spots by the rivers, is Western Skunk Cabbage (*Lysichiton americanus*). This is a beautiful and unique plant, and one of the first plants to bloom in the very early Spring, when the huge yellow flowers are like hooded sentinels watching over the swamps and the rivers. It is easy to identify by breaking a bit off of one of its giant leaves, which will give off a skunky smell. Bears eat the roots of this plant in the early Spring as a cathartic laxative which helps them to clear out all of their accumulated poop and other wastes so that they can shake off hibernation and get ready for the warm season. Individual plants are perennial and can live to be quite old. The plants in general have an ancient and wise feel to them. Harvesting Skunk Cabbage root, which is the part that is worked with as a medicine, is a very difficult process since you have to get down in the freezing cold muddy water in order to be able to get them up and out of it. It is tricky since of the many parts of the rooting structures underground, only the central root makes a workable medicine, which in many cases is a very small amount of material. The abundant rootlets that surround this central root are rich in calcium oxalate, as are the leaves. Calcium oxalate essentially is in a crystalline form in the plant that feels like tiny shards of glass in your mouth if you ingest it. I once had a pleasantly humbling experience early in my teaching career when I was introducing a group of people to Skunk Cabbage. I like to taste the plants when I am talking about them, and if I can I like to also have the people who are listening to me taste the plants. Often I will give out drop doses of the tincture so that we can all get a *feel* for the plant during the lecture. Sometimes I will eat a small bit of the plant in question, and one time while I was talking to a group of people out in a swamp, I casually picked a bit of the Skunk Cabbage leaf and started chewing on it. My mouth promptly began to burn and feel like it was full of fiberglass, and the lecture was delayed for quite awhile as I frantically tried to wash my mouth out with water, to no avail as only time relieves the sting. The small rootlets will also produce this sting, but the central root is not stingy and is rich in a beautiful thick mucilage, which is the medicine you want.

The problem for me is that it is really difficult to tell which plants have large central roots. Often times when I choose a nice plant with large leaves and a few flowering stalks, after taking all the time and effort (and kill this beautiful and old plant in the process) to get the central root out of the muck, it is only the size of my thumb and maybe weighs 20 grams fresh. I have learned that it is best to dig a small trench in the mud next to the plant and feel with your hand for the central

root *before* you start to dig it up. Some of them have nice and
large central roots, and the harvest is worth it, both to me and
(I hope) to the stand of plants. There is no way to lever the
root out of the muck like you can with most terrestrial root
medicines. You have to dig a trench all the way around the
plant in the cold muddy water, then get in there with your
hands and release the many, many rootlets from the surrounding muck and then lift the plant out. The roots look like an
ancient squid type creature and are very beautiful.

I first learned about the medicine of this plant during a
blind plant tasting, which is one of my favorite ways to figure
out how the plants do their work in our bodies. A blind plant
tasting is simply taking a small amount of an unlabeled tincture, ideally with a group of friends, and then sitting quietly
and feeling into your self to try and understand what the plant
is doing. This can sometimes give visions, or be somatic experiences, some people hear things, etc. A friend of mine, who
would later become my partner and the mother of my child,
and I were doing a plant sit just the two of us. We had taken
a plant a few minutes before which had left both of us feeling
amped up in an unpleasant way, kind of edgy and shitty. We
almost called off the rest of the session but decided to take this
other plant. Upon taking our drops we both felt a deep sense
of calm and ease, loosening up the muscles in out bodies and
also relaxing our minds (not that there is really a difference
between these two things, the body/mind split is an Enlightenment fable, of course). I was surprised when I read the label
and saw that it was Skunk Cabbage, who I mostly thought

of as a lung medicine. When I got home that day I did some reading in the older Eclectic literature and found a reference to the Eastern Skunk Cabbage (*Symplocarpus foetidus*), which is analogous in many ways to the Western species in terms of medicinal effects, and found that it was used as a lung remedy, yes, and also as a strong nervine and antispasmodic, meaning calming to the nervous system and loosening to the muscles.

So perhaps my description above has given you a picture of the medicinal actions of this plant, but to be clear I will delineate them here. This plant primarily acts upon the lungs. They are a nice expectorant while also loosening the muscles around the lungs, which can be helpful in asthmatic type symptoms, which have a strong muscular tension component, but also is nice for a dry, spastic, and non-productive cough, since loosening up the muscles around the lungs will help to calm the cough. Even in a person who is not actively sick, working with Skunk Cabbage will help one to take nice, easy breaths, and make breathing feel good in a way that is hard to describe. Stephen Harrod Buhner has a very beautiful description of his experience working with this plant in his lovely book *The Secret Teachings of Plants*, and I would suggest you read the whole thing, which is the prologue to the *Diastole* part of that book, but I will just quote him here on his take on working with this tincture:

> The taste is sweet, earthy, airy. The tincture is mucilaginous, softly coating to the tongue. It moves through the mucous membranes of the tongue and then the breath

comes deeper; a wild, powerful joy surges through the body. It seems as if you can run for miles, without being short of breath, without your lungs puffing-bellows at the end. (128)

Skunk Cabbage is also nicely moistening, which can be good for irritated lungs, and I feel could be nice for bodily pain of a dried out and constrictive nature, dried up and tightened atrophied muscles that could benefit from both the moistening and the antispasmodic action. I work with this medicine only rarely, primarily because it feels precious and is such a difficult harvest both on me and on the plants. I also do not know of a good way to propagate this plant, and until I can learn a reliable way to give back to this plant in that very important way, by helping them to be more abundant out in the world rather than only reducing their populations, I will be very scarce in my working with this medicine. Skunk Cabbage is a *very* nice plant to go and sit with, and ask them to talk with you or give them some of your medicine in a non-physical kind of way, and that is mostly how I work with them.

The final plant that I would like to discuss is not one that I generally find up in the hills, although I imagine that they probably grow in great abundance in some parts of the Black Hills, such as the clear cuts and the open meadows that exist up there. This plant is a wonderful remedy for this time of year (Spring), which within a specific form of Chinese Medicine called Traditional Chinese Medicine is associated with the liver, the gallbladder, the Wood element, the color green, anger, and shouting. This plant is called Dandelion (*Taraxacum officinale*), which is derived from the French *dent de lion* or from the Medieval Latin *dens liones*, both of which translate to "tooth of the lion," from the toothed appearance of the leaf margins. I find the parallel between the Chinese Spring anger/ shouting correspondence with the time of year in which this plant blooms and the common name being associated with a fierce part of a fierce animal to be interesting. Dandelions, by the way, have been worked with as a medicine within TCM for millennia. **Dandelion** is a very widespread and abundant plant. It is considered a "noxious weed" by many people, and many suburban Dads (and of course so many other people) have spent so much of their lives in battle against the humble yet mighty Dandelion in order to gain the mythical "perfect lawn," that it has entered the realm of comic strips and internet memes. I would first of all discourage anyone from killing the Dandelions in their yard, primarily because this plant is one of the first widespread and abundant flowers to bloom, especially around where I live, and is therefore an important source of nectar for the

various bees that live in the area. Bee species across the world are in decline, and the fate of the world as we know it really rests on the fate of the bees and the other pollinating insects, so please do not pull (and dear Goddess please do not use glyphosate/Round Up on) the Dandelions!

Along with the bees, Dandelions are also a great food for humans. They are perennial plants with deep taproots which produce a rosette of deeply toothed, dark green leaves and a number of beautiful yellow flowers. All parts of the plant are edible, but especially the leaves are prized as a bitter green that is rich in many nutrients including vitamins A, D, and K, potassium, iron, and manganese, among others. The greens can be harvested from the same plant year after year, and as long as the taproot is not bothered the plant will survive and keep producing food. The greens are very bitter which some people view as a detriment, but many people's diets, especially those following the Standard American Diet (SAD), which is full of salt, sugar, and bland tasting vegetables, are actually deficient in the bitter flavor. Bitters have a beneficial influence of the digestive system as a whole, specifically they stimulate the release of digestive enzymes and bile from the gallbladder which help to digest the food in the stomach. The bitter flavor also is stimulating and beneficial to the liver, and often helps to move foods through the lower digestive tract, resulting in more frequent bowel movements in some people, especially those who are chronically constipated. This side effect of eating the leaves is a big part of their use as a medicine, same for the root which is perhaps the most prized part of the plant medicinally. The leaves are also nicely diuretic. The root is even more bitter than the leaves, and functions well as a simple bitter. It is also rich in inulin, a polysaccharide that is not digestible by the human animal and serves as a rich source of fiber in the digestive tract, while also serving as food to the microbial organisms that live within the gut and are crucial to the health of the organism as a whole. I like to dig the Dandelions while they are in full bloom, and tincture the leaves, flowers, and root all together. This tincture is very nice to work with in the Springtime when people are moving from eating richer foods and being less physically active to being more active and eating lighter foods. Working with Dandelion at this time of year (or any time) helps to get the digestion going which then supports the person in general. Dandelion is also considered an alterative, like Nettles, and can be helpful at any time of year for people who are living with skin conditions or achy joints, many of which benefit from liver stimulation to help and process some of the waste materials that are involved in these conditions.

The flowers of Dandelions can be battered and fried, which is kind of good and also a little weird/bitter, but people like to do it. It is also a nice Spring ritual to gather Dandelion flowers to make Dandelion wine. Since you do not use any of the green parts of the flowers, only the yellow petals, it takes quite a lot of Dandelion flowers and a lot of work processing them to make a little bit of Dandelion wine, but the final product (which traditionally has citrus peel and other carminative spices in it), is a very nice medicinal product in and of itself. I used to participate in an annual Dandelion wine making party in which we would drink the wine from the previous year, which really helps the workflow.

Propagation of Dandelions is hardly necessary, as they are so abundant and weedy, but it is a very simple process that many children do every day in the Spring and early Summer. Once the yellow flowers have been fertilized, they transform into these beautiful puff balls, and it is a tradition in many cultures that if you blow all of the seeds off of the Dandelion then you are granted a wish. This act is a very nice one, and ensures an abundant crop of Dandelions every year.

This period of the year is very brief, and often hard in a lot of ways. I find that I am often grumpy at this time of year in the same way that I can be grumpy upon trying to wake up after a nice long sleep. It is hard to shake off the Wintertime sleepies and begin to engage with the world again, but going out into the wilds, or into your garden, and interacting with the medicines really helps. While you may not do this work in the Black Hills, it is important to find a place near where you live, get to know it, learn its history, and work with it in a way that feels good and beautiful.

4

ON THE IMPORTANCE OF KEEPING A GARDEN, AND A BIT ABOUT BARKS (MIDDLE SPRING)

HISTORY

As the wheel turns and we move deeper into Spring, with some peeks of Summer here and there, it becomes time to start thinking about the garden. Humans have been keeping gardens for a long time, many thousands of years, and depending on how you define the term "agriculture" the history could be thought of as much older than that. Basically, once humans learned how to help the plants that they liked to eat or work with as medicine to become more abundant in any one place, I would define that as the beginnings of gardening and agriculture. One of the nice things about the plant/human relationship is that in many ways humans help some plants to become more abundant simply by interacting with them. Some examples of this include plants like Burdock (*Arctium lappa*), a lovely herb which has long and abundant roots that humans like to eat, work with medicinally, and make beers out of, and Camas (*Camassia quamash*) which is a beautiful blue flowered plant which has edible bulbs that have been and are still a staple of the diet of many peoples living on Turtle Island. Both of these plants will become more abundant on a landscape simply by humans interacting with them in order to eat them. Burdock has seed pods that are covered with burrs or prickly hooks that can very easily catch and hold onto hair, fur, skin, or clothes. These burrs exist upon the plant to aid in seed dispersal via the animals that move around much faster than the plants do, such as humans. When humans first started to interact with this plant in order to eat it, they inadvertently helped the plant to become more abundant on the landscape since it is very difficult to interact with this plant without spreading their seeds all over the place. Such interactions would have resulted in the plant moving closer to the places where the humans were sleeping or maybe even living full time, as humans tend to groom themselves best once they get back to where they are going to sleep, so a lot of the seeds would have ended up on the ground where the humans in question liked to spend most of their time (which may have been a temporary camp that they would return to since humans are tradionarilly migratory animals) and once they germinated and established themselves there, I would argue that you could call that a garden. It is much easier to have your food and medicine plants growing right next to where you sleep rather than a few miles walk away (although walking is nice), humans would come to realize. This process of domestication went both ways, with the plants coming to enjoy living in the gardens of humans since they were actively tended by them, and with humans coming to enjoy tending plants in a garden as opposed to always needing to go out and hunt for them. There have been some downside for both groups due to domestication but overall I think it has been beneficial (although don't get me started on industrial agriculture).

Camas is another plant that benefits from human interaction, and is a good example of a type of agriculture that was basically invisible to researchers and anthropologists who were of European or Anglo-Saxon or whatever you want to call that lineage (White? "Enlightenment" thinking? WASP? Cartesian?) up until the late 1900s, since it was and is so different from how those people understood agriculture. Indeed, as Nancy Turner says in her seminal book *Keeping It Living*, which is about agriculture in the tribes of the Pacific Northwest of Turtle Island ("USA"): "From the earliest anthropological research on the Northwest Coast of North America to the present day, there has been little debate as to whether the peoples of this region cultivated plants. Most scholars have accepted that they did not" (3). Of course, the tribes in question do cultivate plants, and work with the entire landscape in a way that benefits the plants and animals they like to have around, and they have done this for millennia. This method of agriculture, or

gardening if you will, is I think a much more evolved one and is not based around walls, hedges, enclosures, or plowing, while still acknowledging that specific lineages of humans had the right to work with specific patches of plants. Camas is a great example of how people have and continue to keep wild gardens in simple and complex ways. *Camassia quamash* is a beautiful blue flowered plant in the *Asparagaceae* family that once upon a time was remarkably abundant all across the Western portions of Turtle Island especially in the inter mountain West between the Cascade mountains and the Rocky Mountains. They were historically also very abundant West of the Cascades in the prairie ecosystems of that area, but they are much less common today since the prairies in general are much less common. Lewis and Clark mistook the vast fields of Camas that they came across for blue lakes in the distance. This plant is a great source of carbohydrates which is a boon to humans, and was especially important to tribal peoples living in the Pacific Northwest before crops such as corn or potatoes had been introduced to the area because while the landscape in this area is very abundant in food, especially protein sources such as Salmon, Elk, Deer, and Shellfish and also wild greens, there are not many sources of carbohydrates.

The part of Camas that is eaten is the bulb, which is the root. These large bulbs have smaller bulblets that grow on the side of them. When humans dig up the Camas in order to eat them, they aerate and loosen the soil through digging, often do some weeding either intentionally or not, and replant the bulblets either intentionally or not (they naturally fall off of the main bulb through handling). All these things combine to help the Camas to become more abundant in those areas that are actively harvested by humans. Tribal peoples of this area over time developed a very sophisticated form of agriculture that involved controlled burns, careful harvest, and seed collection/dispersal, that resulted in a landscape that was very abundant in food and game while still maintaining much of its "wild" character.

Hopefully we are all doing this type of work, helping to maintain the wild gardens and increasing the abundance of the plants who live there, but the type of gardening that I am focusing on in this chapter is more of a style that involves the cultivation of plants in clearly delineated spaces near a person's home, this could be called a more "European" type of gardening, but I think that is pretty simplified. This manner of gardening in many ways is developed from European traditions in which people would have access to wild lands in which they would hunt and gather wild foods while also keeping a garden plot close to home, and I am sure that these people historically did engage in similar practices that the tribal peoples of Turtle Island were engaged in but over time the wild places, or the "commons," were enclosed by the moneyed elite and people became more and more dependent upon the food and medicines that they could grow right by their home. This type of plant/human cohabitation is what I mean when I am talking about a "garden." The history of the enclosures is very fascinating and kind of heartbreaking, but I will not go into that here.

PHILOSOPHY

To keep a garden is an act of love and service to the plants. It is also an act of love and service to yourself and to the land upon which you live, as long as you are following good practices. While I like to grow food in my garden, here I am focusing on growing medicinal plants, which is also the aim of most of the gardens that I actually plant. I prefer to grow perennial plants in my medicine garden, which are plants that live for many years, as opposed to annual plants that must be reseeded every year. Perennial plants require much less maintenance than annual plants, and once they are in the ground it is easy to keep them in good health without needing to do much tilling of the earth. There are a variety of reasons why it is good to avoid too much tilling or plowing, but suffice it to say that it helps to keep the topsoil healthy and present. Also, frankly, I am a lazy gardener and would rather not spend too much of my time tilling or plowing, I would rather be able to hang out with the plants. It is also nice to keep perennial plants because you can really develop a relationship with them over the years. I have had some of the individual plants that live in my garden with me for about a decade now, and they are still doing well and setting seed every year. Perennial plants also are great because they are easy to propagate in a variety of ways, which I will go into in the next section of this chapter. Once you get a patch of a perennial medicine plant established, this patch can provide you with plant material to work with as medicine (often so much that you will need to share the medicine that you make) plus propagation material in the form of root divisions, cuttings, or seeds, and if you do nothing to the patch except keep the ground beneath the plants free of weeds and loosen up the soil so that it is in good shape for seeds to germinate in, and allow the plants to go to seed, then next year you will have more baby plants then you know what to do with. In this way a garden can grant you so much abundance, and encourages generosity since you basically have no choice but to get all of those baby plants out into other people's gardens since they would crowd one another out if you left them all in your beds. Giving away baby medicinal plants helps people to become more reliant upon their own hands to take care of their own health, and helps more and more medicine gardens pop up all over the land, and is a good practice of mutual aid in action. I have made a garden in every place that I have lived for the last fifteen years or so, and dug most of it up to take with me when I moved, but whenever I return to these places there are inevitably many plants that I either missed or that are seedlings from my mother plants that have now grown up and are making babies of their own. The medicine garden teaches abundance, sharing, and generosity.

PRACTICALITIES AND SOME PLANTS

These days I like to have my garden made up primarily of raised beds. I find these very easy to install, and I can go from a grassy yard to a garden with very little grass in it in one season by laying down a bunch of cardboard or some other type of weed blocking material, building raised beds on top of that, bringing in soil to fill the raised beds, and heavily mulching the paths in between the raised beds with wood chips. I spent many years digging beds into the ground wherever my garden was and just got sick of spending so much time digging out the runner grasses and buttercup that would steadily and inevitably creep in. I like to make a bed about four feet by eight feet since I can reach every part of that size of a bed without needing to climb inside the bed and therefore compact the soil. I buy an organic "garden blend" soil from a local business and supplement it with compost, composted manure, and rabbit poop from my rabbits yearly or every other year, often applying the compost in the Fall/Winter as a top dressing and allowing it to break down during the rainy season. I also like to mulch my beds quite heavily as this helps them to maintain moisture during the droughty time of year and also breaks down into the soil providing organic material and nutrients. Mulching also helps to keep the soils from compacting. I do not use many liquid fertilizers although I am growing interested in producing my own worm tea/compost teas and working with those. The main downside to raised beds is that they cost some money or at least some materials to build, and are reliant on outside inputs to get started. Also, any wooden raised bed will rot eventually and need to be replaced, but I like to make impermanent things, as all things are impermanent anyway. I am scheming about making raised beds with brick or rock someday for permanence, but maybe not actually, since it is something to do when the beds rot out, and you need to make new ones.

Once my beds are up, I like to plant perennial plants that are already established rather than direct seeding. This results in a productive garden faster. I have been enjoying digging plots and direct seeding them for more long-term projects. There are a few ways that I like to make new plants from preexisting plants to fill up the beds. The techniques that I outline here are best done from Fall to late Spring, but many of them can be done any time of year, if you do not mind some fatalities or to water very heavily while the plants recover from the stress of the process. The rainy season is nice to do these things because the rain takes care of the watering for you, and the lower temperatures are less stressful on the plants.

R OOT DIVISION: Root division is a simple technique to turn one large and well established perennial plant into many smaller plants. Not all plants can be propagated this way, especially not plants that have a taproot and only one flowering stalk per root, but plants that have a taproot and a number of flowering stalks usually can. Also plants that spread by rhizome can be very easily propagated by root division; that is how they propagate themselves anyway.

The basic technique for root division is to dig up a large plant that is several years old. The root ball should be large, and if it is a plant with taproots then there needs to be a large and well developed root crown, which is the place where the stem arises from the root. In many plants the crown will have many points where stems arise from the root mass, and each of these points can become a new plant. To divide roots such as this, simply break the individual root crown along with their associated root off from the rest of the plant. In an older plant with say a dozen individual crowns like this you can break them all apart from one another and produce a dozen new plants. In many plants, such as Elecampane (*Inula helenium*), you can harvest the majority of the root for making medicine and replant the root crowns with only a little bit of root on them. These will recover and go on to become large plants of their own in a few years. Other garden plants that can be propagated in this way include Valerian (*Valeriana officinalis*), Echinacea (*Echinacea purpurea*), and Marshmallow (*Althea officinalis*).

Plants that spread by runners or rhizomes, which are underground stems that have roots coming off of them, are very easy to propagate by simply digging up the rhizome, cutting it into small lengths that have several nodes on them and some true root on them, and then spreading these out and planting them back into the ground. These type of plants propagate themselves essentially by this method, although they often are just growing the rhizomes out from the main body of the plant rather than breaking it up. Many plants that are considered weeds and a nuisance to farmers or gardeners propagate via this method, which makes them really hard to eliminate from a garden or field since any little fragment of rhizome can go on to establish a whole new patch of the plant. Plants such as these also can really benefit from being plowed or tilled, which breaks the rhizomes up into a million little fragments and spreads them all over the place. Some plants that propagate in this way that we work with as medicines and can grow in the garden include Nettles *(Urtica dioica)*, Arnica *(Arnica montana)*, Skullcap *(Scuttelaria lateriflora)*, and Mint *(Mentha spp.)* The most notorious "weeds" that grow in the area where I live that propagate in this way are Bindweed *(Convolvulus spp.)* and Buttercup *(Ranunculus repens)*.

SOME SPRING ROOT PLANTS: I want to go into more detail on some of the root medicine plants that I casually listed above as those that are easy to propagate via root divisions. I like to harvest some of the root medicines from my garden in the early Spring, just as they are starting to wake up. There are two main times when it is best to harvest roots for medicine, the Fall and the Spring. Theoretically you can harvest them at any time between these two seasons, i.e., all Winter long, but I feel that it is really at these two specific times that they are at their prime. In perennial plants, the plant's energies sleep in the roots of the plant all during the Winter, then they wake up in the Spring, when the roots get juicy and lively, then the energies move up the plant into the leaves where they are involved in photosynthesis, then to the flowers for pollination, and the fruits for seed production. Once the plant has set seed the energies and juices move back down into the roots, in the Fall time. The roots are juicy and lively for a time in the Fall, then they kind of go to sleep for the Winter and dry out a bit.

I think that the best times to harvest the roots is in those windows where the roots are enlivened and awake and also are doing the majority of the metabolic processes of the plant. Many people say that medicinal roots that are harvested in the Spring are more tonic and gentle, building, while medicinal roots harvested in the Fall are more potent, pushy, and medicinal. I think that there is some truth to this, and back in my undergraduate days when I was doing some phytochemical research I did find, in an experiment that had many flaws and was never confirmed via repetition, that the plant that I was researching had a different phytochemical make up in the Spring and in the Fall, and the essential oil yield was very different between those two times, which for me lends some weight to the folkloric idea that I outlined above. I often end up harvesting some medicinal roots in the Spring simply because I have free time at that time of year and I am working in the garden anyway, but I do think that a few of the garden roots are better when harvested in the Spring.

One plant that I love to grow in my garden and usually end up harvesting in the Spring is Elecampane (*Inula helenium*). This plant originated in Eurasia, where they grow wild from Spain to Western China. Elecampane has been worked with as a medicine by all of the cultures in which they have lived, being referenced in Chinese medicine (*Inula Xuan Fu Hua* is a Japanese species of *Inula*) and having a long tradition of use in a variety of European cultures. Nicholas Culpeper, an English herbalist who lived in the early 17th century, mentions Elecampane in his *Culpeper's Complete Herbal*, in which he also calls the plant Elfwort since they have a long history of being associated with the fairies and spirit worlds. I really like Elfwort as a name for this plant, but people often don't know what you are talking about when you use it, so I go with the standard common name of Elecampane. In all of the cultures in which this plant is worked with the medicinal virtues are basically the same, they work very nicely to improve the digestion and the lungs in a warming and stimulating kind of way, which can lead to better health in general. I was first introduced to *Inula* as an herb that could be helpful for asthma, and they are indeed very helpful for this condition, a little bit during acute attacks but more so when taken regularly over a long period of time, which leads to stronger and more supple lungs. I have also liked taking Elecampane when I was a tobacco smoker for smoker's cough and to help get some of the accumulated tar out of my lungs. Elecampane is a nice warming expectorant, and helps to warm and thin the mucus in the lungs while also helping to push it up and out. They are much less pushy in this regard than say *Ligusticum* or *Lomatium*, and I regard Elecampane as more of a tonic herb that can and should be worked with for a long time to really see the benefits. Like many expectorants this plant can promote menstruation and I would be somewhat cautious working with them with a person who is pregnant that wants to stay that way, although I think it could be done safely.

The Latin name for this genus of plants, *Inula*, is derived from a polysaccharide that the roots of the plant are particularly rich in, called inulin. Inulin is a very large and complex polysaccharide, and is beneficial to the human digestive system because it serves as a source of fiber, which is not digestible as a sugar by the human body but serves as a bulking agent to the eliminative function, leading to nice bowel movements, and also is digestible as a food to the bacteria that live in the lower gastrointestinal (GI) system. People call inulin a pre-biotic, which is a substance that serves to feed the beneficial microorganisms that live in the human digestive tract and are crucial to good health. This is similar to a probiotic, which people are often more familiar with, which is a food or supple-ment that contains beneficial microorganisms that people eat in order to populate their guts with such. It is a pet theory of mine that it is the prebiotic nature of the inulin found within *Inula* that is a part of why this plant has long term benefits for the lungs, since the health of the lungs is very much tied in with the health of the gut. This is made explicit in Chi-nese medicine in which the lungs and the large intestine are partnered with one another. Also within this system, both of these organ systems are associated with the emotions of sad-ness or grief. Elecampane is in the *Asteraceae* family of plants, which it shares with the Sunflower (*Helianthus*), and the flow-er of Elecampane looks very much like a sunflower, large and bright yellow. I like to work with this plant to bring this solar energy in to people who are feeling gloomy, down, or are in grief. Grief can really take up residence in both the lungs and the intestines, leading to physical issues in those places, and helping someone to get things moving in those body systems will often help them to get the grief moving. Many times tobacco smokers are working with tobacco, which is a sacred medicine by the way, to stuff their grief down into their lungs, and part of the way that elecampane helps with the smoker is working on these stuffed emotions. I have not worked with the plant in this context, but there are many studies suggesting that Elecampane can be really helpful in aiding diabetics to regulate their blood sugar, which I also think can have a strong correlation to fear and grief in the body. This plant is great to work with since it is tonic yet strong, and is simple to grow in abundance, and of course they are very beautiful in the garden.

Another garden plant that I love to harvest in the Spring is *Althea officinalis*, also called Marshmallow. This is another Eurasian plant that is now grown all around the world. They originally lived in the part of the world now divided into Europe, Western Asia, and North Africa, and have been worked with as a medicine since ancient Egypt and Greece, so since at least the ninth century BCE. The roots have been prepared into a sweet treat since for about that long. They were mixed with honey and dried fruits to make a dessert for Egyptian nobility, and today we have the dessert that is made almost entirely out of sugar that is called a marshmallow, that has its origins with this plant. It is possible to make the candy called marshmallows out of marshmallow root, but I cannot say that I have ever tried it. *Althea* is a root medicine, although the aerial parts of the plants work just fine as medicines themselves. I like to make an infusion of the leaves, stems, and flowers in the Summertime when the fresh root is not available to me and I really need the medicine of this plant, which is basically to soothe and moisten the body. I will quote Peter Holmes here, from his book *The Energetics of Western Herbs*, since he gives such a nice general statement about *Althea* and their abilities as an herb:

> *Demulcents* such as Marshmallow work partly through the actual presence of mucilage and partly through the mucus-generating (*mucogenic*) effect that mucilage engages as a result of its indirect, reflexive action. Marshmallow's sweet taste has thick, heavy, cool qualities and is responsible for *moistening, soothing, slowing,* and *calming* effects both locally and, to some extent, systemically. (470)

This is a very nice summation of how *Althea* does their work in the body. They are very rich in a type of polysaccharides known as *mucopolysaccharides* (which are now technically known as *glycosaminoglycans,* but I find that much harder to remember), which essentially function within the body to lubricate and absorb shocks. These are mostly found in the body within the joints and other places where these actions are required, but they are also beneficial to any mucus membranes that they come into contact with since they provide a soothing protective layer to those mucus membranes, and also seem to serve a *vulnerary* (wound healing) function when they come into contact with those surfaces. As a result of all these actions, *Althea* is very nice to work with for a variety of conditions that are hot and dry in their presentation. Marshmallow root is the part of the plant that is most commonly worked with, and I think that the fresh root harvested in the

Spring is the most gooey and tonic, but it can be harvested in the Fall or Winter and still be very nice. Taking the fresh root, chopping it up, and soaking it in hot or cold water overnight results in a nice, sweet, thick beverage that is very soothing and slimy. This is nice to drink for people with irritated lungs such as smokers, people with COPD type conditions, people with bronchitis or dry coughs, or everybody during the massive wildfires that we have been experiencing all over the world with greater and greater frequency as climate change progresses. I also really like working with *Althea* for people with various GI irritability conditions such as heartburn, GERD, or a "sour stomach." Marshmallow will also sooth and moisten an inflamed urinary tract in the case of a UTI or just for general pain and discomfort. Culpeper states that *Althea* "opens the strait passages, and makes them slippery, whereby the stone may descend the more easily, and without pain, out of the reins, kidneys, and bladder..." (224), although I personally would send someone to a Doctor if they are dealing with any stones at all. Of course, oftentimes after going to a Doctor a person is sent home to pass the stone themselves instead of having any kind of intervention, and I would certainly give *Althea* or a moistening herb, although I have never actually worked with a person with this condition.

I like to give *Althea* as a moistening herb in any herbal formulation that is too drying or warming, as they provide a nice simple moisture without many extraneous actions, and I like to give *Althea* to people who are dried out in any number of ways that could broadly be termed *yin deficiency,* but I don't really understand Chinese medicine enough to use that term very precisely. This can look like any of the conditions that I have mentioned above, and could also include dry skin, chronic muscle tension, and joint pain, all of which would benefit from some soothing lubrication. The herb can also be applied as a poultice directly to external irritations such as rashes or cuts to soothe and promote healing.

G ROWING FROM SEED: By far the easiest way for the plants to reproduce themselves is via seeds. The seed is the baby of the plant, it comes from the pollination of one plant by another and is genetically distinct from its Mama, unlike plants that are created via clonal propagation such as root division or by cuttings. This is nice for the populations of plants since it is good to have some genetic diversity in terms of disease resistance, and it keeps the evolutionary process happening. The plants are always growing and changing at the species level after all. Growing from seed is also preferable for the plant because it is the least traumatic method for them to reproduce. The process of you digging up a plant by their roots and then tearing them into little pieces to then replant might be very easy for you, but it sure seems like a hard thing for the plant to go through. The plants, of course, are great models for resilience through trying experiences, and I do not pretend to really understand how they perceive pain or dismemberment, but I am sure that they like to make brand new babies, just like us humans like to make brand new babies: they are *so* cute!

Growing from seed can also be a way to really create a whole lot of new plants. Many plants will produce hundreds or thousands of seeds in one flowering cycle, I assume because they are anticipating many of the seedlings not making it. If you as a gardener can take an active role in germinating the seeds and tending to the seedlings then basically 100% of those seeds can make it into viable adult plants, which is quite a lot of plants.

Seeds are also very cheap to buy, and once you have mature perennial herbs they will flower and set an abundance of seeds every year at no cost to you other than the effort you put in to watering, etc. It can be tricky to get seeds to mature in my climate, the rainforest, without them starting to mold since the rains start right around the time when the seeds are done maturing, but if you keep your eyes on them and wait until the flowering stalks of the plant in question have entirely browned and died back, then harvest the whole flowering stalk and place it upside down in a paper bag and hang it from your rafters or otherwise store it in a cool and dry place, the seeds will dry out and you can shake them out of the seed heads at your leisure and then store them in glass jars until it is time to sow them out.

Even easier than this is to simply cultivate the ground beneath your plants so that the soil is loose and free of competition in the form of weeds, and then allow the plants to make their own baby seedlings in the beds where they live. In the Spring once the babies have grown up to the point that they are a couple of inches tall and have several sets of leaves you can transplant them out of the bed either into a new bed, into pots, or into your friend's garden.

Different seeds have different parameters that they need to germinate. Some like to be sown in the Summer when the soil is already warm, some need to be sown in the Fall or Winter so that they can go through a period of extreme cold or even freezing which they require to germinate (this is called cold stratification, and you can mimic it in a freezer if need be), some like a lot of moisture and to be babied while some need benign neglect and dry conditions. If you are purchasing your seed from a good supplier then the seed packet should have all the information that you need to germinate your seeds. If you are collecting your own seeds, I have found that I have the best success with simply spreading the seeds out in a flat, or more preferably in a deep yet wide planting pot, and leaving them outside all Winter so that they germinate in the Spring. It is nice to place them on the side of a house or outbuilding so that they don't get too much rain, which can wash the seeds out, but they still get some moisture on them. This neglect technique can yield failures of course, but it is very easy and very often works great. Some wild species have seeds that can take years to germinate, and sometimes you will forget that there is anything planted in that pot that is tucked up against the garage until one day when you go to empty in out in order to put it to use and discover that you have one hundred baby plants in there. Learning to collect, preserve, and germinate your abundant garden seeds will also train you to be able to do the same with the seeds of plants that live out in the wild that are much less abundant. I would suggest not harvesting seeds from wild plants unless you are sure that you are going to do something with them since the plants are very good at making their own babies, but once you have some experience with germination you could be really very helpful to the wild plant populations by harvesting (some, not all) of their seeds and either getting them planted in a new spot out in the field where they can establish a new patch, or bringing them home where you germinate them under close supervision and then either grow them out in your garden or reintroduce them to the field once they have grown up a little bit. Please note that plants that have been doted on in a garden or especially greenhouse setting can really suffer if they are planted out in a wild place and have to fend for themselves, so please do be conscious to harden them off and help get them ready for their new environment before you plant them out in the woods or the desert. This work of seed saving and seeding out the wild gardens is crucially important, and I encourage all of us to get on it and get better at it. A great person to research who has done so much work with sowing the seeds of the wild food plants is Finisia Medrano, who recently sadly died. Her book *Growing Up in Occupied America* is a great place to start.

Once all of your seeds have germinated and you have a flat or pot crammed full of seedlings, it is important to get them out of there and either into the ground or into their own pots before they start to crowd one another out. There is a fine line here, and I would suggest actually letting the seedlings get pretty big before you transplant them, even if they are crowding one another, since they are also helping one another to stay moist and to be safe. Some plants will die from transplant shock no matter what you do, and these should just be direct seeded wherever they are going to live, and then thinned at a certain point. If you separate out all of your seedlings and put them all in small pots, be aware that they will take up quite a lot of space, and that small pots dry out very fast in the droughty part of the year, so they will need some space and watering from you. At this point I really suggest giving the majority away (or selling them if you need to) to reduce the burden on you and increase the likelihood of the majority of them living.

Some seeds require very specific techniques in order to germinate, such as being scarified with sandpaper, soaking them in almost boiling hot water, or soaking them in various acids and hormones to simulate them passing through the digestive tract of a bird or other animal (some people germinate berry seeds by eating berries and then pooping where they want to have a berry patch. This is a controversial practice for a number of reasons, but I hear it can be very successful). I find that I often do not have the patience for these techniques. If you do then I applaud you, and this is a place where people who like to obsess over minutiae can really shine. I like to buy baby plants from these people, and plant them in my garden, and when it comes to seed grown plants I mostly let my plants do it themselves or I work with species that are very easy to grow from seed that I gather, such as Tobacco (*Nicotiana rustica*), Motherwort (*Leonorus cardiaca*), or Angelica (*Angelica archangelica*). It is very satisfying to grow a plant from seed, and especially to grow baby plants from a plant that you grew from seed, making your their grandparent.

This past year the only plant that I intentionally grew from seed was Angelica, specifically *Angelica archangelica*. The genus *Angelica* is in the *Apiaceae* family, which also contains Oshá (*Ligusticum spp.*), Lomatium (*Lomatium spp.*), and Carrot Queen Anne's Lace (*Daucus carota*). Members of the *Angelica* genus are found circumglobally in the Northern hemisphere of the planet. Several members of this genus are indigenous to Turtle Island/North America and Canada, and there are members all across the Eurasian continent from England to Japan. Wherever they grow, the Angelicas are treasured and utilized by the humans that live around them. They are very beautiful and striking plants, some of which can grow to be eight feet tall (*Angelica archangelica* will do this)! They are very fragrant and are therefore rich in essential oils, and they have been used in medicines, cooking, perfumery, and in the creation of various liquors including the famous Absinthe. *Angelica archangelica* is indigenous to Northern Europe, and has an especially long history as a medicine within the Sami culture of Scandinavia. Today, they are grown all across the world, and are so commonly incorporated into gardens that one common name for this specific species is Garden Angelica. This plant has long been thought of as having a strong connection to the spirit world. They have a hollow flowering stalk, which many people have associated with the *axis mundi*, world tree, or world axis which connects the three worlds (upper, middle, lower) to one another. The common name Angelica also refers to this concept as it shows the plant's connection to the angels. This herb has been worked with as a medicine in many different cultures, and the various species are all worked with in similar ways. They are a warming and expulsive plant which can be helpful for lung conditions and infections. They are also very helpful to bring on menstruation, and the Chinese species *Angelica sinensis* is cured in a specific way to produce an herbal medicine known as dong quai, which some call Women's Ginseng. This preparation is utilized as a general tonic for women's health including reproductive health but not at all limited to that. Angelica is a very nice digestive herb, warming the stomach and serving as a carminative (relieving gas). They also help to open up the pores and warm the interior which helps to bring on sweating and push out toxins. At the time of this writing (May 2020) I am in the middle of the COVID-19 pandemic, and I think that this herb could be really useful in working with that virus, which causes a fever and a buildup of very sticky mucus in the lungs, so warming the interior while opening the pores and pushing the mucus up and out is just the ticket, not to mention the improved digestion will help to eliminate toxins and mucus through the stool. Many people are reaching for Oshá (*Ligusticum spp.*) for these specific actions, and while Oshá is certainly very good at doing these things, that plant is not easily cultivated and has been over harvested quite badly in many wild places. I planted these Angelica seeds from a plant of mine that had gone to seed at my last garden that

I gathered seeds from on a whim, but I am happy that I will have potentially hundreds of Angelica plants that will be ready to harvest next year, when I am sure we will still be dealing with this virus. It is the root of the plant that is worked with as a medicine, although the stems and seeds have been taken both as a medicine and also as a food. This is a very nice one to have growing in the garden also just because they are so beautiful. The bees really love them.

H ARDWOOD CUTTINGS: We are a little bit late in the year right now to do hardwood cuttings, but we are coming up on the time to do softwood cuttings. These are both methods of propagating woody trees and shrubs by cutting off branches and rooting them out. Hardwood cuttings are taken in the Winter, when the sticks are free of any leaves, are dormant, and any of last year's fresh growth has hardened and become woody. Hardwood cuttings are very nice to work with because they are very easy to do once you get the hang of them. Not all trees or shrubs can be propagated via hardwood cuttings, but it is worth trying it with species that are not known to propagate in this way because sometimes it works anyways. The basic technique is to find a tree or shrub that has some nice long and straight branches coming off of the main part of the trunk. One way to promote the creation of sticks like this is by *coppicing* the tree, which means to cut it down about six feet up from the ground, and ideally right above a node. Not all trees will coppice, but those that do will produce a dozen or so new shoots in the place where the tree was cut down. Coppicing can be really annoying if you are just trying to cut a tree down and kill them, since they just turn right back into a big tree in a few short years. Many fruit bearing trees will do this, and swampy trees like Willows (*Salix spp*), Cottonwoods (*Populus trichocarpa*), and Maples (*Acer macrophyllum*) will also. In many cultures trees such as Willows have been maintained as coppiced trees for generations or centuries since the straight, young, flexible sticks can be utilized for a number of uses such as making baskets, houses, or furniture (this process of weaving with flexible branches is often called wicker). A coppiced tree, especially some specific trees such as Willow, can be coppiced every few years and will keep on producing new sticks again and again, which is a very sustainable way to produce building materials (or herbal medicines, if the bark of the sticks is medicinal). Coppicing a tree is also a very nice way to have an endless source of sticks to use as hardwood cuttings, and many people or companies that are involved with wetland reclamation or stream conservation make a business out of coppicing large tracts of Willow or Cottonwood to then harvest hardwood cuttings year after year. In this way one Willow tree may produce hundreds or thousands of new Willow trees with some help and work on the part of the humans around them. Once your tree has been coppiced and given two to three years to produce a bunch of nice, straight, thick sticks to plant, you cut those sticks off, cut them into six foot lengths, cut off any side branches and remove the spindly growth near the tip, and then plant the whole stick into a spot where you want there to be a new tree.

I have had the best luck with putting fully half of the cutting (so three feet in this example) into the ground, and doing it in a pretty wet spot such as a swamp or next to a river. A nice tool to use in planting is an iron digging bar, which you can use to create a narrow and deep hole that you then shove the hardwood cutting down into. There is also a tool called a dibble bar which is basically a metal bar with a cross bar on it, kind of like a Pogo stick but with no spring, that you can jump on and make a narrow deep hole to slide the stick into. Hardwood cuttings are nice for a number of reasons. It is best to take the cuttings and plant them in the Winter, which gives you a nice reason to get outside and do some physical labor at that slow time of year, which really helps improve my mood. They also take very little maintenance once you have cut them and planted them since it is the wet season so the rain takes care of watering them while they are rooting, and hopefully they are well rooted enough to survive the dry time of year once it arrives. Look out for beavers!

Once you get the technique down, which admittedly takes a bit of trial and error, you can get close to 100% success on these cuttings (mostly with Willows and Cottonwoods, which are rich in rooting hormones that help them to root easily from this type of cutting) which means you can coppice one tree and turn them into a hundred trees which can provide shade to a river that was clear cut over the course of just a few years, with only six or seven days of work total over that period of time. The only real downside to hardwood propagation is that it does not work with many species of tree or shrub, although if you use Willow tea or rooting hormone on these species you can sometimes get them to take (I don't recommend using rooting hormone on sticks that you are planting outside; root them in a pot and then transplant them later). For many of those species that do not take to hardwood cuttings, however, you can switch to a different style of propagation.

SOFTWOOD OR GREENWOOD CUTTINGS: Softwood cuttings are taken in the Summer, and are taken from that year's new growth on the tree or shrub in question. This new growth is often bright green and still soft or pliable, hence the name. Softwood cuttings are much trickier than hardwood cuttings mostly because the cutting is much more fragile and tender, and it is the hot and dry time of year which means that the cutting can die of drying out unless you are really taking care of them. It is best to use some kind of a rooting hormone on softwood cuttings, which can be Willow tea or a synthetic (careful not to get the synthetic on your skin!). Also if you water the cuttings with Willow tea each time you water, you will have much better luck with getting them to root. The professionals use something called a misting table which is essentially a table with built in misters that is either connected to a timer or just constantly mists the cuttings in their rooting substrate. The constant moisture helps the roots to form without promoting algae or fungal growth the way that standing water can, and especially if the cuttings start to leaf out, they lose a lot of moisture through the leaves. You can mimic a misting table by misting by hand several times per day. A pretty simple way to keep them happy is to take a cutting which should be pretty small like six inches long or so. Cut off all the leaves except for the top one or two, dip the base of the cutting in rooting hormone and immediately pot it in some kind of well draining soil or substrate. It is best to then place the cutting into some kind of a clear plastic or glass container that will trap in the moisture and keep them warm while still allowing sunlight in, and then regularly bottom water. I have a friend who works a job in which he is often visiting people's gardens. He keeps a big pot of potting soil that is wet, premixed rooting hormone, and a clear plastic dome that fits over the pot that he stores inside his car. He just takes cuttings, with permission, of any plants that he thinks are cool in people's gardens and gets them rooting right away. If you have ever grown *Cannabis* and made clones of that plant, or if you know someone who has, the process of cloning that plant is essentially a greenwood cutting. There are also a lot of resources about making clones of that specific plant all over the web, and you can adapt those techniques to a number of different plants. Again, it is really nice to practice these techniques on plants that are known to do well through greenwood cuttings that you already have growing in your garden or something like this, so that when you inevitably fail at first it will not be too heartbreaking, and you can just try again. Some common garden plants that propagate readily from softwood cuttings include Roses (*Rosa spp.*), the Butterfly Bush (*Buddleia davidii*), and Sages (*Salvia spp.*). Some medicinal plants that can be propagated easily from green-wood cuttings from the wild around here include the various Elders (*Sambucus spp.*) as well as Pacific Dogwood (*Cornus nuttallii*).

B ARK HARVEST, AND SOME MEDICINAL TREES: At the same time that the roots in the garden are getting plumped up and ready for Spring harvest, the sap in the trees is starting to move from their roots up the trunks to start working on producing leaves. It is at this specific time when it is best to harvest medicinal barks, while the sap is running. This is also when people harvest tree saps for the use of making sweeteners such as Maple syrup from Sugar Maples (*Acer saccharum*) some species of Birch (*Betula spp.*) and a few others, although I think that sap harvest is actually a little bit earlier in the year than bark harvest. I have been taught that the best time to harvest bark is when the deciduous trees are just starting to leaf out, but before the leaves are fully developed. The leaves are a vibrant green and very tender at this time, and the color is easy to spot. I do not think that this very specific timing of bark harvest has much to do with the medicinal potency of the bark, although at this time of year the bark is certainly very plump and juicy, but rather the timing is crucial because there is only a brief window in which the bark will "slip," which means that it will peel off of the underlying wood very easily. When the bark is no longer slipping, peeling bark is a pain in the ass and involves basically scraping it off with a knife, draw knife, or hatchet, but if you can get to the bark when it is slipping all you really have to do is use a knife to make deep enough cuts that they go all the way through the bark and into the underlying wood, and then get your fingers under the bark and peel it off by hand. Underneath the bark when it is slipping is very wet and it usually smells very good, and there are honestly very few things that I find more satisfying than peeling bark when it is slipping.

It is really important to be careful and selective when it comes to harvesting bark from living trees. Many people will harvest small strips from the main trunks of standing trees, that is for example how many Coast Salish people harvest Red Cedar (*Thuja plicata*) and Red Alder (*Alnus rubra*) bark. This is a very nice method as long as you know what you are doing. If you harvest off the bark all the way around the tree, even if it is only for an inch, then you have *girdled* the tree, and they are going to die because all of the vascular tissues are in the bark and the cambium layer. The vascular tissues of a tree have the same function as your vascular tissues, to move fluids around in the body, and if you cut off all of the vasculature in one area then the fluids can no longer get from the roots to the leaves and vice versa, and the tree will die. Taking a single long strip that is six inches wide or so from an individual tree is totally fine, and the tree will recover.

When I am harvesting barks my preferred method is to look for trees that have fallen over, which happens quite a lot with the trees that are growing in the streams and along the sides of rivers. These fallen trees are still rooted and will often start putting up new growth all up and down the length of the fallen trunk. If you cut the trunk just above the first of these new leader branches then the energy of the roots can just focus on supporting that one point of growth and will basically be able to re-form themselves into a tree that can reach the sunlight at the canopy. You have done that tree a favor and now you can harvest as much of the bark as you want off of the remaining trunk, which is probably a lifetime's supply for you and everyone you know if the tree was of any size at all. I will also do some selective pruning of some trees, removing branches that have partially broken off, or branches that are rubbing against other branches or otherwise causing some problem for the growth of the tree. Learning how to spot branches like this basically means learning how to prune trees, which I learned over many years of working as a land-scaper and ornamental gardener. It is too much for me to cover here, but if you know what I am talking about then great, and if not ask your friend who is an arborist or landscaper, or get a book about pruning. I think that making a nice clean cut and removing a damaged branch or two off of a large tree is probably less stressful than taking strips off of the main trunk of a tree, but I do admit that Coast Salish traditions and knowledge far surpass mine, and they like taking strips.

There are two main trees that I want to talk about in terms of bark harvest, and these are Cascara Sagrada (*Rhamnus purshiana*) and Willow (*Salix spp*). Both of these trees can be found in some abundance in the swamps right around me, and they both have their own tips and tricks for working with them. Other trees that I like to harvest barks from include

Red Alder *(Alnus rubra)*, who I discussed in a previous chapter, and Pacific Dogwood *(Cornus nuttallii)*, who I hope to discuss in a future chapter. Cascara Sagrada means "Sacred Bark" in Spanish, which should give you some idea of the esteem in which this tree has been and is held by many people. Another traditional name for this tree is "Chitticum," which is I believe an Anglicized version of a Coast Salish name for the tree. I am not aware of, say, the Lushootseed name for this tree, but I am trying to find out. Cascara is indigenous to the area in which I live in the Northwest of Turtle Island by the Salish Sea. They have been worked with as a laxative by the indigenous people of this area for a long time, and when the Spanish colonizers reached the area they adopted them into their herbal knowledge, and the knowledge has been passed on within and without dominant culture. Cascara was so widely popularized even with the fairly phytophobic culture of late 1900s "America" that the Cascara industry in 1999 had an estimated value of $400 million. Many European people in and around this area would harvest Cascara bark as a way to make some extra money. My partner's beloved Grandfather Don was a longshoreman, and a union man, and when they would have to go on strike he would supplement his income by picking Cascara bark, which I find really charming.

Unfortunately, as has been the case with so many medicinal plants when there is a global demand for them, Cascara ended up being over harvested to the point that the populations were suffering badly, mostly due to the practice of harvesting all of the bark off of a living tree, which kills them. The trees that did make it through this period were, somewhat ironically, the ones that people cut down in order to harvest the bark. Cascara, like Willow and Cottonwood, coppices very easily, so the trees that were cut down back in the day have all coppiced and now are big trees with many trunks coming our from a central stump at their bottom. This actually makes it much easier to harvest bark from these trees in such a way that you are doing them a favor since the many trunks are not ideal. They rub up against one another, which can be a source of infection, and the trunks on the inside are shaded out by the ones on the outside which stunts their growth and therefore the growth of the whole tree, so by doing some selective pruning out of some of these trunks you can actually increase the health and vigor of the tree while still getting plenty of bark for yourself.

Cascara Sagrada is a very effective herbal medicine. They reliably do what we want them to do, which is to get us to poop. I enjoy tasting Cascara tincture in a group of people because it shows the way that people's bodies can inherently know what kind of herbs will work well for them. For example, I love taking herbs. I take all kinds of extremely bitter and otherwise strong tasting herbs all the time. There are very few tinctures that I think taste bad, which is not true for many people I know. Cascara tincture, however, tastes SO VERY BAD to me. It is the bitterest thing I have ever tasted, which is saying a lot, and the taste will remain acutely unpleasant in my mouth for over half an hour after I take it. I do not have any troubles with constipation, at least this far in my life. If anything, I am prone to loose stool and diarrhea when I get out of balance. When I first made a Cascara tincture and tasted it I thought I had done something wrong because it tasted so foul to me, so I had my partner at the time taste it. This person is prone to constipation, and especially at this stage in her life she mostly had little rabbit pellet type poos when she would poo, which she was generally unsatisfied by. She thought the Cascara tincture tasted sweet and wanted more. I have seen other people have this same reaction to the taste of the tincture although most people find it hard to handle. In order for Cascara bark to be an effective but gentle medicine, it is important to age the bark for at least one year before processing it.

Cascara bark contains hydroxyanthracene glycosides which are the molecules that are thought to cause the main effect caused by ingesting the medicine, which is to increase peristalsis directly through an increase in the volume of bowel contents through the reduction of electrolytes and water. This is different from how, say, bitters can help with constipation, which is more by increasing the gastric juices and especially bile flow in order to get the whole system moving. If Cascara bark is not aged before it is prepared it can cause severe diarrhea and vomiting, it is a strong and cathartic purgative. A teacher of mine who I love very much named Scott Kloos is the only person that I know who has intentionally ingested fresh Cascara bark, and he reports that he vomited and diarrhea'd until he was void of anything else to get out, and then dry heaved and had the equivalent of dry heaves in his bowels, all night. This is not recommended and a good reminder to age your bark! A tincture made from the dried and aged bark at a 5:1 volume:weight ratio makes for a nice laxative that is not too strong. Having people take ten drops before bed should lead to a nice bowel movement the next morning, and if that does not work you can have them slowly work up their dose until it does. I like to work with Cascara at drop doses or simply by sitting with them because I think they are teaching me about letting go and release.

It is only in the last several years that I have really gotten to know Willow *(Salix spp.)*. I recently began taking Willow cuttings from the swamp behind the farm upon which I live and planting them along the Black River where there is not enough shade for the baby Salmon, and at the same time I have been working with some friends of mine who harvest Willow cuttings for a living, at least during the Winter months. The patches that these friends work in are amazing Willow swamps, and I have met some ancient and giant Willows that have basically propagated themselves by growing up on a central trunk, growing out in large branches until the branches split the trunk in several directions, then these branches root in the swampy muck and continue to grow out until one Willow tree occupies a circle that is at least one hundred feet in diameter. I never knew they could be that way. I love this job because in a good workday we produce hundreds or up to a thousand Willow cuttings that will theoretically all turn into new trees. Willow teaches a lot about resilience, and in being able to survive anywhere, and in rooting yourself down even if the circumstances are not ideal. I also love working with Willow in basketry and have begun coppicing some trees near where I live for long term basket projects. Willow also teaches about abundance. The genus *Salix*, which is the Willows, grows across the globe in the Northern hemisphere. Over four hundred species readily hybridize with one another, and there are in addition many ornamental hybrids. They range in size from the diminutive Dwarf Willow (*Salix herbacea*), which only grows to be a few inches tall to the White Willow (*Salix alba*) which can grow to be fifty or sixty feet tall. They all like to live in wet and cool climates, and can be considered a good indicator that there is water nearby if you find them growing in the wild. Humans and Willow have a very long history with one another due to the ease with which the flexible yet strong branches of Willow can be woven into various things such as baskets, fish traps, houses, and boats. There is evidence for humans working with Willow as far back as ten thousand years ago in the form of fishing nets in Finland. The net size seems about right for fishing for Salmon.

In terms of medicinal use, Willow is the source of one of the most utilized pharmaceuticals in the world, or at least the inspiration for it. Aspirin is the brand name for a chemical called acetylsalicylic acid and is a Non-Steroidal Anti-inflammatory Drug, or NSAID, which is commonly used for all sorts of pain, such as headaches, all over the world every day. Acetylsalicylic acid is a synthetic drug that was developed as a replacement for extracts of Willow bark, which contain a chemical called salicin or salicylic acid. Willow has been worked with in a similar way to Aspirin for thousands of years, as a simple remedy for pain and fevers. The bark also has a nice bitterness to it which can be helpful to get the digestion going. One issue with people taking Aspirin is that if large doses are taken for a long time, serious stomach damage can result, while whole plant extracts of Willow do not seem to have this effect (although I doubt many people have taken as much Willow as it is possible to take Aspirin in the modern world). I usually blend Willow tincture in with other plants in a formula when I am working with pain or a fever as there is usually more going on that I want to address than simply pain or a fever, but Willow bark as a tea or tincture by itself can be helpful for mild aches and pains. It is easy to find Willow in abundance, but not all species or even all individual trees of the same species have the same level of medicinal constituents. Some individual Willow trees are not very strong. Luckily it is very easy to test for salicin content by simply peeling a bit of the bark off and chewing it up. If it is very bitter and tastes/feels like you just bit into an Aspirin, then you have a winner. It is easy to find branches that have snapped off of the tree in a windstorm, or to find a Willow in someone's yard that they are wanting to cut down, and with a little bit of coppicing to the right tree you can provide yourself with a lot of medicine for the rest of your life or at least as long as you have access to that swamp. It is much easier to peel the bark off of larger branches, like at least an inch in diameter, but you can theoretically just chop up the small twigs and use them bark, wood and all. I imagine you would need to use slightly more material in weight than if you were just using bark, but they are basically interchangeable. I have not looked into whether Willow shares the blood thinning properties of Aspirin, which is taken daily by some people to help and prevent strokes, but I am really curious about that. My favorite way to prepare this plant is by tincturing the freshly peeled bark, which can make a product that is a little bit sweet and fragrant, but dried bark as a tea, tincture, or powder also works well. I mostly am engaging with willow these days by planting them all over the place and making wicker baskets out of them. When the willow sticks have been dried, then rehydrated, and are being worked with and bent into baskets there is a sweet smell that reminds me of the smell of Black Cottonwood bud resin (which also contains salicylates) which I am pretty sure is the smell of salicin. I have noticed that my fingers do not get as sore as I would expect them to after working on a pack basket for several days which I am pretty sure is the medicine seeping into my fingers as I work.

CONCLUSION

I hope that this chapter inspires you to build a garden and to start tending some of the wild gardens and wild plants. It does not take much time, effort, or commitment to start doing some of the propagation techniques outlined here. This is a hobby that can be richly rewarding in a number of ways, and the plants will appreciate it. It is possible to do some level of gardening or plant propagation even if you live in an apartment building, are incarcerated, or even if you live on a boat.

A friend of mine and I spent an entire Summer living on a 24-foot sailboat named the Sette Belle, and we were both plant people so we had several potted plants that just lived out on the deck in the middle of the bay with us. It is hard to express the many things that I have learned while working in the garden, or just sitting there and watching the plants. Same with doing wild tending–type work, the plants really notice this work and it seems to bring luck and good fortune to many of the people I know who engage in it, or at least a sense of good cheer and optimism, because at least if everything else is falling apart you can always engage with someone's garden or create your own in some way. Please get in touch with me for seeds or baby plants if you are reading this. I usually have some extras laying around.

5

PHYTOCHEMISTRY, ALCHEMY, PERFUMES, AND CRATAEGUS (BELTANE)

NOW IT IS BELTANE. This is the cross quarter between the Spring Equinox and the Summer Solstice. Beltane sits directly across the wheel of the year from Samhain, which in "American" culture is generally called Halloween. Beltane is generally said to take place on May first, which is also called May Day, but I think of the two holidays as separate from one another although they both share the same spirit in a lot of ways. I personally celebrate May Day on May first and Beltane on the full moon that is closest to May first, it usually comes about a week after May first. This can be called "Lunar Beltane" and feels more appropriate to the older calendar which was lunar based rather than based upon the Julian calendar. Much like Samhain, the veil is thin around the time of Beltane, and the spirit world is closer to the physical world at this time of year than others (of course the spirit world is always pretty close). Things get weird around Beltane (much as things gets weird around Samhain). This is the time of year, at least around where I live, where we really turn the corner and start to feel like we have officially entered Summer. The days start to get exponentially longer, the frosty nights are mostly over, and all the flowers are starting to bloom. This is the time of year when the Hawthorns

(*Crataegus spp.*) begin to bloom, and that is traditionally what announced that it was Beltane in European pagan traditions. I will get back to the Hawthorns later.

SOME HISTORY AND ETC

Beltane is a time of awakening, a time when life is fecund and death sits on the back burner, although they are all intertwined of course. Beltane celebrations are traditionally times of feasting, dancing (especially around the Maypole), and sex. Beltane is a celebration of life. May Day, which is a newer tradition, is a worker's holiday. May Day is a day of international solidarity amongst working class peoples all over the world. It is a day when people take to the streets to demand fair treatment in the workplace and to celebrate and demonstrate the might of the working class. May Day is also called International Workers' Day, and was created to commemorate the Haymarket massacre which took place on May 4th, 1886 at Haymarket Square in Chicago, Illinois. This event started off as a peaceful protest by the working class peoples of Chicago who were fighting for the eight hour workday in solidarity with other similar strikes that were going on all across the country. These workers had been on strike for a time and had been violently attacked by the police, which resulted in many injuries and at least two deaths among the workers at the McCormick Harvesting Machine Company plant, which had been in a state of strike for months. The workers were demonstrating in response to these events mostly by very peacefully listening to various people give speeches during a mild and rainy evening.

Near the end of the rally, around 10:30 p.m., the police showed up en masse and demanded that the people disperse. An unknown person threw a bomb into the police, which detonated and did some damage, but the resulting gunfire immediately after that caused the majority of the deaths and injuries that night. There are varying accounts as to who started the gunfire, the police or workers in the crowd, and many people dispute whether anyone in the workers' crowd fired any shots at all or whether all the injuries sustained by the police took place from the police officers firing wildly, which resulted in casualties from "friendly fire." Either way, within about five minutes after the shooting started, the square was empty except for the injured and dead. Four workers and seven police officers were killed, along with about 60 police officers being wounded and an unknown but large number of workers being wounded (the number of injured workers is not recorded since the wounded people who were with the workers feared going to the local hospitals out of concerns about being arrested or otherwise harassed due to their involvement with the event, so they sought aid outside official channels).

This event resulted in a crackdown on unions, anarchists, and communists in the city of Chicago and across the country. Police would raid houses of suspected anarchists with or without a warrant, and many innocent people were incarcerated. Eventually, eight people were put to trial for the bombing, who came to be known as the Haymarket Eight. Seven of these people were sentenced to death by hanging although there was little to no evidence that they were directly involved in the bombing. One of the defendants commited suicide before he could be executed, two of them had their sentences lowered to imprisonment, and the remaining four were hanged pretty close to Samhain, on November 11th, 1887. They sang the *Marseillaise*, the anthem of the international workers' revolutionary movement, one announced that "The time will come when our silence will be more powerful than the voices you strangle today," two called out "Hurrah for anarchism!" and one was attempting to give a speech when he was cut off by the opening of the trap doors of the gallows. The hangings were sloppily done, and the four people slowly strangled to death.

Ever since this event the people have taken to the streets on May Day the world over in an attempt to gain a more just world and bring about the end of Capitalism. In many ways May Day and Beltane have the same general themes going on, being that of life against death. The pagans celebrate this time of new life by making love and feasting, while the workers celebrate this time of year by marching and riots, both of these currents are a movement of the forces of life against the forces of death.

Within the Chinese calendar the period around Beltane is thought of as the movement from Spring, which is a time of birth and represented by the element Wood, into Summer which is the time of growth and represented by the element of Fire. Yang is ascending and becoming the more prevailing force while Yin is descending (not that I mean to associate Yin with the forces of death, it is more complex than that).

PHYTOCHEMISTRY

Around Beltane I like to teach about phytochemistry for a number of reasons. At this time of year most of the plants are awake and easy to interact with, and I like to show people the different plants that contain some of the various chemical families that I like to cover when discussing phytochemistry. This time of year is also one of the best times around me to harvest evergreen trees in order to distill essential oils from their needles, which I like to do as the lab portion of learning about phytochemistry, but I will get back to that later. Also I think that phytochemistry, and chemistry in general, is a very beautiful and fun discipline to be involved in, which is often not how people feel about the subject after studying it in high school or something like this, so I like to present this information out in the garden, or in an outdoor laboratory, when the flowers are blooming and the Sun is out, to bring a bit of Eros back into the subject.

Phytochemistry is the study of the chemistry of plants. The plants were the first chemists, and are still the best chemists. Many of the most complicated and intricate molecules that humanity knows about were discovered within the bodies of plants, and many molecules that plants make within their own bodies apparently with great ease are impossible for human chemists to recreate synthetically in the laboratory. A good example of this is the antimalarial drug known as artemisin, which is created abundantly within the body of the plant known as Sweet Annie, *qinghao*, or *Artemisia annua*. This plant is very easily grown and has a long history of use within

Chinese herbalism mostly to treat fevers. At some point one chemical that this plant produces, known as artemisin, was shown by studies to be especially helpful in treating malaria, a moisquito borne illness caused by single celled organisms in the genus *Plasmodium*. Malaria is widspread in the tropical parts of the world and can lead to fever, headaches, and in severe cases seizures and death, so there was a strong desire to be able to create antimalarial drugs in huge amounts. **Artemisin** is a beautifully elaborate molecule which is unique in that it contains an endoperoxide 1,2,4-trioxane ring, which is thought to be a big part in the molecule's efficacy as an antimalarial. While it is simple enough to extract artemisin from *Artemisia annua*, which is very easy to grow, chemists tried to figure out if there was a way to produce artemisin synthetically. It quickly became apparent that the synthesis would be far too technically difficult to make it economically feasible to produce the molecule for medicine. The total synthesis of artemisin became a kind of holy grail for many synthetic chemists and was finally figured out after many years, at great expense and with a terrible yield (the first successful total synthesis by Schmid and Hofheinz has a yield of about 5%). All this time and effort to create a molecule that a weedy and abundant plant just produces without seeming to even need to try. It is easy to think of chemistry as being a boring discipline, or as being part of the death machine, especially within herbally oriented subcultures who often have some distrust of the pharmaceutical and chemical industries (with good reason), but it is important to remember that the scent of a rose is

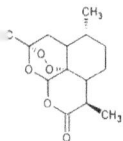

made up entirely of chemicals, as is the color of the petals and the parts of your body that are able to apprehend these things.

I will not attempt to introduce the complicated subject of chemistry here, and I would honestly encourage you to take an undergraduate level general chemistry and organic chemistry course if you are ever able to do so. Phytochemistry is basically a subset of organic chemistry, the branch of chemistry that focuses on carbon-based molecules. All organisms that we generally consider to be "living" are based upon carbon. My own body, the bodies of all plants and mollusks and bacteria, etc., are made up largely of carbon, which is an element that has four electrons in its valence shell. The other main elements that I will talk about here are: oxygen, which is crucial for the respiration of most living beings and is present in our atmosphere in nice levels; hydrogen, also found in our atmosphere, is the smallest of the elements and is highly explosive; and nitrogen, which is also found in abundance in the atmosphere and is the main food for plants and therefore humans. These elements combine with many others to make up various types of molecules, which could be called secondary metabolites in plants, which we interact with as medicines when we extract them from plants. There are four classes of molecules that are worked with by herbalists quite a lot in the context of herbal medicine, and those are the terpenes, the polysaccharides, the alkaloids, and the bioflavanoids. I will go over each of these in turn, and talk about the types of herbs that they live in, and how to extract them out of the body of a plant so that you can most easily ingest or interact with them.

HYDROCARBONS/TERPENES

The simplest family of chemicals in organic chemistry, and therefore phytochemistry, are called *hydrocarbons*. As the name implies, these molecules are made up of two types of atoms: hydrogen and carbon. These molecules are made up of a carbon chain as a backbone, with a bunch of hydrogen atoms radiating off of that chain. The main hydrocarbons that most people are familiar with at this time in history are the petrochemicals which are derived from crude oil through a process of distillation which are utilized to generate the majority of electricity and energy in general to help and drive the force of our current world culture.

Two of these types of hydrocarbons that most people are familiar with are called gasoline and diesel. These types of fuels are refined from crude oil through fractional distillation and are each a complex mixture of hydrocarbons. Gasoline is slightly lighter and more volatile than diesel, and it is a mixture of hydrocarbons that have between four and twelve carbon atoms in their backbones (the more carbon atoms in the skeleton of the molecule, the heavier and less volatile is the hydrocarbon). Diesel has between nine and 25 carbon atoms in the various hydrocarbons that make it up. These fuels are used to make cars and trucks run through a series of controlled explosions within an internal combustion engine.

The lightest of the hydrocarbons is called methane. This hydrocarbon has only a single atom of carbon surrounded by four atoms of hydrogen. This molecule is very light and volatile. It makes up a lot of the energy source that we call natural gas. Methane is generated by a number of natural processes including the belches and farts of cattle. Another light hydrocarbon that many people are familiar with is propane, which has a three-carbon atom backbone with eight carbon atoms attached. This molecule is also very light and flammable, but is a little bit denser and therefore safer and easier to store and transport. Many of us utilize small five-gallon containers of propane, which is a liquid when stored under pressure, to cook on our outdoor grills. Once the carbon backbones get longer and heavier, the molecules are a liquid at normal atmospheric conditions, such as the aforementioned gasoline and diesel, although they will very readily volatilize or evaporate in the presence of warmth and sunlight. Once you get above 50 carbon atoms in the backbone of a molecule, you get very thick solids that are still pliable. One example of this that many people are familiar with is asphalt, which is a sticky black tarry type material that naturally occurs in deposits in the Earth and is also a portion of the oil refining industry calls *residuum*, which is the black sticky sludge left behind after all of the more volatile hydrocarbons have been distilled out of crude oil. Asphalt is the main material used for the creation of roads, which all of the cars and trucks that run on the finer distillates drive around on. The comparison of asphalt, which is the road that you drive on, with the gasoline, that is in the gas tank, is a good lesson in how different a substance can be based solely on the number of carbon atoms in its molecular skeleton.

Within herbalism, the main types of hydrocarbons that we work with as medicines are a specific subtype that are known as *terpenes* or *terpenoids*. This class of compounds is named after turpentine, which is a distillate from Pine resin. Like all hydrocarbons, terpenes vary from light and volatile molecules that have a relatively short carbon backbone to heavy and dense molecules that have a long carbon backbone. Unlike the hydrocarbons in petrochemicals which can have molecular backbones of any number of carbon atoms, all terpene structures are made up of a certain number of a five carbon atom structure called **isoprene** (although in nature the creation of terpenes is a bit more complex than this).

The smallest and most volatile of the terpene types are called *monoterpenes* and are composed of two isoprene units, so ten carbon atoms as their backbones. Most of these are cyclical in their structure, as opposed to being straight chains of carbon atoms, but there are some exceptions to this. Since monoterpenes are so light and volatile, they can easily leave a plant and enter the atmosphere, and are therefore fragrant. The herbal products that most people are familiar with that are composed almost entirely of terpenes are known as essential oils, which are the volatile substances that live within fragrant plants that make them fragrant. Some of the monoterpenes that most people would recognize the smell of include menthol, which is a large component of the fragrance of the various Mints (*Metha spp.*) among other plants, **limonene** which is a key component of the fragrance of many Citrus fruits including Lemons (*Citrus limon*) and Oranges (*Citrus sinensis*) (you have perhaps also run into Limonene in a purified form in any number of "eco friendly" cleaning

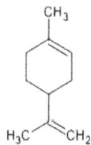

products that smell like oranges as it works very well to cut grease), and thymol which is one of the main components of the smell of Thyme (*Thymus vulgaris*). Many monoterpenes have a quick and profound influence on the functioning of the human nervous system simply through the act of smelling them. Since they are such small hydrocarbons they can very easily pass through the blood brain barrier after gaining entry through the mucus membranes of the nose and get to work regulating and changing various processes in the human body. This fact has led to the discipline known as *aromatherapy*, which is the utilization of various essential oils to help bring about desired changes in people's mental (or otherwise physiological, the line is blurry for me) states through the simple act of smelling them. Some simple and probably recognizable examples of this is the way that the essential oil of Lavender (*Lavendula spp.*) can help to calm people down and induce sleep so it is often put into soothing bath salts or used in a diffuser in a person's bedroom, or how the smell of various Citrus (*Citrus spp.*) essential oils have been shown to brighten people's moods and increase productivity so these oils are sometimes diffused throughout workplaces to help with productivity, or how the smell of Mint (*Mentha spp.*) can help to quell nausea so people can smell the essential oil or simply crush some fresh Mint and inhale it if they are suffering in this way, without having to put anything into their upset stomach. Many monoterpenes are also antiseptic, anti-inflammatory, and anti-carcinogenic.

The next heavier set of molecules in the terpene family

are called *sesquiterpenes* and are made up of three isoprene units, for a total of fifteen carbon atoms in their molecular backbones. These types of terpenes are a little bit heavier and denser, but are still pretty volatile and therefore fragrant. Some examples of sesquiterpenes that you may be familiar with by smell include **zingiberene** (top left), which is a component of the essential oil of Ginger (*Zinziber officinalis*) and **(alpha-)bisabolol** (lower left), which is a main component of the essential oil of Chamomile (*Matricaria chamomilla*). A subtype of sesquiterpenes called *sesquiterpene lactones* are a large part of the bitter flavor in many herbs, which is important to their function as digestive stimulating bitters. This subtype of sesquiterpene is found in such common digestive herbs as Dandelion (*Taraxacum officinale*), Burdock (*Arctium lappa*), and Artichoke (*Cynara cardunculus*).

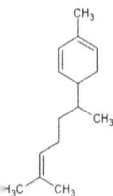

The next classification of terpenes are called *diterpenes* (this always confuses me since it seems like diterpene should come after monoterpene in my head). These are composed of four isoprene units, for a total of twenty carbon atoms in their skeletons. These molecules are generally too large and dense to be volatile and are therefore not fragrant. They are followed by *triterpenes* which are composed of six isoprene units, therefore 30 carbon atoms in their skeletons, and these are surely too heavy to be volatile. While these heavier terpenes are not ones that people can immediately recognize by smell, and are not generally found in essential oils because they are so heavy, they are nevertheless very important molecules that

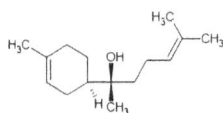

influence the medicinal properties of many herbs including Black Cottonwood (*Populus trichocarpa*), Ginko Biloba (*Ginko biloba*), and Baneberry (*Actea rubra*).

A nice example of a natural product that is a combination of the various terpenes all in one is tree resins or tree pitch. Many of the coniferous trees that grow in the woods around me such as Douglas Fir (*Pseudotsuga heterophylla*), Sitka Spruce (*Picea sitchensis*), and out in the desert Juniper (*Juniperus occidentalis*), produce very nice resins, often at the sites of old wounds but sometimes they just seep out of cracks in the bark. Two well known tree resins that have great significance in Christian history include Frankincense (*Boswellia sacra*) and Myrrh (*Commiphora spp.*), both of which are often used as an incense or smudge.

All these resins are nicely fragrant and can be burned to smudge or cleanse a space. They are all antimicrobial, and it has been suggested that burning these resins in a house will kill of many microorganisms in the air, thus being helpful in the case of sickness. The smoke from these resins often has an uplifting or psychoactive property to the humans around them, which makes them especially useful in religious or spiritual ceremonies. Many of these resins, including a type from further south known as Copal (*Bursera spp.*), have been worked with internally as medicines usually as anti-infective or immune stimulating agents. All these resins are complex mixtures of various terpenoids of various densities. When you find the resins out in the field they can be anywhere from gooey/sticky to rock hard in their physical feel, usually dependent on how long they have been exposed to the air. You can take these resins and hydro-distill them, placing them in the water of the mother flask of a still and heat the water, forcing the resulting steam through some kind of a condenser, in order to separate the lighter and more volatile terpenes from the heavier and denser ones. At the end of the distillation process you will end up with a very nice, light and fragrant essential oil floating on top of some hydrosol at one end of the still. The essential oil always smells brighter and more piercing than the smell of the original resin. This essential oil is the monoterpenes and sesquiterpenes fraction. Left behind in the mother flask is the diterpenes and triterpenes, which will be a thick viscous fluid when it is still hot but will solidify into a substance that is very hard and brittle, almost like a type of plastic in feel, as it cools. If you do not pour this substance out of your still while it is still warm, you will have a *very* hard and long time of cleaning up.

This brings me to the topic of distillation, which is the main way that we can extract terpenes as essential oils from plants in a pure form. The type of distillation that is used to do this is called either *hydro-distillation* if you are putting your plant material in direct contact with the boiling water in the mother flask of the still, or *steam distillation* if the steam from the boiling water in the mother flask is forced through the plant material without the boiling water itself actually coming into contact with the plant material. Distillation in general is an important process in chemistry, which serves to separate lighter and more volatile molecules from denser and less volatile ones in a complex mixture. Most people are familiar with distillation as the technique by which "hard" alcohols, often called liquors, are made. All alcohol is originally produced by yeasts (*Saccharomyces spp.*) which essentially eat sugars and excrete alcohol. This is how beers and wines are made, but the strongest that these alcoholic mixtures can get to is ten to maybe twenty percent alcohol by volume since the presence of alcohol at that ratio kills off the yeasts. To get a more purified form of alcohol (also called *ethanol*) it is necessary to distill the ethanol off from the water and other components of the beer or wine. By heating the complex mixture (beer or wine), the ethanol will boil off earlier than the water because it has a lower boiling point, which is the temperature at which it goes from a liquid to a gas. This vaporous ethanol can then be turned back into a liquid by cooling it down, which is generally done with a condenser, a long tube that is cooled by cold water running through it. A process akin to this is how gasoline is extracted from crude oil, and it is also how essential oils are extracted from plants.

To make an essential oil, it is necessary to distill the plant material along with water. As the steam from the boiling water passes through the plant material, it cooks and forces the volatile components of the plant (the essential oils) out of the plant material. These essential oils are then carried along with the steam into the condenser, where they together condense back into liquids. Hydrocarbons and water are not miscible, meaning that they do not mix with one another (a good example of this principle is in the creation of an oil and vinegar salad dressing in which the olive oil, which is a hydrocarbon, floats on top of the vinegar, which is water based). Once you have collected the distillate in some kind of receiving vessel, the essential oils will float on top of the water and can be drawn off with a pipette or something similar. The water that comes over with the essential oils is, however, impregnated with a small amount of the essential oils and presumably some of the denser terpenoids and other chemicals. This water is called a *hydrosol* and is pleasantly fragrant. I like to see people making use of hydrosols because quite a lot of hydrosol is produced in the distillation of essential oils. They make very nice room sprays, etc. There is a long history of the hydrosols of various plants being utilized as internal herbal remedies. Hydrosols would often be referred to as *floral waters* in this context, and many households in earlier centuries had their own still in order to produce them. I know very few people who have investigated hydrosols as internal herbal preparations, and I would love to see more research done in this area.

I would be remiss to discuss the creation of essential oils without mentioning that I have serious concerns about their mass production, or more specifically with the international marketing of essential oils. It takes quite a lot of plant material to produce a small amount of essential oil. The still that my distillation partner and I use is pretty big all things considered, with a mother flask that is made out of a 55-gallon stainless steel drum. We put about five gallons of water in the bottom of this and fill the rest with plant material, usually some fragrant coniferous tree that is abundant around us such as Douglas Fir

(Pseudotsuga heterophylla) or Western Red Cedar *(Thuja plicata)*. Oftentimes we get this plant material when people have decided to cut down some of these trees in their yards, which makes it so that we can harvest a bunch without needing to bother living trees to do it. A still load of this material, so envision a 55-gallon drum stuffed with fresh plant material, will yield at most 200 to 250 milliliters of essential oil at the end of the process (this is 6.5–8.3 fluid oz. for those of you not into the metric system, or less than half a pint).

There are several essential oil companies (Young Living and DoTerra come to mind) which are essentially pyramid schemes, convincing people that essential oils are the best way to utilize herbs, and that they work either by smelling them or by taking them internally (it is a *bad idea* to ingest essential oils internally, there are concerns about kidney damage over the long term, among other things) in order to take care of any number of very common health complaints. These philosophies are dangerous in a number of ways. As I mentioned above, essential oils are very strong and concentrated extracts of plants, and ingesting them for everyday ailments can have negative consequences. Furthermore, many of the conditions that people end up taking essential oils internally for could be handled quite nicely with a simple cup of tea of the herb in question. It is an unfortunate tendency of modern, Western, peoples to like to take very strong extracts of medicines.

Beyond the concerns about toxicity for the humans, many of these companies promote the frequent use of essential oils from plants that are not very common and that have a poor yield of essential oil, which is really pushy on the populations of these plants. The global essential oil industry is dependent either on industrialized mono-cultural farming of plants as source materials or on unsustainable harvest practices of wild plants. I do not mean to poo poo on people's love of essential oils—I love them too clearly—but I would encourage the reader to do their research on where their essential oils are coming from. If you can please invest in some distillation equipment and only work with essential oils that you have carefully and sustainably created yourself.

Beyond distillation, essential oils can be extracted out of plants using ethanol, which they are miscible with. If you want to work with a fragrant plant such as Rosemary (*Rosmarinus officinalis*) or Sage (*Salvia officinalis*) and the fragrance is part of the medicine, it is most effective to extract the plant into ethanol by making a tincture. You can still make a tea of these plants, but the heat of the hot water will drive the essential oils out, and they are not water soluble anyway, so theoretically you will not get much of the essential oils that way. Making teas of fragrant plants does work, so it is more complex than mere solubility, but these are good things to think about.

Essential oils and other fragrant molecules bring us to perfumery, which is an art unto itself. I will not go too deeply into this process but I want to mention it as a subset of herbalism via aromatherapy. Most perfumes are essential oils and other plant extracts, often combined with some animal products such as civet or castoreum (both of which are tinctures of a paste that is produced in the anal glands of a cat and a beaver, respectively) which are all dissolved into a base of ethanol. Perfumes are created much as herbal formulas are created, and a well-balanced perfume will have top notes, heart notes, and base notes. This division into top, heart, and base notes is a division of the molecules by their volatility and therefore how long they will stay on the skin. Top notes are light molecules. They are often very sweet and floral, sharp or bright. They are the first ones that you smell upon applying a perfume, and they dissipate quickly. Think monoterpenes. These are often essential oils. Heart notes are deeper in their smells, often spicier or woodier. They are the next scent that you notice after the top notes have volatilized and they linger much longer. These may be essential oils (probably more of woody plants than of flowers) or sometimes they are very concentrated tinctures or otherwise concentrated extracts of the plants such as concretes. The base notes are often funky and animalistic, or at least very woody. They are often derived from animal products which gives them a certain animalistic erotic smell to them (there are a lot of valid concerns about how these products are produced). These linger the longest on the skin, often for hours, and you need to get closer to the skin in order to smell them. Making perfumes and wearing perfumes can be a really great method for people to take some control over their own feelings, as the way that you smell influences your emotions and how you carry yourself in the world. I would encourage you to do more research in this subject, and to experiment with wearing perfumes and creating your own. Perfumes are very nice during the Beltane season.

ALCHEMY

Discussing essential oils, ethanol distillation, and perfumery is a good time to also discuss a little bit about practical, laboratory based alchemy. In many ways I am hesitant to discuss alchemy because I feel that it has been debased from a beautiful science to some New Age bullshit in the modern era. Whenever people think that a subject or discipline that they are studying is profound they like to say that it is "like alchemy," which always makes me cringe. Just because you put fancy ingredients in your artisinal chocolate bar does not make it "the Alchemy of chocolate" in my humble opinion. Alchemy is an intricate and beautiful way of working with plants. Of course the vegetable work is just one aspect of the alchemical path, and is traditionally thought of as the simplest and safest way to learn the techniques. People will then move on to working with minerals and animals.

I first bought Manfred M. Junius' *The Practical Handbook of Plant Alchemy* when I was maybe eighteen years old, and it went entirely over my head. I am not sure what made me buy that book but it came in handy many years later when I was making tinctures and especially after I took a general chemistry and an organic chemistry course with lab components in them and became familiar with lab equipment and how to work with it. Once you have a basic understanding of how to work in a lab this book becomes very straightforward and gives very nice and practical advice on how to make various alchemical preparations from plants. The main type of alchemical preparation that I have made and that is pretty simple to make is called a *spagyric*. There are two types of spagyrics, the *spagyric tincture* and the *spagyric essence*. A spagyric tincture is very simple to make while an essence requires more specialized equipment, mostly you need to be able to distill. The general idea in working with alchemy is the maxim *solve et coagula*, which means to break something down into its simplest parts and then recombine them, often in a more "refined" state. In the alchemical worldview three basic elements make up the entirety of the world, similar to the Chinese yin/yang concept in a way. These three philosophical principles, as they are called, are *sulfur, mercury,* and *salt*. These correspond to fire, water, and earth or soul, spirit, and body, respectively. In the body of a plant the sulfur is the essential oils, the mercury is the ethanol, and the salt is the minerals. Spagyric preparations basically extract these three priciples, purify them, and recombine them. Making a tincture by macerating fresh plant material in ethanol is one way to extract two of the priciples from a plant, the mercury (ethanol, which is provided from the outside when you are making a tincture) and the sulfur (essential oils which are soluble in ethanol). Once the tincture has macerated long enough, all you have to do is purify the salts and add them back into the tincture in order to make a spagyric tincture.

The salts are extracted and purified in a process which is called *calcination*. To calcine means to burns down to a fine ash. So to make your salts for your tincture, you press the tincture and save it. Take the *marc* which is the spent plant material, and burn it down to a fine ash. This ash is burned for a long time until it is a fine white color. The ash is then dissolved in distilled water, the water is filtered to remove the *caput mortuum* or the "death's head," which is the non-water-soluble constituents in the ash and are considered toxic. The water is then evaporated which reveals the salts in the form of beautiful clear crystals. These salts are then ground and added back into the tincture to make a completed spagyric tincture. These are very nice, adding the minerals back in kind of grounds and strengthens the medicine in a way that is hard to define.

A spagyric essence is a more involved process, and results in a potent final product. To make a spagyric essence, you first distill the fresh plant material to extract the essential oils, also called the sulfur. These oils are set aside in a brown glass bottle. The hydrosol and the plant material along with any remaining liquid that is left behind in the mother flask of the still are then all combined together and placed into some kind of a carboy, like you would use to brew beer or wine. Some people do not add sugar or yeast, and some do. Either way, put an airlock on the carboy and allow it to ferment into a wine. This often takes months. Once the wine is done fermenting, distill it and rectify the distillate, producing a purified ethanol from the plant. This is your mercury; put it aside as well. Then, the remaining plant material and tea left behind in the still are all burned down to an ash and calcined to produce the salts of the plant as outlined above. This is the salt. Finally all three of these purified essences are combined, and this becomes a spagyric essence. They are clear in color and very potent to taste.

A whole side of alchemy is astrological in nature. Each plant has multiple planetary correspondences, often based upon their appearance and also their medicinal qualities, etc. Lab workings are timed so that the planetary ruler of the plant is in an auspicious place in the heavens while the operation is taking place. I will not get into this in this book, but I would encourage the interested reader to check out Junius' book, or the writings of Robert Allen Bartlett, who is a living and practicing alchemist who lives pretty close to me here in "Washington State." While I love to make spagyrics, and the discipline of alchemy in general, I have to admit that I have not found a good way to incorporate alchemical medicines into my practice as a clinical herbalist. I think that the process of making spagyrics is a great spiritual process and helps the practitioner to get deeply and intimately involved with the plants that they are working with, but spagyric essences especially take a lot of plant material to make a little bit of medicine. They are basically essential oils dissolved in ethanol which people take orally, so they are very strong and concentrated and I am hesitant to give them to people regularly. I love them in drop doses to get in touch with the spirit of the plant. Especially if you love intricate laboratory operations, alchemy is a very rewarding path to embark on, remember to not lust after results and to focus on process not progress.

POLYSACCHARIDES

The next class of phytochemicals that I would like to talk about are the polysaccharides, which are a subset of the molecular class known as carbohydrates, or sugars. Carbohydrates, much like terpenes, are divided into several classes based on their size and complexity. All carbohydrates are composed of individual units which are called *monosaccharides*. Monosaccharides are ring shaped structures that are composed of carbon, oxygen, and hydrogen atoms. Monosaccharides are often called *simple sugars* and that is how most of us will be familiar with them, as sweeteners. The two most common monosaccharides are glucose and fructose, both of which function as some of the most basic fuels of our bodies. They are very abundant throughout the plant kingdom and we eat them quite a lot. Fructose has come to be implicated in many health problems in much of the world, where it has entered the diet in a whole new way in the form of high-fructose corn syrup, an industrial product used to sweeten many cheaply mass produced foods that can lead to a number of health complications. Fructose is also found in honey and is found within the disaccharide sucrose where it is paired with glucose. Sucrose is table sugar.

This brings us to the *disaccharides*, which are molecules that are composed of two monosaccharides bound to one another. These are also present in a number of plants, but not many of them are utilized as medicinal constituents, although table sugar can be added to herbal teas or elixirs to provide some sweetness and as a moistening agent.

Oligosaccharides are short chain polysaccharides, having some three to ten, but sometimes up to fifteen or twenty monosaccharide units in a single molecule. The most important of the oligosaccharides in my opinion are the *inulins*, a conglomerate of insoluble oligosaccharides that are found in a number of plants including Burdock (*Arctium lappa*) and Elecampane (*Inula helenium*). Inulins were first isolated from Elecampane in 1804 by German scientist Valentin Rose, and they are named after the Latin name for that plant, *Inula*. The inulins are indigestible polysaccharides that are abundant in certain plants that humans like to eat as foods or medicines. They serve as bulking agents since they are a form of fiber, and as such are beneficial to the digestion by promoting nice healthy bowel movements. The inulins are also thought to be a *prebiotic*, which is a type of polysaccharide that is not digestible by the human organism directly but does feed the microbes that live within the human digestive tract and bowel. We are becoming more and more aware over time of the importance of having a healthy gut microbiome in order to be generally healthy, and eating foods or medicines that are rich in prebiotics are one way to help and achieve this goal. I have written more about this concept specifically in conjunction with the medicinal aspects of Elecampane in an earlier chapter.

After the oligosaccharides come the *polysaccharides*, which are simply molecules that are composed of more than the ten to fifteen monosaccharide units that make up an oligosaccharide. There are several classes of polysaccharides present in plants, but I want to focus on two specific groups that we work with quite a lot as medicinal constituents, namely the *mucilages* or *mucopolysaccharides* found in many moistening herbs and the *immunomodulating polysaccharides* that are found in medicinal mushrooms and several other immune influencing herbs. Mucilages are very important constituents for the herbalist to consider, and I am coming to incorporate them in my own herbal practice and in my own personal healing formulas more and more as the years go on. Mucilages are basically polysaccharides that are water soluble and form a nice slimy gloopy substance when they are extracted out into water. This slime is thick, cooling, soothing, and vulnerary, and can be used on any inflamed or irritated tissues throughout the body.

There also seems to be an effect that especially some specific moistening herbs have—Solomon's Seal (*Polygonatum biflorum*) and False Solomon's Seal (*Maianthemum syn. Smilacina racemosa*) both spring to mind—in which they can bring moisture to dried up, tense, and atrophied connective tissues within the body, such as the *fascia* which is a web of connective tissue composed primarily of collagen that wraps around all of the various internal parts of the body, holding them together and also allowing them to move smoothly in relation to one another.

Many health care providers and body workers are just starting to become really interested in the fascia and the crucial roles that it plays within the body. I think that when the fascia becomes too dried out or stiff, this can lead to a number of health issues including chronic pain or chronically tense muscles. Moistening herbs seem to have a beneficial effect on the fascia by helping it to remain moist and supple. It has also been hypothesized that many of the moistening herbs, again with a specific nod to *Polygonatum* and *Maianthemum* although there are many others that work in a similar way, may help to encourage the production of synovial fluid, which is a thick fluid that is present in the joints that helps to lubricate them and protect them from shocks. I do not believe there is an understanding as to how this happens physiologically, but subjectively many people have noticed that working with these moistening herbs can help quite a bit with creaky, painful joints as well as chronic pain and a generally stiff body. A supplement that can be nice for these same sorts of conditions is called hyaluronic acid, which is one of the main components of synovial fluids in the human body and you can buy in capsules to take in order to make sure that you have plenty of it on board.

Beyond the above uses, moistening herbs have traditionally been worked with to soothe and promote the healing of inflamed or damaged mucus membranes within the body, from the lungs to the stomach to the urinary tract. Marshmallow *(Althea officinalis)* is a great example of an herb with a long and successful history of being worked with in this way, and is very nice for chronic stomach inflammation up to and including GERD (Gastroesophageal Reflux Disease, or acid reflux/heartburn) and has even been helpful when working with people who are living with ulcers. Mucilaginous herbs are also really nice for irritated lungs, and are great to incorporate into formulas for people with acute or chronic lung issues. Some plants that are rich in these mucilages include Plantain *(Plantago spp.)*, Comfrey *(Symphytum spp.)*, both species of Coltsfoot (*Tussilago farfara* is the Eastern species, *Petasites palmatus* is the Western species), and Calendula (*Calendula officinalis*), as well as the species discussed above.

The final class of polysaccharides that I would like to discuss are the immunomodulating polysaccharides. These are found in a number of different types of medicinal herbs. The ones that I am most familiar with and have worked with the most are those which are found within the various medicinal mushrooms such as Reishi (*Ganoderma spp.*), Cordyceps (*Cordyceps spp.*), Lion's Mane (*Hericium spp.*) and Red Belted Polypore (*Fomitopsis pinicola*), among others. I will discuss these mushrooms in much greater detail in in the chapter around Samhain, but suffice it to say that some polysaccharides that are found within these mushrooms, especially those known as the (1,3) Beta-D-Glucans, have really interesting and profound effects on the human organism that can be helpful in so many health conditions, up to and including cancer. Many of the other immune stimulating or modulating herbs such as *Echinacea* and *Baptisia* have some immunomodulating polysaccharides as a component of how they do their work within the human organism.

Polysaccharides are water soluble, and not very alcohol soluble. They are best extracted from their plants with water in one way or another. In the case of the mushrooms, a prolonged cooking of them in water, known as a decoction, is the best way to get the polysaccharides out. Many people say that the mucilages such as those found within *Althea* are damaged by exposure to heat, and that the gooey nature of the medicine will break down if you decoct them or even use hot water to make an infusion, and therefore I was taught that to best extract *Althea* or *Ulmus rubra* which is Slippery Elm you steep the fresh or dried plant material in *cold* water overnight, which does result in a very nice slimy water by the morning that is great to work with. I have to admit that one time I was in a rush and so I used hot water to steep my *Althea*, and it came out just as slimy if not more so! I have since discussed this with a number of other herbalists who have confirmed that using hot water does not seem to break up the polysaccharides and may even lead to a better extraction. I will leave it up to the reader to do their own experimentation. You can make a nice tincture out of these plants, especially with fresh plant material and a low percentage of alcohol in your menstruum. I make a nice slimy *Althea* tincture by tincturing the fresh Spring-dug roots at a 2:1 volume:weight ratio using 50% alcohol and 50% water as my menstruum.

ALKALOIDS

Alkaloids are a fun and interesting group of herbal constituents. Alkaloids are the first group of phytochemicals to be discussed in this essay which have nitrogen as a part of their molecular structure. Indeed if a molecule does not have a nitrogen atom somewhere in their structure than they cannot be classified as an alkaloid. The discovery of alkaloids in the laboratory led to so many advances in the health sciences because they provided purified extracts of many of the strongest effects that some medicinal plants can have. The first alkaloid to be discovered by being isolated and purified in the laboratory was morphine, which is one of the constituents of the Opium Poppy (*Papaver somniferum*) that gives this plant their sedative and pain killing properties. This alkaloid was discovered by Friedrich Sertürner, a German chemist, in 1804. He named the chemical **morphine** (he actually called it "morphium") after Morpheus, the Greek god of sleep. Like morphine, many plant derived alkaloids are very potent and physiologically active. They are all crystalline powders when they are isolated from plants, at least in their acid salt form. The main way that many people have encountered isolated alkaloids in their "pure" state is in the form of illegal drugs taken for pleasure. If you have ever interacted with a purified form of cocaine, methamphetamine, MDMA, or heroin then you are familiar with what an alkaloid looks like in isolation.

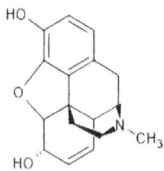

Most alkaloids taste very bitter, and tasting for bitter can be a method to determine if a plant you are interacting with may have alkaloids in it. Alkaloids are not easy to generalize in the same way that, say, polysaccharides are in terms of their medicinal applications within the human body other than to point out that they are often very strong and direct in the ways in which they do their work. Almost all psychoactive plants have alkaloids as their main chemical constituents, from "magic mushrooms" (*Psilocybe spp.*) to Coffee (*Coffea spp.*) and tea (*Camelia sinensis*). Alkaloids can also be wound healing (allantoin), bronchiodilating (ephedrine), or antimicrobial (berberine). I will look at a few plants that grow around me or that I like to work with that have alkaloids as a part of their chemical make up to show some examples of the various actions that they can take.

One group of alkaloids are known as the isoquinoline alkaloids. These are found in hundreds of different plant species and there are thousands of known molecules in this chemical family. The main ones that I know well and have worked with the most are known as the *protoberberines* which are found in a number of plants but I know them best from Oregon Grape (*Mahonia nervosa*). Oregon Grape is a very abundant herb in the understory of the forests around where I live. The main species that I like to work with spreads via rhizomes throughout the forest and can be propagated by pulling up a rhizome that connects two plants to one another, cutting out the rhizome that connects them in order to make this into medicine, and then re-planting the individual plants with a goodly amount of rooty rhizome still attached to each so that they will root back into the soil and begin sending out new rhizomes. I mostly work with Oregon Grape lotion? in three ways: as a cooling bitter to promote digestion, as a liver stimulant, and as an antimicrobial herb to kill off unwanted microbes on the inside or outside of a human's body. All these medicinal effects are directly attributable to the alkaloids that live under the bark of the roots, rhizome, and stems of these plants. You can see the presence of these alkaloids by peeling back some of the bark which will reveal a bright yellow color. The yellow is the medicine, which is the alkaloids. There are several alkaloids present in this yellow color, but they

are all variations of **berberine**. Berberine
is a bright yellow, water soluble alkaloid
that has a number of physiological effects
within the human body. It has been studied as an antifungal, antiamoebic, antibacterial, antifungal, anti-inflammatory, and
as an anticancer agent. This alkaloid is a great one to get onto
mucus membranes that are infected, which is how many of the
herbs that contain it are applied in practice such as *Mahonia*
or the better known but over harvested Goldenseal (*Hydrastis canadensis*). Berberine has also been worked with to lower
blood sugar in many people when taken as an isolated alkaloid,
with some people comparing it to the common diabetes medication Metformin. Berberine has one of the cutest molecular
structures around, to me it looks like a caterpillar with that
little methylenedioxy face!

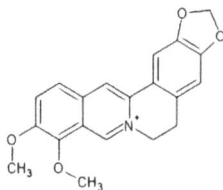

Another plant that I love to work with, is abundant
around me, and is rich in alkaloids is Pacific Bleeding Heart
(*Dicentra formosa*). This is a beautiful, low growing perennial herb that has tiny purple flowers that bloom in the early
Spring and look like little hearts. There is an ornamental hybrid that people often grow in their gardens which I am sure
many of you readers have seen. Bleeding Heart can best be
propagated via root divisions in the Fall or early Spring. They
like to be planted into a shady spot in the garden, where they
can very quickly get established and spread by both runners
and by seed. I would encourage people to find places where
there is going to be development or a clear cut is slated to

occur to transplant these plants out of and into their gardens, grow them out for a few years, and then harvest that material rather than wildcraft, as while this plant is very abundant in the woods around me, they do not have a very large range. The roots of Bleeding Heart, and to a lesser extent the aerial parts, are rich in many alkaloids including **protopine**, dicentrine, glaucine, and corytuberine. Many of these alkaloids are found in other plants in the *Papaveraceae* (Poppy) family. Protopine is found in the Opium Poppy *(Papaver somniferum)*, for example. Like many other plants in this family, which include *Corydalis spp* and California Poppy *(Eschscholzia californica)*, Bleeding Heart is a strong anxiolytic and pain killing herb. I think that of all the anxiolyitc (anxiety reducing) herbs that I work with, Bleeding Heart works the best and the fastest for me. This herb is certainly a low dose herb, especially if the roots were extracted into the tincture. I like to harvest the whole plant, aerial parts and roots, when they are in flower in middle Spring. I find that the roots alone make for a pretty narcotic and pain killing extract, which has its uses but can be overwhelming. For a long time, in the name of sustainable harvest, I would only pick and tincture the aerial parts in flower to make medicine, and this is a much gentler and more tonic but still very effective preparation. Since learning to cultivate this plant I have moved on to making medicine out of the whole plant which I feel is nicely strong while still keeping some of the tonic qualities.

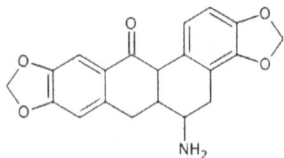

Many people, especially in the West Coast herbalism community, have a lot of concerns about Bleeding Heart in terms of both harvesting it and it also being too strong of an herb for people to work with safely. Some people have reported that taking even a couple of drops of the tincture causes them to become uncomfortably sedated and to have strongly confusing, drug-like experiences. That has never been my experience, nor have I seen it in any of the clients that I have given this herb to, but I suggest that if someone is going to start working with this herb, start off at a very low dose, like one drop of the tincture, and work up gradually from there until they find a dosage that works for them. Bleeding Heart is a great herb to carry around an ounce bottle of in your pocket just in case, for times of crisis. Often a few drops, or a dropper full or two if you are a hardhead, will calm and soothe the nervous system quickly and reliably. This can be super helpful for people who are working with mental health issues, working through old traumas, getting off of hard drugs, or some combination of all the above. I have found

that **Bleeding Heart** has a restorative effect on the nervous system when they are worked with for an extended period of time. I think that part of this is just knowing that you have a reliable way to settle down your anxieties when they flare up, which leads to feeling safer in the world, but I think there is a physiological thing going on too. Bleeding

Heart also works pretty well for pain, both acute and chronic. Many of the alkaloids that are found in this species have been shown to be analgesics in animal testing at least. A tincture of the fresh root is nice internally for pain, and also can be applied directly to the place that hurts as a liniment. such as to an aching tooth (essential oil of Clove [*Syzygium aromaticum*] works well to numb tooth pain, also). Bleeding Heart also helps with heartbreak and emotional wounds, helping the emotions around them to come up and out safely.

I once had an experience when working with this plant in a meditation where I took a drop while laying in a patch of the plants. I was having a hard time at this stage in my life and had a lot of emotional pain. I had a vision of giant Bleeding Heart flowers all around me, dipping their heart shaped flowers down and drinking a fluid I was excreting like sweat, which they explained to me was my emotional pain which they loved to drink as it is like food to them. I felt a little nervous about this but once I came out of the meditation I felt renewed with a much calmer state of mind.

While I'll save discussion of psychedelics for the Samhain chapter, I like to talk about a group of alkaloids known as the *harmala alkaloids* when I teach phytochemistry. These are a group of alkaloids, the two best known being **harmine** (top)and **harmaline** (bottom), that are mainly found in two plants: Syrian Rue (*Peganum harmala*) and the Ayahuasca vine (*Banisteriopsis caapi*). These alkaloids are not

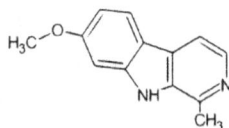

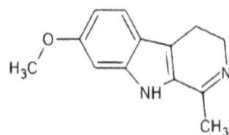

what you would consider classical psychedelics, but they do cause an interesting alteration of consciousness that is more dreamlike and trancey, with none of the bright colors and geometric patterns of the classic psychedelics, such as LSD or mescaline. These alkaloids are legal in the "United States of America," first of all, which makes them much safer to work with than most psychedelic alkaloids. They are mostly known for their effects as reversible Monoamine Oxidase (MAO) inhibitors.

Monoamine Oxidase is a beautiful little enzyme that lives all throughout the human organism, where it helps to defend the organism from the effects of ingesting of certain chemicals, specifically monoamines, which are alkaloids with a single amino group. There are several toxic monoamines such as tyramine which is found in many foods and can cause severe hypertension. Many human neurotransmitters are also monoamines such as **serotonin** (top), dopamine, epinephrine (adrenaline), melatonin, and histamine. MAO thus also has an affect on how the human nervous system is regulated, by breaking down these compounds via oxidation. Pharmaceutical MAO inhibitors were some of the first drugs used in the treatment of a variety of mental health conditions such as depression and anxiety, where they are believed to hep by preventing the breakdown of some of the "feel good" neurotransmitters in the brain too quickly. Another alkaloid which is a monoamine is called **N-n, dimethyltryptamine**, often abbreviated to **DMT**.

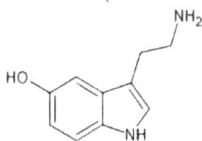

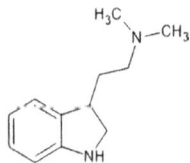

This molecule is a powerful psychedelic in the classical sense, working primarily on the 5-HT2a receptor subtype and causing visual changes, a sense of connection to a larger self, etc. This molecule is not active if it is swallowed by a human being because the MAO living in that human will break it down before it can cross the blood brain barrier. The visionary medicine known as Ayahuasca, which is worked with traditionally in the Amazon rain forest and has recently become quite popular (too popular) all over the world, is a tea that is made out of two plants. One of them is the aforementioned *Banisteriopsis caapi*, often called the Ayahuasca vine, and the other is any of a number of plants that contain DMT within their beings, the most common being called Chacruna *(Psychotria viridis)*. *Banisteriopsis* is rich in harmala alkaloids, which function as MAO inhibitors, which enable the DMT in the admixture plant to function as a psychedelic within the human body even if it is drank as a tea. This is an amazing bit of psychopharmacology that the Amazonian plant people worked out, and one that has baffled Western scientists for decades, specifically how people would figure out how to combine these two specific plants out of the hundred-thousands of possible combinations in the extremely biodiverse rain forest. The Amazonian plant people in question, of course, know how they figured out that particular combination of plants, which is that the plants told their ancestors how to do it.

Lately, quite a lot of attention has been paid to Ayahuasca and the many benefits that it can have on people who work with them. Studies are showing that drinking Ayahuasca can help with depression, addictions, and other similar afflictions. Closer to where I live, we have another source plant for harmala alkaloids: Syrian Rue *(Peganum harmala)*, a plant that is native to the desert regions of North Africa and the Middle East, where it has a long history as an herbal medicine. The plant is often called *esphand* in the context of being discussed as a medicine. This plant has become naturalized in some parts of Southwest Turtle Island to the point that they have been declared a "noxious weed," and routinely have poisons sprayed on them and the landscape to try and eradicate them. What I am trying to say is that this plant is an abundant and readily available source of these alkaloids.

A simple and kitchen-friendly method of extracting and purifying these harmala alkaloids is called the Hafenfratz technique after the scientist who first published the process of isolating them from *Peganum harmala*, which he called *telepathine* since they were known to encourage telepathy in people who worked with them. This technique is easy to find on the web, and it involves cooking the seeds in water that has some white vinegar in it, filtering well, then adding common table salt to precipitate the alkaloids. The process of filtering and precipitating is repeated several times until the alkaloids are nicely purified. This is a very easy, inexpensive, and fun do-it-yourself experiment on alkaloidal extraction, and I encourage people to try it. Once isolated, the alkaloids can be worked with in small doses to get some of the antidepressant effects. I find that working with these alkaloids or just the seeds as a decoction, improves mood in both the short and long term.

Alkaloids are soluble in water and alcohol, so teas (especially decoctions) and tinctures extract them pretty well. It is often suggested that a tincture needs to have some acidity in it, often by adding some vinegar to the menstruum, in order to efficiently extract alkaloids. This is often done when making a tincture of Lobelia (*Lobelia inflata*), a nice alkaloid-rich, anti-spasmodic herb, but I honestly don't think that it is necessary. Just alcohol and water should do the trick with most alkaloidal plants.

FLAVONOIDS

The final class of phytochemicals that I will discuss in this chapter is the flavonoids, which are a subset of the polyphenols. These are a class of large and complex molecules made up mostly of carbon, oxygen, and hydrogen atoms. They are characterized by the frequent occurrence of double bonds among the carbon chains, which are a type of electron bond that can enable a chemical to act as an antioxidant. The main purpose that flavonoids serve in the bodies of plants is protecting them from free radical damage that can result primarily due to the effects of UV light from the Sun. All the flavonoids are brightly colored (except for some that are clear). They are present in all green plants, especially in the flowers and fruits but also in all parts of the plant including the leaves and stem. When the leaves of deciduous trees turn from green to yellow, orange, or red in the Fall that is a process of the flavonoids in the leaf becoming exposed as the green of the chlorophyll goes away while the leaf begins to enter senescence. The bright colors of flowers are due to the presence of flavonoids, and many of these molecules have pigments that are not visible to the human eye but are visible to bees and other pollinators, who they serve to call in.

Much as they act within the body of the plants, flavonoids are valuable for humans to ingest due to their antioxidant capabilities. Much of the accumulated damage that happens to the human body over the course of a life that causes many of the signs of aging is caused by oxidative damage, which is also implicated in many disease states. This oxidative damage is caused by what are called free radicals, which are molecules that have an unpaired electron within them. An unpaired electron is highly unstable, like many of us they really want to be in relationship with the other beings around them, and they will break the bonds of other molecules to get some electrons to bond with, which results in damage to the molecules in question and also the creation of more free radicals. Left unchecked, this process can wreak havoc on the body of any living organism. It is one of the many interesting paradoxes of living on this planet that oxygen both keeps us alive and slowly kills us. Flavonoids, with their many double bonds, have the ability to bond with a free electron without having to break their own structure apart and therefore neutralize the free radical's ability to do damage. There are many antioxidant chemicals that are created by the body and taken in via the diet, but the more of them that we can get into us the better. This is part of the reasoning behind the diet philosophy that suggests "eating the rainbow," meaning that you should strive to have a food on your plate that is every color of the rainbow for most meals. By following this diet you are ensuring that you are ingesting a goodly amount of flavonoids with your meals, thus helping with oxidative damage.

Dark berries such as Blackberries (*Rubus armenianicus*), Blueberries (*Vaccinium spp.*) and dark Cherries (*Prunus spp.*) are all particularly rich in flavonoids and are great to incorporate into your diet. Flavonoids are also found in Tea (*Camelia sinensis*), Coffee (*Coffea arabica*), and a number of other herbs including Licorice (*Glycyrrhiza glabra*), Yerba Santa (*Eriodictyon californica*), Baikal Skullcap (*Scuttelaria baicalensis*) and Hawthorn (*Crataegus monogyna*), among many others. Along with their abilities as antioxidants, flavonoids also function as anti-inflammatories, anticancer agents, antispasmodics, antiparasitics, and venotonics (meaning that they strengthen the capillaries).

This last function of flavonoids—that of increasing the strength, suppleness, and permeability of the capillaries of the body—brings me to the final plant that I want to discuss in this chapter: Hawthorn (*Crataegus monogyna*). This tree has a long history as an herbal medicine all across the world with a strong connection to the spirit world and the fairies. They have been studied more than many other herbs, and it is well established that working with Hawthorne over an extended period benefits the cardiovascular system, often leading to lowered blood pressure and preventing cardiovascular events. Hawthorn flowers, leaves, and berries, all of which are worked with medicinally, are all rich in flavonoids. I have generally heard that it is these constituents that give Hawthorn their heart healing abilities through their encouraging the health of the capillaries, which are the tiniest little blood vessels at the extremities. If these capillaries are healthy, supple, and permeable then the blood can move through them very easily, which cuts down on blood pressure, and thus takes much of the strain off of the cardiovascular system as a whole, and the heart in particular. As the years go by, I feel that some other mechanism is taking place other than simply the presence of flavonoids in Hawthorn, or else you should be able to have the same medicinal effects by taking an extract of Blackberries daily for a month (although I am sure that if you did this there would be some benefit to the cardiovascular system).

Hawthorn is a precious and powerful plant. The flowers open up around Beltane, usually closer to lunar Beltane than to May Day around me, and their smell is both sweet and a little bit rotten or funky—some people compare it to the smell of sperm. This smell is due to the presence of **triethylamine**, an alkaloid that is also found in rotting meats and human sexual fluids. This is only appropriate for this tree which serves as a bridge between the worlds of the living and the dead. We harvest the leaves and flowers around Beltane, and the berries which are produced in great abundance, close to Samhain, on the opposite side of the wheel of the year and the other time of the year when the veil is very thin. In this way a complete extract, which combines leaf, flower, and berry, holds both of these key times of year, holds life and death.

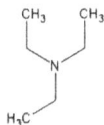

Along with their cardiovascular properties, Hawthorn is a softening and strengthening nervine and trophorestorative. Taking an extract, especially of the flowers, is immediately calming and grounding. They are a great plant to work with for frazzled humans, or for humans who have been through big traumas.

In many European traditions the Hawthorns are thought of as entrances to the Faerie realm and are treated with great respect and some fear. It is suggested to not fall asleep under a Hawthorn tree unless the fairies come and take you away. Hawthorn groves do have this tendency to cause people to enter into a kind of liminal and altered state. It is really easy to get turned around and lost while picking Hawthorn flowers, which is some classic fairy stuff. It is considered really bad luck to cut down a Hawthorn tree, which someone should tell to the city workers of the City of Olympia who have begun to systematically cut down the European Hawthorns in all of the city parks because they have decided that they are an invasive species. Hawthorn trees very readily propagate themselves from seed, and the easiest way that I have found to grow this plant is to dig up some of the many seedlings that can be found under older trees and bring them home to plant in your garden.

There are two species of Hawthorn that are indigenous to the PNW of Turtle Island, namely *Crataegus douglasii* and *Crataegus columbiana*. These are both species who like to grow along the rivers and in other wet places. The fruits of these trees are very dark, verging on black, and so both of these species are sometimes called Black Hawthorn. They are very profound medicines although I usually only gather the European species because they are so abundant, are considered an invasive species, and have a connection to part of my lineage (that part which is from Ireland and England). Hawthorn is an herb that could benefit just about everyone. Most people could use some heart support, either for their physical cardiovascular system or for their aching and sometimes broken emotional heart. The only people who could theoretically be harmed by working with this herb would be people who already have low blood pressure to the point that it causes some negative symptoms, although it takes working with Hawthorn in high doses daily for at least a month before they will start to have an effect on the blood pressure, so even for these people working with Hawthorn occasionally for the nervine, calming, and strengthening aspects of their medicine should be fine. Hawthorns have mighty thorns, as the name implies. They have traditionally been called Whitethorn in England and Ireland. These thorns are very long and strong. They point towards the protective nature of this plant, which can be very helpful for times when a person is feeling vulnerable. I like to place a few thorns in my jars of macerating berries or flowers for the energetic protection that they provide. I include Hawthorn in many of my formulations, along with Reishi who they pair with very well.

CONCLUSION

The study of chemistry is ruined for so many people in a public school type environment, but chemistry can be so beautiful and rewarding, and can teach us so much about the world around us. It is especially important to begin doing some practical laboratory work to really start to fall in love with chemistry. Any herbalist who makes their own herbal preparations is a practicing phytochemist since they are extracting phytochemicals in that process. The many chemicals that make up the world around us are sentient beings and their own people with their own worlds in which they are engaged, and to try to interact with them as living beings with their own wants and desires instead of dead building blocks that move around only as machines or automatons will really cause a whole level of the world in which we live to come alive and begin to teach you new things. I would really encourage the interested student to find their way to a class that teaches practical organic chemistry lab skills, just to be able to learn the various techniques and become familiar with how to work in a laboratory and the various tools that are available there. At the very least learning the art of distillation is a lifelong process that almost anyone I know who has gotten involved with it has quickly become a devotee of. I incorporate this material into the Beltane class to help remind us that chemistry too is a sacred act with which we can bridge the worlds.

6

SUMMER SOLSTICE IS THE TIME OF YEAR in which the days are at their longest, with the solstice itself being the longest day and shortest night of the year. At this time of year we are often very busy as humans in general and especially as herbalists since all of the plants are very active and blooming if they are flowering plants so we are frantically running around trying to pick all of the various flowering herbs that all seem to bloom at the same time (at least to me, trying to make medicines and fill orders). This time of year is when yang is ascendant and yin is resting. There is a lot of Sun and the rains are just starting to end, although in my specific area the solstice is often still in the more gentle part of the summer, there are still some rains and the temperatures are still cool at night. It is not until mid to late summer that it really starts to get hot and droughty, although I assume there will be longer and longer drought periods as climate change advances. Weirdly the last summer (I am writing this in 2020, what a weird year this has been) was actually pretty wet overall, and so far this summer has had a lot of precipitation. As usual global weirding seems more appropriate than global warming for this process that we are all living through.

At this time of year I do a goodly amount of picking in the prairies around me, and also by the rivers. I like to talk about the prairies since they are so crucial to this area and are great examples of landscapes that have benefited from human interaction and maintenance, in the form of harvesting and intentional burns for millennia, although they are suffering currently for a variety of reasons that I will go into. I will also discuss flower essences as a form of herbal medicine, their history as well as some practicalities around making and working with them, as well as some plants that live by one of my favorite rivers, the Skokomish.

PRAIRIE HISTORY, ANCIENT

While many people think of the area where I live, at the southernmost tip of the Salish Sea, which is also called the Puget Sound, as being primarily lush temperate rain forests, this place is also home to a unique system of landscapes which are drier and more open. They have specialized plant species that live upon them and nowhere else. These are often referred to as the *South Sound Prairies*, and they exist in the lowlands that are surrounded by various hills and mountain ranges including the Black Hills, the Cascade Mountains, and the Olympic Mountains. As a result of their geography, these lowlands lie in a variety of rain shadows and therefore are drier and hotter than the surrounding landscape. This trough in which the prairies live was created by the movements of glaciers, which grew and shrank, up and down between the Olympic mountains and the Cascades over the course of ancient history. This area has been glaciated more than a dozen times, as far as geologists have been able to learn. The most recent glaciation event occurred some 16,000 to 17,000 years ago: the Puget Lobe of the Cordilleras Ice Sheet made it as far south as the Rochester-Maytown area (Chehalis Territory), where I currently live, before retreating North again after only a few centuries.

The glaciers scoured the landscape as they traveled across it, and upon receding they left behind a ground up mix of minerals known as *glacial till*. Many massive floods and movements of water during these periods brought in additional materials, which all combined to form the prairie soils, which are rich in minerals and generally poor in nutrients and organic material. Following the retreat of the glacier, the area became much drier and hotter during what is called the Xerithermic period, which lasted from about 10,000 to 5,000 years ago. In this period, fires broke out in the landscape with increasing frequency and intensity, which allowed many of the plant species that now define the prairies to first become abundant in the area, as many of them are adapted to hotter and drier conditions and benefitted from periodic fires. One keystone species who became abundant at this time and still lives in this area are the Garry Oaks (*Quercus garryana*). During this Xerithermic period, the prairie ecosystems occupied a much larger area of space than they currently do. About 5,000 years ago the climate began to move towards being cooler and wetter, and the plants species that thrived upon the landscape began to shift towards many of the species that are common today, such as Red Cedar (*Thuja plicata*) and Sitka Spruce (*Picea sitchensis*).

As the rainforests began to expand and occupy the majority of the landscape, the prairies began to shrink and therefore to become more precious to the humans living upon them, who were the ancestors of the Chehalis, Nisqually, Cowlitz, and other Coast Salish tribal peoples. As I have mentioned before, while the landscape in this area is abundant in food, especially in proteins in the form of fish, shellfish, and wild game, the prairies provide only two main carbohydrate sources, the bulbs of the blue flowered Camas (*Cammasia quamash*) and the acorns created by the Oaks (*Quercus garryana*). The prairies are also places where berries can grow in great abundance since they get plenty of Sun, unlike in the depths of the forests, and they are also places where game animals will congregate and are easier to spot and hunt from a distance.

The prairies are also abundant in many medicinal herbs that are hard to find in the forests or the lowlands in general, you would need to either go up in elevation to alpine habitats or go across the Cascade mountains into the more desert habitats to find herbs such as Yarrow (*Achillea millefolium*), Oshá or Kishwoof (*Ligusticum spp.*), Balsam Root (*Balsamorrhiza deltoides*), and various species of Lomatium (*Lomatium spp.*). The Lomatiums could be worked with as carbohydrate rich foods in the form of the roots of some species, as a flavoring agent in the forms of the seeds of some species, and as a medicinal herb in the form of the roots or seeds of some species. As the climate slowly shifted and forests began encroaching on the prairies, the Indigenous peoples living in this area began intentionally setting fires to make up for the lack of "naturally" occurring fires, as well as utilizing various harvesting and replanting practices in order to increase the abundance of the plant species that they liked to work with and to maintain the prairie ecosystems for themselves and the plants and animals. These practices enabled the prairie ecosystems to continue to thrive for millennia, and without those human interventions there would be much less prairie ecosystems around today than there currently are.

Following the shift in climate, the next big change that caused the prairies to suffer was, as usual, the arrival of European colonizers. Starting in the mid 1800s the government of the "United States of America" began to give the land in what was then called "Oregon Territory" away to white farmers and their families as a way to "settle" the "wilds" of the area. Of course, these lands had already been occupied and were still occupied by the Indigenous peoples of this area, although at this point in history the populations of these Indigenous tribes were at an all time low due to the devastating effects of disease brought over by the European invaders, which by some accounts killed some 90% of the Indigenous populations of Turtle Island in just a few decades, as well as by a genocidal campaign on the part of the occupying government and military.

The prairies were just the sorts of landscapes upon which the farmers wanted to farm. They were not covered in trees (the old growth forests were often considered a nuisance or even an evil presence by the colonizers and were cut down and burned at an astonishing rate), got plenty of sunshine, and often had rivers or streams nearby which could by used for drinking and irrigation. These colonizers did not appreciate the prairies as unique and special places, and they could not see that these places were maintained by the Indigenous peoples who lived upon them and worked with them, rather they assumed that God had essentially created these spaces for them to build farms. Their ideology was largely focused on farming and capitalist accumulation through resource extraction from the land, which is an inherently destructive mindset. The use of root plows decimated the many perennial plants such as Camas and the various Lomatiums, while the suppression of Indigenous fires enabled the forests to begin encroaching on the prairie habitats. Domesticated livestock also greatly damaged the prairie plant species, especially pigs who love to eat Camas, apparently. Farmers also began to plow up the prairies and plant them with introduced grasses to serve as fodder for grazing animals and to produce hay. The land upon which I live is a former prairie that was turned into hay fields and cattle grazed upon it for over a century, although I am pleased to say that there are still some Camas living in the hay fields. A number of Eurasian plants were also introduced which have become weedy in the prairies such as Scotch Broom (*Cytisus scoparius*) and tall oatgrass (*Arrhenatherum elatius*).

Today the South Sound Prairies are greatly reduced in their size and occurrence in the area, with forests, farms, and urban development occuping much of the land upon which they used to live, and especially due to the severing of the relationship of the indigenous peoples to these lands. A number of prairie habitats have remained in tribal hands, especially the Chehalis and Cowlitz, and these prairies are doing well or are being actively restored. There has also been a growing interest among botanists and conservationists towards restoring and maintaining the prairie habitats that still exist. One really interesting and ironic fact is that there are thriving prairie ecosystems within the land that has been occupied by the "United States" military in the form of the Joint Lewis McChord Airforce Base (JBLM), which was established in 1916 and today occupies some 86,000 acres and is located East of the Salish Sea between the modern day cities of Olympia and Tacoma. Much of the base is maintained as open areas so that the soldiers can practice their war games there. While these activities are largely destructive on the immediate environment (not to mention the environmental devastation all over the world that is wrought by the "United States" military), the base is also home to some two thirds of the still existing prairie ecosystems in this area. Military drills often involve live ammunition and explosives, which do significant damage to the landscape but also set frequent fires which have helped certain prairie plant species to thrive. The base is also involved with conservationists in habitat restoration projects and with the Chehalis and Nisqually tribes in traditional harvest and maintenance practices. It is funny and heartbreaking that the military's claiming of the land has "protected" it from development by other arms of the military-industrial complex, but here we are, and I am grateful for the prairies that live in this especially occupied zone. There are many groups who are working to protect and restore these ecosystems, and I would encourage you to reach out to them and get involved, especially any projects that are tribally led or that are focusing on getting prairie habitats back into the hands of indigenous peoples.

SOME PRAIRIE PLANTS

A number of plants grow in the lowland prairies that normally can only be found in alpine or desert areas. I do not encourage people to harvest plants from the prairies since these places already have so much pressure placed upon them. Several of the plants that live in the prairies also live or have analogues in the arid lands East of the mountains and will be covered in a later chapter. One plant that is very abundant in the prairies, and can be found in developed lands and even in people's yards that are adjacent to the prairies themselves is Yarrow (*Achillea millefolium*). Yarrow is a very common herb, and is found all across the globe in the northern hemisphere. They have a long history of being worked with as a medicine in all cultures with whom they have lived and are quickly adopted into medicine traditions in places that they are not native to. For a long time I was taught that Yarrow was a Eurasian plant that was introduced to Turtle Island, and therefore could be considered an invasive weed, but it is clear that Yarrow has existed on Turtle Island for millennia. It seems that there are two species, one is native to Eurasia (*Achillea millefolium*) and one is native to

Turtle Island (*Achillea lanulosa*). The two species are identical in terms of their phenotypic presentation and can only really be differentiated by examination of their chromosomes, with *A. millefolium* being haploid while *A. millefolium* is diploid. Both species are common all across Turtle Island and have a long history of use upon this land, where they are called "Squirrel's Tail" in some languages. The Anishinaabe names for this plant include *Waabanoowashk* and *Ajidamoowaanow*. Yarrow is a perennial herb with beautiful white flowers and a dreamy, characteristic fragrance. Humans have loved this plant for as long as we have lived around them, as evidenced by the presence of Yarrow in the grave of a Neanderthal man in Iraq that dates to some 60,000 years ago. This person was laid to rest on a bed of flowers, and one of them was Yarrow.

The Latin name for the genus, *Achillea*, refers to Achilles who is one of the main characters in Homer's *Iliad* and a great warrior in the Trojan War. In one story, Achilles was dipped by his Mother into a great vat of Yarrow tea when he was a baby, which provided him with lifelong protection during battle. Since she was holding Achilles by his foot when she dipped him, his foot and ankle did not get dipped and so that was the only vulnerable part of his body, which is where he was hit by an arrow (supposedly also made out of Yarrow) which finally killed him. This story provides one good indications of one of the main ways that humans like to work with Yarrow, which is for wounds and bleeding.

Yarrow is a strong astringent, meaning that they will tighten up and toughen tissues that they come into contact with, and they will also contract blood vessels that they come into contact with. This makes Yarrow nice to apply externally to toughen up skin that is going to be put through a rough process. Keewaydinoquay, an Anishinaabe herbalist who was also a great teacher and wrote several books, talked about how her mother would soak her hands in Yarrow tea in order to toughen up the skin so that she could weave lots of baskets, which she sold to make her living. Yarrow is also great for wounds or cuts after they happen. Yarrow will staunch the bleeding of even deep cuts, which is a great first step to dealing with a cut, since the blood really gets in the way and promotes panic. Yarrow is also antiseptic so helps to prevent infection, and will encourage the wound to heal quickly without leaving as much of a scar. I have heard stories of packing even very deep and serious wounds, in a situation in which getting to the hospital was not an option, with Yarrow which stopped the bleeding and functioned as a bandage until the person could get to more first aid options, but I have never done this myself. There is also a pain killing quality that Yarrow holds which is nice externally for wounds, sore muscles, or for tooth pain.

Internally, Yarrow is worked with in a number of ways. Internal bleeding of all sorts can be helped though ingesting Yarrow, similar to applying them externally. This makes Yarrow a very nice herb to work with for people who menstruate, as the plant has been shown to both staunch excessive bleeding and also to break up stagnant blood and help to get it out. This herb should be avoided in the first trimester of a desired pregnancy since this ability to bring on menstruation could also lead to losing an early pregnancy. Yarrow is a bitter and increases digestive secretions, so they can be worked with like any number of other bitter plants to help with a person's digestion. Yarrow is also nicely sedating and pain killing, especially if taken in larger doses. They contain a number of constituents including thujone, which I believe is involved in the mild psychoactivity of the plant. Even the smell of Yarrow is nicely settling and opens a person up. Yarrow stalks are how the Chinese oracle called the *I Ching* was and is worked with for many people, although coins are often used also. The stalks are thrown and the way that they lay determines which of the hexagrams are to be looked at in the divination. I like to think that the mildly stoning effect of smelling the stalks helps to get practitioners into a good space for divination, which is an idea I first heard from Ryan Drum who is an herbalist living up on Waldren Island.

When taken as a hot tea, Yarrow is nicely diaphoretic, meaning that they will bring on a sweat in the human body, and they are worked with quite a lot in this capacity to help to break a fever, often in combination with Elderflower (*Sambucus spp.*) and Peppermint (*Mentha x piperita*). While it is often wise to let a fever run its course, in situations where the person in question in getting too exhausted, or for any of a number of other reasons why it might be beneficial to break the fever, having a person drink a big mug of hot Yarrow tea, wrap up in a bunch of blankets, and then go to bed for the night will often result in lots of sweating and the breaking of the fever by the morning. I like to drink Yarrow before going into

a sauna in order to really get the sweat flowing, especially if I am a little bit sick. In the places where they grow, **Yarrow** is often very abundant, and since the main part of the plant that people work with as a medicine is the flowers, you can harvest Yarrow without doing much damage to the stand that you are interacting with. Although if someone was to pick all of the Yarrow flowers in a stand that would certainly keep the plants from being able to set seed and make babies. I strongly encourage people to grow their own Yarrow, as they are very easy to start from seed. You can either harvest seed from a wild patch in the late summer and early fall, or Yarrow seed is cheap and common to find for sale by either flower or medicinal herb seed companies. I have had the best luck clearing a patch in the garden of grass and other plants, breaking up the soil, spreading out the tiny Yarrow seeds, tamping them in and covering with some rotted leaf mulch in the winter or early spring. The seeds will start to germinate by mid spring and you can transplant the young plants in the fall.

Another plant that grows in abundance in the prairies that I *do* feel good about harvesting is St. Joan's Wort, also called St. John's Wort (*Hypericum perforatum*). This herb is a Eurasian native that has become weedily abundant all across the globe, especially in the northern hemisphere. They are often found growing in the prairies, where their presence is not ideal, so harvesting them from these places will provide you with medicine and also take some of the pressure off of the wild plant communities living in the prairies. St. John's Wort is perhaps one of the better known herbal medicines as they have become accepted in more mainstream circles as being beneficial for depression, which here in the late-capitalism Anthropocene is a condition that many people live with. St John's Wort is a plant of the summer, and they begin to bloom right around the solstice. The traditional time to harvest this herb is on the Feast of St. John the Baptist, which is June 24, just a few days after the solstice. The bright yellow flowers of this plant are very solar in appearance. If you pinch off some of the flowers and squish them between your fingers they will stain your fingers purple, which tells you that they are medicinally potent, since the purple color seems to correspond to the presence of many of the medicinally active constituents within the plant, such as the hypericins and various flavonoids. This purple juice is also a good way to determine if you have picked the correct plant. Another nice defining feature of the plant's appearance is to hold a leaf up to the sunlight and look for the perforations. *Hypericum perforatum* is named after these perforations, or small holes, found in the leaves, which let the sunlight stream through when the leaf is held up to the Sun. I like to make a fresh herb tincture from St. John's Wort, and you can tell that it is good if the menstruum turns a bright blood red. The herb can also be extracted into oil for external use, and you want to see the red color there as well.

All these solar correspondences point towards to most common way that people like to work with this plant, which is as an anti-depressant. St. John's Wort lets the light in to the dark places. I have found St. John's Wort to be most helpful in mild or transient depression, especially so-called Seasonal Affective Disorder, or SAD. Here in the temperate rainforest the winters are long, dark, and some would say dreary, especially if a person lives in the forest where the trees block out what little sunlight may be available. Many people have a hard time with the dark season here, especially if they grew up in a sunnier locale. While one of the main things I actually recommend for this condition is to supplement Vitamin D3 throughout the dark season, St. John's Wort can also be really helpful to work through the winter glooms. The plant brings in some sunshine and can help to alleviate this kind of mild seasonal depression. St. John's Wort is also a nice uplifting nervine that can be worked with any time of year to bring a calm sense of peace. I have found that while they can be helpful, St. John's Wort often will not be enough to address more chronic or deeply entrenched depressions. I like to work with Black Cohosh (*Actea syn. Cimicifuga racemosa*), among others, for these kinds of conditions.

It is very well documented that St. John's Wort has a strong effect on the functioning of the liver, specifically increasing the activity of the cytochrome P450 pathway, which is a big part of phase one of liver detoxification. For this reason it is important to *not* work with St. John's Wort with people who are on any number of different medications, as the herb can increase the functioning of the liver to the point that the medications may be processed too quickly through the body to be able to do their job. For this same reason St. John's Wort can be nice for people who work or live in conditions in which they are exposed to potentially toxic materials that may be taxing on the liver or that can be detrimental if they linger in the body for too long. I think that the liver stimulating aspects of this herb are part of the antidepressant aspects also, helping to clear out detritus and stress hormones.

The nervous system in the body is clearly affected by working with St. John's Wort in terms of helping to deal with depression, but this herb can also be worked with internally and especially externally to help with nerve pain or physically damaged nerves. I like to have people trace the length of an inflamed, painful, or pinched nerve with an infused oil of St. John's Wort to help with pain and promote healing, while also having the person take some of the herb internally in the form of a tincture.

FLOWER ESSENCES, AND A FEW MORE PLANTS

While I do not like to harvest plants from the prairies, other than the ones that I have outlined above, I do love the plants that live in the prairies and want to be able to work with them as medicines. For this reason, and also because the prairies are places where there are lots of flowers and also sunshine, I have taken to teaching about and making flower essences when I am introducing people to the prairies.

Flower Essences are a type of herbal preparation that can be created without causing much damage to the plant that you are extracting, the most harm being picking some flowers off of the plant, and in many cases flower essences are made without doing any physical damage at all. For this reason if you are feeling called to work with a specific plant that is rare or endangered, or a plant that is too toxic to work with internally, a nice way to get around these things is by making a flower essence with the plant, which is essentially an energetic extraction.

Perhaps the best-known flower essences are the Bach Flower Essences, a line of 38 distinct essences, each of which have a specific emotional or spiritual ailment that they are supposed to be good for. Many people who are not really into flower essences have interacted with Bach's product known as "Rescue Remedy," which people give out for all sorts of shock and trauma, and as a calming agent. The Bach flower essences were developed by Dr. Edward Bach, who invented the flower essence as an herbal preparation. Dr. Bach lived in England from 1886 to 1936. Bach was medically trained and worked mostly as a homeopath. At the age of 43, he decided to find a new method of healing, as he felt that the models being worked with at the time were inadequate for getting to the roots of disease. He and his family abandoned his practice and went to the countryside to learn how to heal from the plants. His methods were intuitive and involved him noticing that when he was having certain negative emotions in his body, he could hold his hands over specific plants and they would alleviate his suffering. He determined that the warming action of the Sun shining on the dew of a plant, allowed it to absorb the plant's healing qualities. His first essences were made by collecting this dew and preserving it with brandy (I will point out here that dew is an important substance within the alchemical tradition also). Since this technique did not provide enough material for him to work with, he developed a method of putting the flowers of the plant in question into a bowl of water and allowing the Sun to shine on this for a period of time, then preserving this with brandy as his mother tincture, which would then be diluted in a similar method to how homeopathic preparations are diluted to make the actual essences for people to ingest.

Now, clearly, a heavily diluted solution of brandy and water, that has had some flowers briefly steeped in it, does not have much if any of the plant in question in the final product. Bach believed that it was the energetic essence of the plant that was extracted, which you could perhaps call the plant's spirit. Today many people all over the world create and work with flower, plant, stone, and place essences. I am not much of a flower essence person, I really need to be able to taste the plant in order to get a good feel for them, even if I am working with a tiny drop dose with the intention of doing plant spirit type work. For many people, however, flower essences seem to promote emotional and spiritual healing, and supposedly they can be worked with to address the same physical maladies that a tea or tincture of the plant in question will work for (but this has never worked for me in practice).

Two of my mentors and teachers, namely Joyce Netishen, who lives near me, and Mimi Kamp, who lives in the Sonoran desert, are prolific essence makers and work with essences alongside other herbal preparations in their practices. I can say without a doubt that these people are effective practitioners. Mimi often makes her essences by not even putting any part of the plant at all into the water, at least not cutting or picking anything. She might dip the flowers that are still attached to the plant into the water, or she will just place a jar of water next to or on the plant in question and ask the plant to move into the water, allow it to sit for awhile, and then call it good.

Joyce makes her essences in what I think of as a more traditional way, which consists of getting some clean water and a glass or crystal bowl which has no writing or characters on it. This bowl is filled with water and placed next to the plant which is to be made into an essence on a bright and sunny day, ideally without a cloud in the sky. Using scissors she will cut the flowers from the plant, being careful not to touch the plant with her hand so as to not contaminate the essence with her own energies, and float them face down on the water, cutting enough flowers to cover the surface of the water in the bowl. This is then allowed to sit in the Sun for several hours, at which time the flowers are removed and discarded and the water is filtered and then preserved with brandy. This becomes the mother tincture. This version of the process ends up getting some of the physical stuff of the plant, since the water will often take on a bit of color and flavor. This mother essence is then diluted, often one part mother essence to ninety nine parts water/brandy, to make a stock bottle, which is then further diluted to make the final product which is what people take.

I love the process of making flower essences, and I have had some profound experiences working with them in my own body. Some people seem to be called to working with the plants in this way; often they are very sensitive and they work with the plants in a spiritual way. As I said before, I like to make flower essences primarily with plants that are not very widespread or that are too toxic to take in physiological doses. When I am working with flower essences it is often for more emotional or spiritual reasons than, say, to help someone get over a cold.

Two plants that I have made flower essences of in the prairies are Camas (*Cammasia quamash*) and Death Camas (*Toxicoscordion venenosum*). I have spoken of Camas before. This plant is and traditionally has been a crucial food for many indigenous peoples on the western part of Turtle Island. Their roots are harvested and eaten after being baked for a very long time, often utilizing a pit bake, which involves digging a big pit and lining it with sword ferns or other vegetation, then either building a fire in the pit or heating rocks in a fire, which are thrown in the pit. Then cover the heat source with more ferns and pile Camas bulbs on top. This whole thing is buried and left overnight, during which time the Camas bulbs are thoroughly cooked until they are translucent and sweet. Death Camas is a plant that lives in the same habitats that Camas live in, and they are similar in their general shape including that they have a bulb type root. The easiest way to tell Death Camas from Camas is by their flowers. Camas have purple/blue flowers while Death Camas has white flowers, also the size of the flowers and the way they are arranged on the stalk are very different. Death Camas is deadly poisonous, they contain a number of neurotoxic alkaloids including zygacine, indeed they are one of the very few deadly poisonous plants that live in this region. Including even a few Death Camas bulbs in a large Camas pit bake could sicken everyone who eats the Camas and maybe kill some of the people, and for this reason Camas is harvested in the summertime while they are in bloom rather than in the fall which is when most edible roots are harvested.

I have never eaten Camas, and I never will unless I am specifically invited to by a tribal member, so I decided to make a flower essence of this plant, as well as one from Death Camas, which I will not ever eat (I hope) for obvious reasons. In my workings with these essences I have found that the Camas essence is deeply nourishing, calming, and helps me to connect to this land upon which I live. The Death Camas essence is pushy, feels a little bit scary, and helps to kill off the things that I am holding on to or that are attached to me that I don't want anymore. They are very nice to work with in conjunction, first taking the Death Camas for the purge and then taking the Camas to heal and soothe after the intense experience.

In my practice as an herbalist I rarely work with flower essences, but when I do it is usually to call in a specific emotional, spiritual, or felt aspect of the plant in question. This process is more intuitive and can be guided more by the spirits or my deep unconscious or whatever you want to call that, than my process of choosing tinctures for someone which is more logical. I like to add a few drops of a flower essence to a tincture formula in order to bring in some of those emotional or spiritual components (not that a tincture does not also carry these things). I once saw a flower essence practitioner who chooses their essences entirely by guidance from their spirit guides. This person is partnered to Mimi and comes from a line of indigenous healers from northern Mexico. He would lay out a box full of hundreds of different essences that Mimi had made and just slowly pass his hand back and forth over the box. Much like dowsing for water, his fingers would sort of twitch downwards when they passed over a specific essence, and he would pull that one out and hand it to Mimi to explain to me without ever reading the label. The two times that he chose essences for me in this way the description of what things the essences were worked with were amazingly appropriate to what I was going through at that stage of my life.

SKOKOMISH RIVER

High summer is a great time to go to the river. My favorite river to visit at this time of year is the Skokomish river, which is the southernmost of the many rivers that run on the Olympic peninsula. The Skokomish river flows from the crest of the Olympic mountains down into the Hood Canal. It is composed of three main tributaries, the North Fork, the South Fork, and the main body of the river. The Skokomish is the largest river in the Hood Canal watershed. The waters of the Skokomish are clear, cold, and beautiful. There are so many great spots to sit, and you can find this beautiful grey clay that forms perfect rectangles in the depths of some parts of the river. Traveling up the Skokomish you are also traveling up in elevation, which essentially means traveling back in time in terms of what herbs are harvestable or blooming. I like to go up the Skokomish to do some last minute bark harvests since the bark of the trees will still be slipping up there into mid summer, long after they have stopped slipping in the lowlands around where I live. The Skokomish is also home to many flowering and herbaceous medicines that I like to gather, especially the Roses that grow right along the river.

SKOKOMISH TRIBE

The Skokomish river is named after the Skokomish tribe, who are the descendants of the Twana people *(tuwa' duxq)*. Prior to colonization, the Twana people's territory extended from marine and estuarine environments along the Hood Canal up into the eastern slopes of the crest of the Olympic mountains in the heart of the peninsula. The valleys of the three forks of the Skokomish river were where the Skokomish Twana *(sqWuqWu'b3sH)*, called "the people of the river" lived traditionally. There was also a community of Twana peoples who lived along Vance Creek, which runs into the Skokomish near the forks, who were called *ct'welq'we'li*. These people have lived in this area for millennia, indeed they have lived there for so long that they have recollections and stories of events that took place in the deep past such as the Great Flood:

Skokomish tribal member Frank Allen recounted a version of the story to the anthropologist William W. Elmendorf in the 1930s: "The Skokomish people had a flood. My grandfather said about eight or nine generations before his time. The Skokomish all put food and their belongings in canoes and then the rains and the waters began to rise. They rose and rose until the mountains were covered. All except one back of *e'lo'at*, (Mount Ellinor) called *duxwxwe'kw' adebetebad*, 'Where You Tie Yourself'. Just the top of this mountain was showing." (Wray, 66)

The Skokomish Twana were blessed with a huge salmon run on the river as well as shellfish along the Hood Canal and abundant game and berries up on the mountains. The Treaty of Point No Point of 1855, which was met with great resistance, eventually forced the Skokomish Twana, now designated the Skokomish Tribe, to a small reservation at the mouth of the Skokomish River on the Hood Canal, which they would share with members of the S'Klallam, Twana, and Chemakum tribes. While the federal government claimed that they would still have access to their traditional hunting and fishing grounds, over time much of this land was bought by white settlers. Furthermore, industrial and agricultural developments resulted in the loss of many species of plants and animals that had once been abundant in these areas, especially the damming of the North Fork of the Skokomish river, which is where the ancestors of the Skokomish landed their canoes and made their first homes after the Great Flood caused further damage. Two dams were built for hydroelectric power, which decimated the mighty Salmon runs of the Skokomish, most of which originated in the North Fork, while also flooding vast areas of land that were traditional villages. The damming of the river also resulted in a lower water flow, which caused sediment to build up in the main fork, raising the bed by more than four feet. This has resulted in more severe and frequent flooding in the valley, resulting in homes being flooded as well as groundwater being contaminated by septic systems, and damaging the estuarine environment at the mouth of the river.

Through all this the Skokomish have maintained a strong tribal community, and they continue to fish the Skokomish river as well as gather traditional foods on the peninsula. One of the main people to come to national attention from the Skokomish tribe was Gerald Bruce Miller, also called *subiyay*, who was the tribe's cultural and educational director for more than thirty years. Miller helped to revitalize tribal practices that had been made illegal by the "United States" government, was a story keeper, an artist who especially focused on basketry and textile weaving, and an herbalist who worked with both traditional medicinal herbs as well as introduced weeds. *Subiyay* also served as a bridge in many ways to the white community in and around the Skokomish reservation, he taught and was friends with many faculty members of The Evergreen State College, the local and pretty liberal college in Olympia where he introduced many young people to the indigenous cultures and practices of the area in which they

lived. Much of my own knowledge of indigenous lifeways began from information that my teachers got from *subiyay*. He
died in 2005 just after a movie was made about him, called
Teachings of the Tree People: The Work of Bruce Miller, which is
a wealth of information and inspiration.

PLANTS

The Skokomish is the place to go to harvest any barks
that you did not get around to in the springtime. There are so
many Red Alders (*Alnus rubra*) along the many streams and
rivers that have fallen over and are easy and sustainable to
harvest, and Willows (*Salix spp.*) galore, but the main tree that
I end up harvesting bark from up on the Skokomish is Pacific
Dogwood (*Cornus nuttallii*). The reason I like to harvest the
bark of this tree here is because when you drive up towards
the river, before you get to the national forest in which most
of the river lies, you pass through a bunch of land "owned"
by various logging companies such as Green Diamond and
Weyerhauser. These areas are basically either clear cuts or
Douglas Fir (*Pseudotsuga heterophylla*) monoculture plantings,
but the Dogwoods manage to grow in them, presumably because the birds eat their fruits and poop the seeds all around.
When the Dogwoods are in flower you can easily spot their
distinctive and beautiful white flowers peppered throughout
the Doug Firs. There is this interesting phenomenon where
the Dogwoods often grow right at the edges of the clear cuts,
where the clear cut meets the surrounding forest. Often the
soil in this area is churned up and formed into a kind of hill

or berm of very loose soil. The Dogwoods germinate in this loose soil, grow up for awhile, and once they get to a certain age and height, they become too heavy for the loose soil to hold them in place, and they fall over. I have found probably half a dozen Dogwoods in one specific spot along the edge of a clear cut and the forest where they have all fallen over. The fallen over Dogwoods then begin to sprout new leaders all up and down their trunks which turn into almost a line of new trees, but the tree will often start to die back from the old tip which is now on the ground.

I have been in a many year process with this one tree where I will cut down the outermost of the new upright leaders and then cut the main trunk, which is on the ground and rotting from the tip down, to the next leader. I harvest all the bark off the leader that I cut off, and come back a few years later when I need more. Inevitably the rot has progressed and I will do the same process again. The goal is to eventually cut off all of the leaders except the lowermost one, essentially pruning the main trunk down until it does not go beyond the lowermost leader. I hope that at that point the tree can put all of their energy into that one leader and turn themselves back into an upright tree, so they can get to the sunlight, and hopefully the rot will stop. I think that this specific harvest method is beneficial to the trees that I am working with, although I have not completed the process to actually know. At the same time, I have been working on figuring out how to germinate the seeds that are in the fruits that the Dogwoods produce so abundantly in the fall, and also buying baby Dogwoods from commercial native plant nurseries and planting them around my home. I know at a certain point all of the Dogwoods that I have been building relationship with will be destroyed, when the forest they are in is clear cut by the "owner," although I pray that things change so that day never comes.

The Dogwoods live in the shadier parts of the forest, although they are almost always leaning out from that shade towards the sun. When in full sun, they can really fill out, as evidenced by the Dogwoods that people grow in their yards.

The **Dogwood**s bloom just after the Hawthornes most years. Their flowers are huge and white with usually four "petals" which are really modified leaves called bracts. The actual flowers are tiny and in the center of the bracts. The flowers look in many ways like a single open eye, and they point upwards towards the sky. The bark of this tree is the part most often worked with as a medicine. The bark is bitter and a little bit sweet in taste, and like most Cornus species the bark of Pacific Dogwood can be worked with in many ways as a substitute for quinine or Cinchona (*Cinchona officinalis*) bark, from which quinine is derived. During the Civil War, when the Confederacy was cut off from being able to access medicines from other countries due to the northern army blocking the ports, the bark of the local Dogwood in that place (*Cornus florida*) was used in place of Cinchona which was imported in the treatment of malarial fevers. So like many bitter barks, Dogwood can be thought

of as a cooling and calming remedy. Like most of the other barks in this category, Dogwood is nice for aches and pains. I have heard that this plant contains salicylates, and I have also heard that they do not, and I have not been able to find any published analyses of the constituent make up of this tree. The bark is very rich in tannins and is therefore astringent and antiseptic. There is also a nice bitter action, aiding in digestion and calming a gassy belly.

I was first introduced to Dogwood in a blind tasting led by a good friend and teacher of mine. I took the bitter tincture, and laid down under a tree and closed my eyes. I was still very new to blind tastings and also to plant meditations in general and would often feel underwhelmed by them. I was surprised when I almost immediately started to go into a dreamlike state in which I found myself in some kind of subterranean space, with walls and pillars made out of ancient, shaped bricks. I was just starting to look around when we were all called back to share our experiences. This was weird for me because I was not then and am still not today the type of person to very easily have visions, even when I take traditionally visionary or psychedelic plants. As we went around the circle sharing our various experiences, several other people were surprised because they had *seen* things. The teacher, Scott Kloos, revealed that the mystery plant was Dogwood, which he told us is a plant that has a strong affinity for psychic perceptions and the seeing of visions—third eye stuff you could say. The signature of the single open eye in the flowers is a good one for this. I still like to work with Dogwood from time to time in a very intentional way to open up my second sight a little bit. Dogwood can also be helpful for people who are too psychically sensitive, or people who have psychic abilities but they are very chaotic and hard to control, in order to settle things down and help the person to get some control over how the process is going. I like to think of them as a psychic modulator. They can be really nice to add in small amounts to a formula for people with anxiety or who are looking for a nice nervine blend.

Many of the Dogwoods around here have a fungal infection called Dogwood Antracnose which is caused by *Discula spp.*. You can tell when the trees have the disease because their leaves and flowers will be covered in brown spots. This infection inhibits the tree's ability to grow, in some cases infecting the trunk and preventing new sprouts from reaching maturity. If you are harvesting or pruning more than one Dogwood tree be sure to clean and bleach your tools between trees so that you do not accidentally spread the infection from one tree to another.

Along the rivers and streams right around the solstice and blooming well into the summer is *Stachys cooleyai,* which does not seem to have a generally accepted common name but is sometimes called Dead Nettle. This species of *Stachys,* which is one of the largest genera in the *Lamiaceae* family of plants, is pretty abundant in wet spots in the forests and looks very much like the Stinging Nettle (*Urtica dioica*), the only difference being that *Stachys* will not sting you and indeed has a soft, fine fuzz on all surfaces of the plant. The flowers of *Stachys* are a bright magenta style color and look like mint type flowers.

They are very showy unlike the flowers of Stinging Nettle which are pretty nondescript and easy to miss. While *Stachys cooleyai* does not have much information out there about working with them as a medicine, many people in my circle of herbalist friends work with them in analogous ways to the closely related *Stachys officinalis*, whose common name is Wood Betony. Wood Betony is a Eurasian native with a long history of medicinal use, almost as a kind of panacea. An old Italian proverb goes: "Sell your coat and buy Betony," to give you an idea of how loved this herb was. I have mostly worked with Wood Betony, and also with *Stachys cooleyai*, as a remedy for pain and inflammation with a nice calming effect on the mind. I like *Stachys* for joint pains especially, old injuries that flare up every once and a while, things like this. I will often combine *Stachys* with a more potent analgesic such as Bleeding Heart (*Dicentra formosa*) or California Poppy (*Eschscholzia californica*) which helps to further ease the pain and allow the *Stachys* to do some deeper work to the injured joint, where they seem to help speed healing and strengthen the tissues. One easy way to tell if the plant that you have found is *Stachys cooleyai*, after you have checked that they do not sting you, is to crush a leaf and smell it. *Stachys* has a very distinctive odor that many people do not like, it is a little bit funky or animalilstic. I have not done much work around cultivating this plant although I would like to, and I imagine that they would transplant very well, in much the same way that Stinging Nettles do. Thankfully, harvesting the flowering tops of this plant and leaving several sets of leaves and the majority of the stem will not kill the plant, which is a perennial and will come back next year.

Once we finally make it to the Skokomish river and are walking along their banks, we will find the final herb that I would like to talk about in this chapter which is Rose (*Rosa spp.*). Several species of wild Rose grow in this area including the Wood's Rose (*Rosa woodsii*), the **Nootka Rose** (*Rosa nootkatensis*), and the Baldhip Rose (*Rosa gymnocarpa*). These wild roses are not nearly as showy as the hybridized cultivated roses that people are used to seeing in gardens, but while they may not be very showy in terms of looks they are all very fragrant and really tough plants. Wild Roses will often form impenetrable thickets in areas along the rivers where they get enough sun, and some of the Rose species that are feral or weedy, especially the Dog Rose (*Rosa canina*) can form thickets that are twenty feet tall. Roses are precious for medicine since the rose petals are so light, and it takes quite a lot of petals to make a little bit of medicine. They are pretty simple in their physiological workings, being a gentle, cooling, astringent, but Roses have such strong symbolic associations with people that working with them as a medicine can have really profound effects.

Roses are associated with love, beauty, and sweetness while at the same time being a symbol of strength and protection. The taste and smell of roses is so sweet and soft,

calming and cloying. I like to tincture Rose petals fresh off the plant, which is much easier to do on some of the garden varieties which produce an abundance of large and fragrant flowers than by picking the sometimes sparse flowers of the wild plants, although sometimes you can get in to good picking with them. The tincture is sweet, cooling, and calming. Whenever I vend my tinctures at an herbalism conference or farmer's market I always have an open bottle of each type of tincture available out as a tester so that people can get a sense of how the plant feels in their body before buying. My Rose tester is the one that people always come back to, and when they first taste it they smile and sigh. I don't work with Rose much as a simple for any specific ailments, but I mostly like to incorporate them into teas or tincture formulas to bring the protection and to bring the love. They are very nice in heartbreak formulas and for people who are wanting a strong heart. Most Roses propagate very well from greenwood cuttings or especially from root divisions or by cutting off suckers with a bit of root attached. They are a joy to have in the garden and, once established, are hard to kill.

When I take people out to the Skokomish river to learn about plants for the summer solstice, usually we will pick some Roses, then do a tasting of a Rose tincture sitting by the river in the sun, and then we jump into the freezing cold and clear water, so that is where I will leave you.

7

GOLDEN LIGHT,
LATE SUMMER IN THE GARDEN,
AND TAHOMA

ONCE WE HAVE MOVED PAST THE SOLSTICE, the days begin to become shorter again. The Yang begins to descend and yin begins its ascent, although this is not immediately clear since this time of the year is often the beginning of truly intense heat in this part of the world. The light begins to take on a specific golden hue, which only intensifies as the season progresses towards Fall. This season can be called many things, either Late Summer or just Summer, depending on who you talk to (some people think that Summer starts on the Solstice, which is not really my belief but to each their own).

This part of the year can also be called the Dog Days of Summer, as the great star Sirius begins its heliacal rise, appearing just before sunrise for the first time since being below the horizon at night for a time. Sirius is the brightest star in the night sky, and has been revered by humans for most of recorded history. In ancient Egypt it was noted that the annual flooding of the Nile often took place when Sirius first returned to visibility, which was a crucial event for the agrarian peoples at that time. Later on, the Greeks noticed that the hottest and driest period of the Summer corresponded to the return of Sirius to the night sky, and they attributed the additional energy of that bright star with the uptick in heat. The Greeks also believed that this time of year was one in which fevers and madness were most common, dogs were more prone to bite, men were at their weakest and "women are most wanton," thunderstorms were frequent, people were exhausted, and bad luck was common. This is still a theme in people talking about the this part of the Summer, with the "Dog Days" mostly just referring to those days in the late Summer that are miserably hot without having any reference to Sirius. Sirius, of course, is the eye of the constellation Canis Major which is the hunting dog of Orion, the great hunter, and follows him across the night sky. The Dog Days have been described as occupying a wide variety of times in the calendrical year but are generally believed to extend from mid July to mid August or so.

Another mark upon the wheel of the year around this hot time is Lughnasadh, a Gaelic holiday which is one of the four including Samhain, Imbolc, and Beltaine. Lughnasadh is traditionally held around August 1st and celebrates the first harvests of the year. This festival is said to have been first held by the god Lugh, who made it up in order to commemorate his mother Tailtiu, who died of exhaustion after exerting all of her efforts to clear the plains of Ireland for agriculture. Traditional activities include the eating of the first bilberries, the first harvests of corn in a ritual fashion, athletic games, visits to the sacred wells, and climbing the sacred hills and mountains. Often there would be the sacrifice of a sacred bull, with all present eating his flesh, who would then be replaced by a new, young bull for the next year.

So this time of year is both a time of exhaustion and disease, while also being a time when the fruits of everyone's labors, the humans and the animals and the plants and the Earth herself, are just starting to be present and abundant. At this time of year some things are at their peak of flower, many are starting to bear fruit, and many are starting to set seed and die back. Where I live in the Pacific Northwest corner of Turtle Island, this is also the time of year when many of the mighty Salmon runs are happening, especially the Bluebacks or Sockeyes (*Onchohyncus nerka*), the Pinks or Humpies (*Onchohynus gorbuscha*), and the Chinook or Kings (*Onchorhyncus tschawytscha*), which are also a time of exhaustion, abundance, and death for the fish and for the people who are fishing them for food. This is a pretty frantic time of year when the work of the warm season is not yet complete, but everyone is starting to get a little bit tired and worn thin already. The veil is thin at this time, and I find that this can be tough to deal with that thinness, since we are all so often paying a lot of attention to the everyday things that are so pressing.

As herbalists, these Dog Days are really busy. The gardens need lots of watering, and it seems like all of the flowering medicine plants start to flower all at once. This is a time of running around trying to get all of the Summer's bounties harvested and stored away, whether it is flowering herbs, or Summer vegetables, or berries, or Salmon. Conversely, this can also be a time of ease if you allow yourself to take breaks. It is funny for many of us who grew up in a city or suburb because summertime was when the schools were out, and for those of us who had no link to agricultural life there was nothing to do except have lots of fun in the sun, go to the beach, drink sodas and enjoy the long days and warm nights. Likewise if you have a job that is not tied to the seasons, the Summer is often when people take their vacations and spend the days hiding out in the shade or enjoying the Sun and taking it easy. I find that in my own life this causes some cognitive dissonance or a strong sense of nostalgia for my childhood when "the lazy days of Summer" was a phrase that I really resonated with, whereas for the past couple decades Summer days I am usually working all day everyday, trying to make money and maintain a garden and harvest plants and harvest food, and it is exhausting, and I get grumpy and irritable.

Luckily this time of year, like most times of year, provides the medicines that we need to be in balance with the season. One of the first harvests out of the herb garden is Milky Oats (*Avena sativa*), which is a perfect medicine for the frantic and frazzled summertime vibes. Oats are thought to be native to the British Isles, or at least to that part of Europe, and they are best known as a wholesome and nourishing food in most parts of the world. Oatmeal is a popular, healthy breakfast for many people and served as one of the staple foods for the European peasantry since this grain is very easy to grow, therefore cheap to produce, and provides deep nutrition. Oats in any form are rich in protein, many minerals (including silicon, magnesium, iron, calcium, and potassium), vitamins (including several

B vitamins, vitamin D, and vitamin E), polysaccharides, flavonoids, oils, and insoluble fibers. Oatmeal is the processed grain of the plant, and is associated with increased heart health, the lowering of cholesterol, and increased gut health. All preparations of Oats are also calming and strengthening to the nervous system. I would highly encourage people to incorporate Oats, especially steel cut Oats, into their diet as a medicinal foodstuff.

Beyond this plant's use as a food, the fruits of Oats have a specific stage that they go through in the mid to late Summer in which they are still green and tender when they plump up and fill with a creamy white liquid which resembles milk. This specific part of the Oat plant at this specific period of the plant's development is what we mean when we say Milky Oats. This is a little bit of a picky harvest as you really need to keep your eyes and fingers on your Oat patch in order to harvest the fruits in the sweet spot when the majority of them are plump and milky. A dozen or two fruits are on each stalk of the Oats, which are a grass, and they become milky one by one over the course of several weeks, starting in my experience with the top-most one and working their way down the stalk. The best medicine is made by only extracting the milky fruits, and it is an easy thing to do the harvest too early in the season when you notice that the topmost of the fruits is milky so you harvest them all and tincture them all together. This will result in a tincture that is mostly green and not rich in milk, which is essentially Oatstraw tincture, not Milky Oat tincture. It is important that, once you have seen the first fruit spurt out milk upon being squeezed, you wait, from several more days to a week or more, and keep on checking the fruits lower down on the plant until the majority of the them are milky, then harvest them. The trouble is that you can also wait too long, and then the milk dries up and the fruits begin to turn into seeds, in which case you have missed it for this year, and you might as well let the seeds mature and sow them in the next Spring to try again.

Once the majority of the fruits are swollen and milky, strip them all off of the plant and tincture them in a pretty high alcohol menstruum (I often do 75%, although I see that some people do as low as 35%).* The real trick to getting a good quality Milky Oat tincture along with time of harvest is to run the plant material and the menstruum through a blender, which breaks up all of the little fruits and allows all of the milk to come out into the menstruum. You will immediately know if your tincture will be good because it will have an electric milky green color to it as soon as it is run through the blender. Once the tincture has been pressed out (I do not filter this one) you will know that it is good if there is a thick precipitate that settles out when the tincture sits in a bottle. You want to have a very visible milk layer at the bottom of the

* See Holmes.

bottle that you shake up very well before dispensing. Many times, I have run into, purchased, or (I regret to say) made myself "Milky Oat" tincture that does not actually have any milk in it, and this extract is inferior. The nit-picky nature of Milky Oat harvest does not help you to be less hectic in the Summertime, since you need to go and check the Oat patch everyday and then drop everything in order to make the medicine the very day that it is perfectly ripe, but the medicine is worth it.

Milky Oats are a mild remedy, more like a food than a drug, with minimal chance of causing long term damage even if taken in huge amounts over a long period of time, indeed that is really the way to get the most benefit from this medicine. They are a deeply nourishing remedy for many of the body systems, especially the nervous system for which they are considered the quintessential trophorestorative. They also benefit the neuroendocrine-immune system, the cardiovascular system, the reproductive system, and the musculoskeletal system. I believe that many of these benefits to the other body systems stem from the strengthening of and relaxing of the nervous system, which has profound downstream effects on the rest of the organism. The specific extraction method I outlined above was first developed (as far as I can tell) by the Eclectics in the late 1800s, who worked with the remedy much as I describe it here. Milky Oats is a great herb to work with for people who are exhausted, stressed out, overworked, depressed, anxious, etc. A certain depletion goes along with living in chronic stress, which so many people do especially in these times of late capitalism, climate change, increased wealth disparity, and the rise of fascism/authoritarianism across the globe. Milky Oats is a great remedy for parents, workers, activists, and anyone who has to overexert themselves in order to get by. Milky Oats is calming but not narcotic or debilitating, and conversely can help provide some energy or support without being stimulating. Milky Oats is a specific aid for mid-summer burnout, I think. Many people have found this herb to be greatly beneficial for people who are in recovery from addictive drugs where they have exhausted and depleted their nervous systems, as the herb both nourishes them and is calming. The nutritional richness of the plant is helpful for people whose diets are made up of foods that are depleted in minerals, which is true for so many people due to the effects of industrialized agricultural practices. They will help people to regain their strength in many ways, and can be thought of as a building herb in general, indeed Peter Holmes says that this herb can be worked with to generate growth and weight gain in the body. The tissue regenerative aspect of Oats are well known in terms of external applications, as many skin care products contain oats, or extracts of them, and there is also the old practice of bathing in oatmeal to relieve the itching and swelling of a Poison Ivy (*Toxicodendron radicans*) rash. After harvesting the Milky Oats, you can also cut the rest of the tops of the plant, being the leaf and stem, which is called Oatstraw and makes a very nice mineral rich and restorative tea.

There is a pleasant parallel between the actions of Oats in the human body and the actions of growing Oats in the garden that I would like to touch upon. Much as Oats are deeply nourishing and rebuilding to the human body, Oats are a very nice cover crop for the garden, where they provide nice root mats which keep the soil from eroding and retain moisture, and can be turned under after they have grown out in order to feed the soil. Growing Oats in the garden can feed both you and the land upon which you work at the same time, protecting the both of you from exhaustion.

Also in the garden at this time many of the various Mint family herbs are flowering and ready for harvest. There are more of them then I really have time to go into deeply in this essay, but I will cover a few of my favorites.

Skullcap (*Scuttelaria lateriflora*) is a lovely, low growing herb in the Mint family that is native to Turtle Island. They grow in the wild in moist places such as marshes, wetlands, and along lakes. The only time that I ran into Skullcap growing outside of a garden, they were growing alongside a boardwalk with their feet in standing water in a swamp type environment, close to a lake. This was good for me to see, since I kept on killing the Skullcap I attempted to grow in my garden since I assumed they were super hardy and drought tolerant like Motherwort (*Leonorus cardiaca*). Once I realized that they needed lots of water, they have done very well for me, and as they are a perennial that spread via rhizome they have become pretty abundant in the garden. Skullcap is a good herb to discuss along with Milky Oats because they pair with one another very well. Like Milky Oats, Skullcap is a trophorestorative to the nervous system and is very helpful for those people who have been under stressful situations for long periods of time and have become somewhat burnt-out and exhausted, while also having accompanying anxiety and agitation. I do not think of Skullcap as being nutritive in the same way that Milky Oats are, they are not really a source of minerals or proteins, but they are more strongly relaxing and pain killing than Milky Oats. They are rich in flavonoids and essential oils, both of which have an effect on the nervous system. They are also very bitter in flavor, which provides some stimulation to the digestive system, which can be nice for people who are stressed out and help them to better digest their foods. There is some evidence that the flavonoids in Skullcap have both anti-inflammatory and sedative effects, with some of the flavones selectively binding to benzodiazepine receptor sites *in-vitro*. Some common benzodiazepines include Valium (*diazepam*) and Xanax (*alprazolam*), which are potent anxiolytics and sleep inducers in humans. Skullcap is a very nice herb to work with to acutely reduce stress in the moment, to relieve pain, or to induce sleep. They can also be worked with over long periods of time for a general trophorestorative effect on the nervous system, although I like to combine them with other, gentler herbs in a formula for working with long term. For some people it is too sedating to work with Skullcap regularly, but for others it can be very helpful to have something on board to take the edge off for long periods of time while the nervous system can put itself back together.

Lemon Balm (***Melissa officinalis***) is another Mint family plant that is in flower at this time of year. This plant is a joy to have in the garden, mostly due to their beautiful flowers and to the sweet, lemony smell that the leaves give off when crushed between the fingers. Lemon Balm can also become very abundant in the garden as they are a perennial that seeds themselves profusely and can thrive in many locations and in a variety of moisture levels, so some people end up getting mad at the Lemon Balm in their garden because they can become quite "weedy." Personally, I am really into weedy medicines because I am kind of a lazy gardener and like plants that can take care of themselves and don't need too much attention from me. Lemon Balm is a European native and has been worked with as a medicine for a very long time, often under the common name Melissa which they were given by the ancient Greeks and is also the name given to the honey bee in that culture, which was and is a very revered creature for their healing capabilities. Lemon Balm was much loved by the alchemists and was often worked with by them in their attempts to create medicines that would prolong life or restore youth. A great example of the marvellous curing properties ascribed to this plant, and to alchemical preparations in general, comes from this quote by a French physician named Lesebure who was the physician for Louis XIV in the late 1600s:

One of my most intimate friends prepared the Primum
Ens Melissae, and his curiosity would not allow him to
rest until he had seen with his own eyes the effects of
this arcanum, so that he might be certain whether or not
the accounts given of its virtues were true. He therefore
made an experiment, first upon himself, then upon an
old female servant, aged seventy years, and afterwards
upon an old hen that was kept in his house. First he
took, every morning at sunrise, a glass of white wine
that was tinctured with this remedy, and after using it
for fourteen days his finger- and toe-nails began to fall
out, without, however, causing any pain. He was not cou-
rageous enough to continue the experiment, but gave the
same remedy to the old female servant. She took it every
morning for about ten days, when she began to menstruate again as in former days. At this she was very much
surprised, because she did not know that she had been
taking a medicine. She became frightened, and refused to
continue the experiment. My friend took, therefore, some
grain, soaked it in that wine, and gave it to the old hen to
eat, and on the sixth day that bird began to lose its feathers, and kept losing them until it was perfectly nude, but
before two weeks had passed, new feathers grew, which
were much more beautifully colored; her comb stood up
again, and she began to lay eggs. (Stavish, 102)

Melissa is rich in essential oils, although it is interesting that
these oils are almost impossible to isolate using distillation.

Whenever my friends and I have attempted to distill Lemon Balm essential oil, all we can ever produce is a hydrosol and it often lacks the beautiful smell of the fresh plant. Like Skullcap and many of the Mint family plants, Lemon Balm is a calming herb, however they have a specific affinity for the heart along with the nervous system and influence them both in a calming and settling way, so Lemon Balm is reached for when a person's anxieties or stress are accompanied by a sense of tension in the heart or palpitations. Lemon Balm also has a nice, gentle but present, mood-lifting or anti-depressant action that is immediate and helpful, somewhat like St. John's Wort, but more jolly. Lemon Balm is a very nice herb to give to children, who often really like the smell and taste and respond very well and quickly to the joy-inducing and grump-dispelling qualities of the herb. They are a nice one for crabby toddlers. Lemon Balm encourages sweating and the movement of blood to the exterior, so they are nice to work with for people who are sick with fevers, especially since they are thought to have a mild anti-viral quality. I like to incorporate Lemon Balm into formulas that address fevers or sickness since they help to calm the person and cheer them up as well as work on the fever itself, which can really be helpful to the healing process. The mood lightening aspects of Lemon Balm come through very effectively just by smelling the crushed leaf, and they are nice to have growing all around just so that, while rushing all about, you can stop and smell the lemon balm and have a pleasure break.

Outside of the garden but still in the lowlands (we will be exploring the plants of the Mountains later on), there are so many plants in flower to harvest at this time, but I want to focus on a specific plant that seems to hold some aspect of this time of year in their appearance. I have mentioned before how the Sun's light at this time of year begins to take on a very specific and golden hue, and this hue is very present in the flowers of Goldenrod (*Solidago canadensis*), which can be found all along the roadsides and in open, disturbed areas such as clear cuts. Goldenrod flowers relatively late in the Summer, starting around mid July, but the flowers continue to develop and then linger until very late in the season. Basically they are in flower for the entirety of the golden light period, and the flowers themselves are of a striking golden color. The Latin name *Solidago* means "to bring together,"* which points to the wound healing properties of this plant. Extractions of the leaves, flowers, or roots all are strong vulneraries that can be applied externally to cuts and irritated tissues or can be taken internally as a tea or tincture to heal the internal tissues that they come into contact with. They have a specific affinity for the urinary tract and kidneys and should be thought of when someone is living with a urinary tract infection, has difficulty with urination for other reasons, or has weakness of the kidneys which can lead to buildup of uric acid in the system, which can in turn cause irritation and inflammation in many different body systems. Goldenrod can heal the tissues in the urinary tracts, lessen tension of the musculature there to allow the free flow or urine, and give some strength to the

* See Wood, 459.

kidneys themselves so that they can do their work of cleaning up the blood and helping to get the waste products out of the body. There is a correlation between the kidneys and fear, which can be seen when in times of great fear or tension it becomes hard for people to urinate, and Goldenrod works on this fear as well. It is nice that this herb shows up in the driest and hottest time of year to help and move the waters within our own bodies.

This hot time of year is also the start of the brief window in which we can get up into the upper elevations in the mountains, and that is the focus of the remainder of this chapter.

TAHOMA/THE MOUNTAINS

GEOLOGY

Mountains are all around me, where I live by the Black Hills in "Washington State," in Chehalis Territory. To the West are the Olympic Mountains, an almost circular chain of mountains that occupy the center of the landmass known today as the "Olympic Peninsula." The Skokomish River, who I wrote about in an earlier chapter, flows outwards from this mountain range. To the East lies the Cascade Range, which is part of a larger cordillera that is often called the American Cordillera, which runs all the way from the North to the South poles, approximately, of the planet. The Cascades begin in Canada and travel down to Northern California, where the Sierra Nevada mountains begin, which flow into Mexico and become the Sierra Madres, which flow into South

America where they become the Andes and eventually the Tierra del Fuego at the Southernmost tip of Chile. From there the mountain ranges flow into the frozen mountains of the Antarctic Peninsula. The Cascades are composed of thousands of volcanoes, some of which are still active, and are a part of a ring of volcanoes encircling the Pacific Ocean, often called the "Ring of Fire." The most recent volcanic activity in the Cascades was the eruption of Lawetlat'la (Mt. St. Helens) in 1980, which was a big one that anyone who lived in the area at the time remembers well, and before that Amblu Kai (Mt. Lassen), which is the Southernmost of the Cascades, erupted several times between 1914–1917.

The Cascades play a huge role in the weather patterns on either side of themselves, since the moisture rich air that comes in from the Pacific Ocean to the West drops that moisture upon being pushed up in elevation over the mountains, which results in the West side of the mountains getting lots of precipitation which is why they host the amazing and unique temperate rain forest ecosystems that they do, home to Red Cedars (*Thuja plicata*), Devil's Club (*Oplopanax horridum*), and Bleeding Heart (*Dicentra formosa*). Since almost all the moisture falls on the West side of the mountains, the Eastern side is a dry, arid desert which is its own marvelous and unique ecosystem home to Junipers (*Juniperus occidentalis*), Sagebrush (*Artemisia tridentata*), and Balsam Root (*Balsamorhiza sagittata*). Locals often refer to the "wet side" and the "dry side" of the mountains. The tallest of the Cascade range, and one of the most beautiful sights on a clear day in many parts of

Western "Washington" is Tahoma, often called Mt. Rainier (or simply "the mountain" by locals).

TΛHOMΛ

Tahoma has been called by many names by Salish peoples, who have lived with this person for a very long time. Other names include Tacobeh, Tacoma, Talol, and Pooskaus. My favorite proposed interpretation of the name of this mountain comes from the Puyallup which is in Lushootseed and translates as "mother of waters," which is precisely what the mountain is. They are covered in glaciers which feed the beautiful rivers that bring water to the forests and all the people that live among them such as the Cowlitz, Nisqually, and Puyallup rivers. The rivers in turn house the Salmon who feed everybody.

The name "Mt. Rainier" was proposed for this mountain by George Vancouver in 1792, who was a good friend of Peter Rainier, then the commander of the British warship HMS *Monarch*. Peter Rainier was a lifelong member of the British Navy and spent much of his career actively involved in the imperialistic expansion of the British empire by fighting the American rebels in the late 1700s and later by commanding Royal Navy operations around the East Indies Stations, which involved violently colonizing people and lands all around the Indian Ocean, such as India, Sri Lanka, Iraq, and Yemen. This brutal subjugation of people in the name of expanding the British Empire is a vile and disgusting history, with many of these lands not regaining their autonomy and independence for centuries, and many of them still deal with the economic fallout of being an occupied people, not to mention the trauma still felt by those who were alive during occupation and their descendants. I hope that we as a culture can move away from naming such beautiful and sentient entities as the mountains after bloodthirsty colonizers. I am inspired by the official return of the name of Denali to the mountain that was for a time known as Mt. McKinley in "Alaska," and am pleased to see that there are some rumblings about officially restoring the other mountains to their true names. In the meantime, I try to call the mountains by their original names whenever I can learn them, and to try and learn the indigenous names for other landmarks upon the landscape such as rivers, lakes, and prairies.

The mountains are very much alive and sentient and are the heart of this landscape, especially Tahoma to the place where I live. My relationship to the mountain shifted in a good way when I started addressing them as Tahoma instead of Mt. Rainier; they recognize that name, and it pleases them to be addressed as such. It is hard to explain the feeling of getting up on the mountain, especially after years of talking to them from a distance, praying to them and trying to become their friend and accomplice. In many ways I think of Tahoma as being the head or brain of the larger organism that is the Cascadian bioregion, perhaps the mountain is the brain, high up in the air and able to touch and feel the landscape all around, while the magma in the interior of the mountain is the heart, providing the heat and the life force. Of course, since the mountain holds all of the glaciers, which in turn feed so many of the rivers, and the mountain generates the rains that feed all of the rivers, and the rivers are in many ways the vascular system of this great being that is the bioregion, in that sense the mountain could be looked at as the heart. I don't actually know, and clearly this is all very speculative and just my own musings.

There is a joy, and a stillness, and a deep replenishment of the life force that happens when you visit the mountain, especially if you can have some intention around the process. Once you start to get very high in elevation, the highest I have ever been is 10,188 feet on the Cowlitz glacier at a spot called Camp Muir, you can watch the clouds be born and roll down the side of the mountain. The mountain will also teach you to respect them of course, and they are not to be trifled with. I once got lost while descending from Camp Muir with a dear friend who was my guide, and my then-partner. We were glissading down and were kind of stoned, and we went into the wrong snowfield, which suddenly became so steep that we had to struggle to stop ourselves from sliding all the way down. The weather had shifted from a bright and clear day to a sudden white out with snow, you could not tell the difference between the sky and the ground. We were trying to climb our way up to a rocky outcrop which was about ten yards above us, but we would climb a little ways up and then slide back down, cursing. My guide began to weep and shouting "I don't want to die, I want to live!" which is not really what you want to hear your guide yelling. That was the moment when I first thought "This is how people die on the mountain," which became a frequently recurring thought. We eventually made it back to the correct area, but remained hopelessly lost. We did not have a compass, a map, any food beyond some trail mix, or any warm clothes, and the Sun was starting to go down. We were just starting to discuss digging a shelter in the snow, that we could all curl around one another inside of, to try and survive through the night when my guide's cries for help brought forth a person who was training for snow camping up on the mountain, bless them. They showed us back to the trail and we made it back to the parking lot just as the Sun went all the way down, and the cold started to set in. I had never been so happy to see a parking lot or get in a car. In many cultures across the world the tops of the mountains are places for the gods and for the dead, and are not places for living people to go. I am starting to think that there is merit to this idea, more and more as I grow older, although my Capricorn self still really wants to summit Tahoma. Mostly what I am trying to say by sharing this story is: know where you are going, tell people you are going there, bring a map, a compass, fire making material, extra clothes, a knife, and more food than you think you will need. The mountain loves you, yes, but it is easy to die on them anyway.

It is also good to remember that Tahoma is an active volcano, in terms of having a great respect for them as a very powerful being. Tahoma is considered a Decade Volcano by the International Association of Volcanology and Chemistry of the Earth's Interior, which means that they are worthy of being carefully monitored because they have a history of violent eruptions and are close to heavily populated areas. If Tahoma were to erupt there would likely be massive *lahars* which are huge and violent mud and debris flows that move very fast and can be very deep, which would destroy anything in their path. If such lahars followed the model set by the Osceola Mudflow, a similar event that occurred about five thousand years ago, many of the cities around the mountain including Kent, Enumclaw, Puyallup, Renton, and parts of Seattle would be destroyed. Such an event could also cause a tsunami in the Salish Sea. There is also the chance that the mountain could produce lava flows, and of course the falling ash would effect people for thousands of miles around. I decided a long time ago that if Tahoma erupted and ended my life, that would be a fine and honorable way to go.

ALPINE HERBS

Another reason that I think of the mountain as the head or brain of the entity that is the larger bioregion is that so many of the medicinal plants that grow there are focused on the nervous system when ingested into human bodies. Alpine plants are a very hardy bunch. They can all be considered ephemerals because they have such a brief growing season since the alpine meadows upon which they live are carpeted in snow from Fall to late Spring, or mid to late Summer in the case of the highest elevations, so the plants need to be able to survive the long Winter covered in snow, and then grow, flower, and set seed in the few months where the snows have receded, often in extreme heat and UV exposure. They are strong plants with big personalities, but they are also delicate in that the whole landscape up there is delicate, and it is important to be delicate and careful when you are interacting with these plants and these places. Think hard about where you are stepping and who you might be disturbing. The alpine habitats are pretty scarce overall, and it is extra important to think about not being too pushy on the plant communities that live there in terms of harvest. Tribal members often harvest these same medicines from the mountains and the patches that you might find up in the mountains might be a patch that someone's family has been harvesting from for generations or millennia, so approach these patches with respect and be extra careful to not over harvest or harvest in a destructive way. In many ways it might be better to purchase or trade for medicines made from some of these alpine plants from someone who has a relationship with the place and the patches and who is keeping an eye on the populations and has good propagation practices. Furthermore, many of the alpine habitats are in National Parks, where the harvesting of any plant material is illegal (unless you are a tribal member). I personally think more about ecology, sustainability, and respect for tribal territories than I do about the legalities imposed by the occupying forces, but it is true that National Parks see quite a lot of traffic and it would be best to find patches of plants in places where not so many people go.

The first plant that I want to discuss is the most visually

striking of the bunch, and they are very easy to identify. This plant has many common names including Anemone, Pasque-flower, Wind Flower, and Easter Flower, the Latin is *Anemone occidentalis*. Anemone grows in moist, gravelly soils in alpine areas, above 6,000 feet or so. They are some of the first of the wildflowers to flower up on the mountains, and in order to find them in flower you basically have to go up to the alpine fields in March or April and climb over snow drifts to get to them. Immediately after the snows melt, the Anemone erupt up through the ground, flowering immediately before they even produce leaves. The flowers are very beautiful and delicate, mostly white with some blue and purple hints here and there. It does not take long for the flowers to fall away and the plant to go to seed, and it is the seed heads that most people recognize. The seeds stay attached to the plant often until the Fall, and each seed has a long wispy tail of fluffy material attached to its base, making each individual seed look kind of like a long sperm cell. The flower head has hundreds of these seeds all over it, and the overall effect is that the flowers look like they have a shock of unruly white hair. The fluff is often blown to one side, which I think is the source of the common name Wind Flower. The Genus name, *Anemone,* means "daughter of the wind" in Greek.

Various species of *Anemone* grow all around the globe in the Northern Hemisphere, primarily in temperate regions. They are worked with as medicines in all of these places, with a long history of medicinal use in European, Chinese, and American herbal traditions. To check and see if the species of Anemone that you found may be workable as a medicine, chew up a little bit of the fresh leaf. If it is acrid and peppery on the tongue, then it is probably good. I primarily work with this plant as a strong, low-dose anxiolytic. Not many other herbs work as quickly and effectively to bring someone down from a really high anxiety state than a few drops of a fresh *Anemone occidentalis* tincture. For many people that I know or have worked with as clients, this plant can really change the way that they exist in the world simply by being a reliable way to stop a panic attack or overwhelming feelings of dread. This plant does not work for everyone, though. They have a strong blood moving quality to them and in those people who already have plenty of fast moving blood Anemone can lead to headache or other unpleasant side effects. In my own practice I break people with severe anxiety into two classes: *Anemone* people and *Dicentra* people. Both herbs strongly reduce anxiety, and I have found that if one of them does not work for the person, then the other probably will. The Anemone person is more of a deficient person, often with poor circulation and cold extremities with a tendency towards depression and fear. I can no longer find the book that I found this description in, and it is a little bit of a patriarchal description, but I once read that Anemone is a specific for a skinny, blonde woman who is prone to having fits of fainting. Clearly this description comes from an Eclectic or Homeopathic practitioner in the 1800s or something, but the image stuck with me and can be expanded upon to paint a picture of the type of person who would respond well to this plant.

I find that *Anemone* has an immediate calming influence on the person, and also can have a long term effect on the person's nervous system if the plant is worked with somewhat regularly over a period of time. I generally do not put *Anemone* into formulas that are to be taken regularly, but I would give the person in question some kind of a nervous system trophorestorative formula with more tonic herbs such as Milky Oats, Skullcap, Hawthorn, and Reishi (I love this specific formula) to take several times a day, everyday, and also give them a simple of *Anemone* to keep in their pocket in case of acute anxiety episodes. Even just knowing that they have something that can calm down the anxiety if it gets bad has a positive influence on people's nervous systems, and I think that the calming aspects of *Anemone* help to retrain the nervous system, especially if the system is being tonified and fed by the more nutritive formula. People who have been long term stimulant users (cocaine, amphetamines, even caffeine) can often really benefit from this plant, either to take the edge off if they are still taking the stimulants (*Anemone* can help when someone is coming down from, say, a meth binge and they are very agitated and still not able to sleep) or for someone who has quit the stimulant in question, but are pretty worn thin and prone to anxiety from the long term use of the substance. Along with stimulants, *Anemone* can be really helpful for someone who is having an anxiety reaction to the over consumption of *Cannabis* or even in the case of anxiety during psychedelic experiences.

While I have not worked with *Anemone* in this way, the

plant does have a long history of being taken for painful menstruation, or to help bring on a delayed menses. PMS symptoms are also said to respond very well to this plant, especially if the person tends to get weepy and headache-y. Within Chinese medicine traditions, various species of *Anemone* are worked with as anti-infective agents, as they are said to be helpful for bacterial, fungal, and even protozoal infections. Within the Chinese traditions, however, the plant is always dried, and the root is worked with preferably to the leaf or whole plant. I am not sure if this alters the anti-infective qualities, but I personally am not willing to dig up these plants and kill them in order to harvest the root.

My preferred harvest technique for this plant is to go up to the *Anemone* fields in late Summer, towards early Fall, when the seeds on the plants are fully ripe and ready to be planted. Sometimes the foliage of the plant is starting to yellow and die back, and while I kind of prefer to make medicine from the still green foliage, the yellowed material still has the correct taste, and that way you know that the life energy of the plant has already moved down into the roots and the organism is not currently dependent on those leaves to create energy via photosynthesis. I will just harvest leaves from one side of each plant, ideally while blowing the seeds off of the plants like they are dandelions. When you find a good *Anemone* patch there are hundreds of plants in close proximity to one another, so even with this dainty harvest technique, it is fast and easy to gather quite a lot of plant material. My belief is that this harvest does little to no damage to the plants, although

I have to admit that I have never managed to mark a plant or otherwise check with 100% certainty that they survive the harvest. I have been watching some of the same patches for many years now and they have not become less abundant in that time. Many people will harvest the whole above ground portions of the plant and tincture it all, sometimes including the seed head. While I realize that tincturing the seed head does result in a macerating jar that looks like it has little sperms floating in it, and that this makes a great picture for Instagram, I really doubt that the seeds or the main stem are very medicinally potent, and it makes so much more sense to me to encourage those seeds to become more plants.

Often growing in the same fields as the *Anemone* are many different species of the Genus *Pedicularis*. In the mountains around me I often run into *P. groenlandica*, also called Elephant's Head since their flowers look quite distinctly like the head of an elephant, trunk and all, *P. bracteosa* which is sometimes called Parrot's Beak, and when I travel more to the Southern end of the Cascades I run into *P. densiflora* which people sometimes call Indian Warrior (which I think is an obnoxious name). Several other species grow around me, but these are the ones that I know the best. They seem to be the most abundant in the areas where I go to pick them, and they are all pretty tall/generally have some heft to them. All these species are interchangeable in their medicinal effects, as far as I am concerned, although some *Pedicularis* aficionados describe the subtle differences between the various species. While the flowers of the various species are pretty different from one another, once you can identify one species of *Pedicularis* you would probably be able to tell if you ran into another species, as they all have similar growth habits and general appearance. They all have very beautiful flowers, are pretty low growing (although some get a couple feet tall, and a few really only grow to be a few inches tall), and are most often found growing in open alpine meadows, often near some kind of water source.

Members of the *Pedicularis* genus grow all over Turtle Island, Europe, and China, with China having the largest number of recorded species. Interestingly, some species of this genus also grow in the Southern Hemisphere, with some species endemic to the mountains of South America. All species of *Pedicularis* are hemiparasitic, meaning that while they do produce chlorophyll and engage in photosynthesis for their energy needs, they also tap into some kind of host species which they rely upon for water and some minerals. There is some concern that *Pedicularis* could be rendered toxic if they are parasitically entwined with a toxic plant. In the areas where I harvest *Pedicularis* the main toxic plants that I see are Lupine (*Lupinus spp.*) and False Hellebore (*Veratrum viride*), so I do not harvest *Pedicularis* that grow in the vicinity of those plants, although I have never gone so far as to dig around and see where the *Pedicularis* roots are going to determine if they are tapped in to those plants or not.

All the *Pedicularis* species have a strong affinity for the musculoskeletal system, specifically they act to relax it. This is a very nice action to have, and this plant can be worked with in a number of ways. If a person has an injury or acutely tense muscles that are painful and stiff, taking a few droppers full of the tincture will help to loosen them up and reduce the pain. *Pedicularis* can also be really helpful for the person who holds their stresses or unwanted emotions by tensing up their muscles, resulting in chronic muscle tension and pain. Working with the herb will loosen up the muscles which, in many cases, will help the person to either let go of or take a look at the emotions that they are bottling up.

I often think of *Pedicularis* as being helpful for working on what Wilhelm Reich (who is considered a quack by much of the medical establishment, but had some thought provoking ideas and techniques) called character armor. The general idea about character armor is that as a person is trained as a child to not express certain emotions, such as being told to stop crying or to stop yelling and screaming, that person learns how to hold in the cries or the screams by tightening up certain muscles, often in the chest and jaw. Over time this muscle tightness becomes chronic and automatic, and this constant muscle tension keep the emotions of that person kind of buried or locked away, inaccessible. Reich also thought that in sex negative cultures, when people are trained to repress their sexual desires and urges there was a similar chronic tightness of the muscles in the pelvis. He thought that by loosening up these muscles, often through pretty intense pressure point type body work, that people's long suppressed emotions could come to the surface (people would often begin crying and screaming) which would help to liberate that person to become their more true self. I find this theory interesting and think of the many ways that humans are forced to ignore their bodies and emotions in order to function in Capitalist/ Patriarchal/Imperialist/Puritanical/Etc. cultures, which sure seems like it would lead to some intense character armoring. Reich felt that the more rigid the character armor, the more willing the person would be to go along with with destructive cultural norms. He was very concerned about the rise of fascism that he watched happen over the course of his life. We have seen how traumatic experiences often end up living in the body in the form of tensions and ways people move or hold their posture, and how somatic therapies that engage the body and help it to work through these things can really help with mental health issues. I think that *Pedicularis* has a place here, as an adjunct to other types of therapies to help the body to relax and let go of chronically held tensions. Massage therapists and chiropractors have reported to me that having a client take some *Pedicularis* before a session, and continuing to take it for some time after a session, helps the relaxation or adjustment to stick and helps prevent the body from falling back into learned tension patterns. The plant is also very nice after a long day of working with your body, either in terms of physical labor such as carpentry, waitressing, or commercial fishing, or in the case of a desk job where you sit and stare at a computer screen all day, typing away. They will help to relieve the tensions and pains of the day as you wind down towards sleep. I really like to incorporate *Pedicularis* into pain relief formulas, formulas to help get to sleep, or formulas for anxiety and worry. It helps to have that very body based relaxation to go along with the other herbal actions.

The final alpine plant that I want to discuss is our local Valerian, often called Sitka Valerian (*Valeriana sitchensis*). You can find this plant in moist open meadows, and also in more shade-dappled areas in the mid to upper elevations of the various mountains, especially on slopes. You generally do not find them above the tree line as they do like a little shade. Valerian flowers are a creamy white to pink to purple and extremely fragrant. Some people do not like the smell of the flowers, which does have a bit of a funk to it, a milder form of the "dirty socks" smell of the roots (I actually really like the smell of Valerian root and don't think it smells like dirty socks at all, but many people do), but I think they are heavenly. The smell is sweet and rich and narcotic, and I am convinced that some of the plant's constituents are released in a volatile form by the flowers since smelling Valerian flowers very quickly settles me down.

Valeriana officinalis, the standard Valerian that is known in herbal commerce and is grown in gardens all across the world, as well as having become feral in many places, has been worked with by humans since at least the time of ancient Greece. Both Hippocrates and Galen recommended this herb, primarily for insomnia. Nicholas Culpeper wrote about it in *Culpeper's Complete Herbal*, which was first published in the seventeenth century. He says of this plant that "it helps in nervous complaints, head aches, trembling, palpitations of the heart, vapors, &c.." (37). The Latin name of the herb is derived from the verb *valere*, which means to be strong and healthy, and is also related to the word valor which Merriam-Webster defines as *strength of mind or spirit that enables a person to encounter danger with firmness.* I like to think that Valerian helps to encourage valor. The root is the part of the plant that is most often worked with as a medicine, and extracts of Valerian are helpful to calm an anxious mind, as an antispasmodic, to help a person get to sleep, and as a carminative or digestive aid. The benzodiazepine Valium is named after Valerian, although it is not derived from the plant. There is some evidence that the constituents of Valerian act on the GABA systems in the body, much like benzodiazepines do, although I am not familiar with anyone becoming physically addicted to Valerian, which is very easy to do with benzodiazepines. Some people have a reaction to Valerian in which it will actually cause them to become more agitated and feel uncomfortable, and can cause insomnia. I think that the warming volatile oils and digestive stimulating aspects of the herbs may have something to do with this, but this is just speculation of course. It is best to have someone try out Valerian during the day before they take it to try and go to sleep at night, just in case it proves to be stimulating. I like to make a tincture of Valerian flowers in the Summer when they are blooming. I find this to be less sedating and more valor inducing than the root. Sometimes I will combine the flower and root extracts for a very well-rounded experience of what the plant has to offer.

Garden Valerian is really easy to grow in abundance in the garden. They self seed like mad and can be easily propagated by root divisions, so that is the species that I have mostly worked with, although I finally found a pickable patch of *Valeriana sitchensis* just a few weeks ago and have a tincture of that macerating right now. I have heard that *sitchensis* is stronger and more sedating than *officinalis*. While interacting with the *Valeriana sitchensis* patch recently, it was clear to me that this plant could be very easily propagated in much the same way that the garden species is, and I did a bunch of root divisions in the patch that I was harvesting from.

I think it is so interesting that most of the herbs that I gather in alpine environments are calming to the nervous system, relieve pain, or both. I like this both because I think of these mountains as being a central part of the nervous system of the landscape as a whole, and also because I have noticed that many landscapes will provide their own corrigent in terms of the plants that grow upon them. The mountains can be really stressful and scary places, especially if you get lost or the weather turns. They are also an environment in which it is easy to overextend yourself or to hurt yourself, and the mountain provides the herbs to help with just those conditions. Many of these herbs are also genuinely helpful in these Dog Days of Summer, when people are worn thin and freaking out. It is a nice late Summer ritual to climb the mountains, much like the people traditionally climb the sacred hills in Ireland for Lughnasadh, and come back with these calming remedies for the people.

ROOT CAMP/
WILD TENDING/
FIRE SEASON

As the Sun moves from the constellation of Leo the lion to Virgo the virgin we truly enter late Summer or early Fall. The leaves of the deciduous trees begin to yellow, brown, and fall to the ground. Many of the plants in the garden are going to seed and starting to die back, browning and crisping up, moving their energy down into their roots where it will slumber until the return of the warmth next spring. All the grasses have died back and the open fields are a golden brown. This is also, especially in the last decade or so, a time of significant drought. I have only lived in this area for about twenty years, and I have noticed in that time that the late Summer droughts have gotten worse and gone on longer as the years have progressed. Leo is a fire sign, and Virgo is an earth sign, and this time of late Summer is traditionally associated with the earth element, at least in some traditions of Chinese medicine. It is a time of calming down, getting grounded after the hectic Summer, and getting ready to settle down for the Fall and Winter. Unfortunately due to climate change, and decades of poor choices about how the forests are to be managed on the part of the timber companies and the government, we now have a new season here on the West coast of Turtle Island, which goes from early to mid August to late September or even into October, which is wildfire season. It is terrible. The wildfires get worse every year it seems, and at least here in "Washington State" so far in this fire season more acreage has burned than in the previous twelve fire seasons put together. As I am sitting here at my desk in "Littlerock," occupied Chehalis Territory by the Black River, the air outside is so full of smoke that it is partially blocking out the sun, and my lungs are hurting even though I am staying inside and wearing an N95 type mask which filters out particulates whenever I go for a walk outside.

FIRE HISTORY

Fire season is just one of the many symptoms that we are seeing of the sickness upon this land that is Capitalism/Neoliberalism/I don't even know what to call it. Prior to European colonization, the forests were thick and old growth, wild fires were allowed to burn when they happened, and many places were intentionally burned annually. These prescribed burns happened in many different places and generally served to increase the abundance of various food and medicine plants. I mentioned in the chapter about the Prairies about how those places were and still are maintained by intentional burns, which clear away the undesirable plant species while leaving behind the desired food and medicine plants such as Camas (*Cammasia quamash*) and Kishwoof/Oshá (*Ligusticum grayi*). This practice would also keep the coniferous trees from encroaching into these areas while leaving the Oaks (*Quercus garryana*) in fine shape and encouraging their seeds to germinate. In the forests, intentionally set fires helped to keep the over story open so that sunlight could get in, and cleared out the under story to keep it open while also encouraging berry plants and other forage plants to produce more abundantly those parts of themselves that are good for humans and other animals to eat. In the high elevation areas, intentional burns helped to keep the berry fields abundant as the Blueberries (*Vaccinium ovalfolium/deliciosum, etc*) and the Huckleberries (*Vaccinium membranaceum*) produce much greater yields of berries in the years after a burn due to both the effect of the burn "pruning" the tops of the plants as well as the fire liberating many nutrients that are locked up in the woody parts of the various plants in the area in the form of ash, thus feeding the soil and the plants. Fires in these areas also kept non desired plants such as the Heathers (*Calluna spp.*) from encroaching on the berry fields. These practices kept these various places abundant in plant based foods that humans could eat, and also provided good forage for the Deer (*Odocoileus hemionus*), Wapiti/Elk (*Cervus canadensis*), and various other animals that humans could then hunt for food. These intentionally set fires also burned up all the standing fuel on the landscape, which helped to keep really out of control fires from occurring. Once the European colonizers showed up one of their first activities was to set about cutting down the great forests. This was both for economic reasons, at first just to clear land for farming and to provide wood for building houses, and for philosophical/genocidal reasons in that there was this Calvinist notion that European colonization was the will of God, and that it pleased God for "Man" to tame the wilderness and bring order and light to the dark and savage places. Of course, there was the technique utilized in so many ways in the genocidal attack upon the indigenous people of this land of destroying the natural environment upon which the people depended for their food, clothing, spiritual fulfill-ment, and general lifeways in order to kill them off or force them to adopt a more "civilized" way of life by embracing the ways of their oppressors and becoming churchgoing farmers. Later on the forests came under a prolonged and intensified attack that is still going on to this day in order to cut them down and sell them as lumber. This extractive process re-sulted in the clear cutting of basically all of the old growth forests on Turtle Island, with a very few exceptions that stand as protected islands here and there. This destruction of the forests made a few people disgustingly wealthy, the "lumber barons," and also became a way that many colonizers and also eventually many indigenous people (I was so surprised when a Quinault friend of mine told me that much of the cut-ting on the Quinault reservation, which does not have much old growth, was done by tribal members in order to make some money, but of course this makes sense) came to make their livings over the decades. There is a strong logger culture still in this region, although logging is no longer nearly as economically viable a career as it used to be because all of the old growth forests have already been cut down. Many of the logging towns that used to be bustling and relatively wealthy communities are now kind of ghost towns and im-poverished. Much of the forests that are standing are "owned" by one of the big logging companies such as Weyerhaeuser or Green Diamond. These forests are actually thickly planted monocultures of fast growing trees that can be easily milled into lumber. Around me the main trees that are planted are Douglas Fir (*Pseudotsuga menziesii*) and a Douglas Fir/Hemlock hybrid that I cannot find any information about. The trees are planted thickly together and the area around them is often "weeded" by either chemical or mechanical means to keep the undesired species from taking up water and sun. After these trees have grown up for twenty years or so, the logging machines come in and cut them all down (often leaving a tiny island or two of standing trees for "wildlife habitat") and remove the big trunks which can be milled into lumber while leaving all sorts of downed branches and other "slash," which is sometimes piled up and burned to get rid of it, but often is just left there as "mulch" or "fertilizer." This has resulted in the forests being thickly crowded with trees that can easily burn anyway (remember that fire was used to keep the Doug Firs from encroaching on the Prairies), which are unhealthy due to their being mass produced on plantations and then planted out in a hurried and often sloppy way by either underpaid workers or slave labor in the form of prison inmates. All this in a landscape that is covered in dead and dry wood left behind by poor logging practices.

These forests are primed to burn, but along with all of these changes to the forests that make them so susceptible to burning, there has grown up a huge industry and tradition of fire suppression. This is mostly due to economic reasons as the forests themselves are "owned" by the logging companies who want to be sure that all of "their" trees grow to be harvestable size so that they can make their money. Also many towns have been built in the middle of the forests or right next to them, and many homes have also been built outside of towns in the woods. Many of these homes were not built with wildfires in mind, and many people who live in these homes do not maintain the land around their home in a way that would help to keep a wildfire from running right through their yard, since the wildfires that we are seeing these days are a new phenomenon. Every year firefighters, many of them also slave labor from prisons who are forced to work a very dangerous job for less than $1 an hour but also people who choose to do that work, spend the entirety of the late summer putting out forest fires. This has been going on for decades in order to protect the "standing timber" and the human houses. If some of these fires had been allowed to run their course in the past they probably would have cleared away some of the underbrush and dry downed wood, but after such a long period of time of bad planting and harvesting practices along with fire suppression, the forests can no longer burn in a slow and controlled way.

This is exacerbated, of course, by climate change. We have been seeing longer, hotter, and drier summers every year for the past many years. New temperature records are broken every year, and while it used to be unusual for the lands West of the mountains in this corner of Turtle Island to see much drought, the past several years with some exceptions there has been widespread drought every Summer. Two Summers ago every county in "Washington State" was in drought according to the state, which is unheard of (or used to be). Additionally, the intense heat and drought is causing mass die offs of many different plant species in the forests of this area. Many of the coniferous trees are dying, even older and well established trees. I first started noticing the the Red Cedars (*Thuja plicata*) were dying off in town about a decade ago, but now the Douglas Firs (*Pseudotsuga menziesii*) are also dying, and it is happening in the forests as well. Even in the deeper forest within the National Parks such as up on the Olympic Peninsula, which has had much less logging and other poor practices inflicted upon them while also literally being a rainforest, the coniferous trees are just turning brown and dying where they stand. In some places the Salal (*Gaultheria shallon*), which is the majority of the under story in many of the forests around here, is experiencing a mass die off as well. All these things together have led to the current situation, namely that the wildfires are getting worse every year and fire suppression is becoming increasingly difficult. The situation is even worse in those areas South of us, such as "Oregon" and "California," which are naturally hotter and drier anyway. These wildfires are devastating for so many people, human and greater than human alike. Humans lose their homes and often their lives, and of course the animals and plants in the forest are killed or lose their homes in huge numbers. I do see again and again how resilient the landscape is and how quickly the plants start to repopulate the burned over areas, followed by the animals and birds, and this is soothing to me. I honestly think that this process is going to continue until the majority of the poorly managed forests have burned, and maybe will continue on after that unless indigenous peoples are able to regain control of how the forests are managed, hopefully with strong support on the ground from the descendants of colonizers without them trying to take over leadership.

Beyond the loss of habitat and the danger of the fires themselves, the main issue with this season is the smoke. The smoke from the fires totally cover the landscape all around, sometimes so thickly that the Sun is blocked out and it becomes uncomfortable to breathe. The smoke is full of particulates as well as carbon dioxide, both of which are harmful to health and can cause trouble breathing as well as stress on many of the other body systems, especially the nervous system. When the fires make it into towns or burn down houses that adds a whole other layer of toxicity to the smoke since all of the insulation, plastics, and other industrial products are burned and add their components to the smoke. Everyone suffers from the smoke, but especially those with chronic lung and cardiovascular issues, the old and the very young. The best thing to do is to keep yourself inside your house at this time with some kind of air filter running. You can buy air purifiers at the store, or simply placing a filter designed for a home heating or forced air system on the back end of a box fan and running that inside the house can be really helpful to clean up the air inside the house, since the smoke gets in no matter what you do. During the fire season it is really important to keep very well hydrated to moisturize the lungs and to help flush out the various toxins that you are ingesting through the smoke. Moistening and emollient herbs such as Marshmallow (*Althea officinalis*), Licorice (*Glycyrrhiza glabra*), Slippery Elm (*Ulmus rubra*), or Solomon's Seal (*Polygonatum biflorum*) are really great to take quite a lot of at this time to help keep the lungs moistened and to counteract the hot and drying aspects of the smoke and of the season. Mullein (*Verbascum thapsus*) is also a really nice, soothing lung tonic that can be drank as a tea all the time when smoke is bad. Mullein is also pretty weedy, especially in the drier areas where the fires tend to happen, so that is an easy one to procure. I also like to give people calming and anxiolytic herbs at this time such as Skullcap (*Scuttelaria lateriflora*), Hawthorn (*Crataegus monogyna*), Milky Oats (*Avena sativa*), or even stronger ones such as Anemone (*Anemone occidentalis*) or Bleeding Heart (*Dicentra formosa*) since the whole situation is really scary and anxiety inducing. Hawthorn also benefits the cardiovascular system which is working harder at this time to move oxygen around. It can be nice to provide some liver support also since the liver is working extra hard to process the toxins in the smoke, as well as all of your stress hormones, so something like Milk Thistle (*Silybum marianum*), Dandelion (*Taraxacum officinale*), Tumeric (*Cucurma longa*), or Burdock (*Arctium lappa*) is nice to take during the fires. If you have to be out in it, an N95 type mask, or more ideally a respirator and goggles will provide some protection. The main way to try and ameliorate the effects of the wildfires, however, is to change forestry practices and return the management of the lands to the tribes who actually know how to do it.

PLANT/HUMAN ALLIANCES AND CLIMATE CHANGE

The fires bring the reality of climate change and climate disruption home in a dramatic way. It is clear that we are only going to experience more and more of these devastating effects of climate change as the years go on and the landscape in general becomes hotter and drier. We are living through a mass extinction right now, which is the sixth mass extinction event recognized by many scientists as having occurred on the Earth. This mass extinction is unique in that it seems to be caused by one specific species, *Homo sapiens*, largely through economic, religious, and cultural systems that humans created and then took on lives of their own as egregores which have voraciously eaten up the majority of the available resources of the planet while excreting innumerable toxins. Since 1900, which is in many ways the dawn of the Industrial Age, extinctions have occurred at over 1,000 times greater abundance than the background extinction rate. By some estimates about 1/8th of all of the species currently existing on the planet are threatened with extinction. It is always important, but especially at this time, to create and sustain widespread, decentralized networks of mutual aid and solidarity both among the human inhabitants of the planet and maybe more importantly between humans and greater than human beings such as the plants, animals, insects, and the land. As an herbalist I especially focus on creating good relationships with the plants who are our teachers and ancestors and who give us so much. One of the reasons that the plants created humans is because with our hands and our legs we can help the plants to move around the planet and to grow in new places. It is our job and our privilege to help our plant teachers and friends to survive through the current and coming changes. I especially think about this for some of the hard to cultivate plant species that live in specific environments, such as the root medicine plants of the upper elevation deserts that I will talk about next. We are already seeing that plant communities are migrating North and also up in elevation in response to the warming and drying climate. Now more than ever it is important to go out to the plant communities and help them to be more abundant in the places where they are already living through propagation techniques, as well as helping them to move to new areas where they may do well in a warmer climate, or even just to move them away from places that are likely to be destroyed or "developed" by human interests. Keep a garden, try to move some of the "wild" plants into your garden and allow them to live a nice chill life there, take good care of them. Propagate plants out in the woods, move them to new locations, especially by seed. If you have a goodly amount of land that you live on, make it into a sanctuary for plants and animals as much as you can. They are all suffering from climate change, especially at this time of year when everything is burning. Finally, work on mutual aid projects with the humans around you. If you are studying herbalism then you must want to heal humans and I encourage you to offer your services as an herbalist as freely as you can, especially to historically and currently disadvantaged humans.

While you are at it, try to help people get the food that they need, and if you make a goodly amount of money give some of it away both directly to panhandlers on the street as well as to organizations that you trust to do good things with it, especially indigenous- or POC-led organizations. Try to get out there and help people directly, since the only way that we are all going to get through this is by helping one another out. The more that you can give and help the better off you will be in the long run. Self care is important too, and be aware that you can't do it all, but some little actions can really go a long way.

THE DESERT HIGHLANDS

INTRODUCTION & HISTORY

Fire season is also the beginnings of root season, and it is around this time that I like to go to the desert highlands East of the mountains to visit with, propagate, and sometimes harvest some of the plants that live there. There are many places that I like to go, but I am going to focus on one specific place while also being a bit vague in this written piece about where exactly it is, for reasons that I will make clear later on. One of my favorite places to go is a place that one of my teachers first introduced me to which he calls Medicine Mountain. This mountain is in a mountain range East of the big mountains. This range is much smaller than the big mountains, and many of them have flat tops. They have a long and interesting geological history and are part of a vast uplifted plateau that has had a great amount of volcanic activity over the course of millions of years that has shaped and molded this place into the beauty that it is today. The landscape around these mountains is more open desert, filled with Sagebrush (*Artemisia tridentata*) and Junipers (*Juniperus occidentalis*) with scattered towns here and there. Once you get up into the hills there are more Pines (*Pinus ponderosa*) and Aspens (*Populus tremuloides*) along with the Junipers, especially in middle elevations. Once you get to the top of these tabletop mountains there are generally less trees and you are back in Sagebrush type habitat. These mountains have seen a very wide variety of plants and animals living upon them over the millennia, as evidenced by the many animals that were trapped by volcanic mud flows thousands or millions of years ago that have fossilized including horses, camels, and hippopotami. These mountains are amazingly abundant in both medicinal and edible plants, especially roots. Many of the edible tuber bearing species that have been and are still treasured by the indigenous people of this place such as Camas (*Cammasia quamash*) and the various Biscuit Roots (*Lomatium spp.'s*) are abundant in these mountains, as well as a wide variety of medicinal plants which I will discuss in depth later on. These mountains are within the occupied territories of the Paiute, Wascoe, Nez Pearce, and Warm Springs tribes. As usual, these people were violently displaced during European colonization, and many of these disparate tribal peoples were forced to live together on what is called the Warm Springs reservation by a treaty written by the superintendent of "Oregon" in 1855. The tribes relinquished/

had stolen around ten million acres of land while keeping the Warm Springs reservation and the right to hunt, fish, and gather on their traditional grounds. These various tribes who eventually came to be called the Confederated Tribes of the Warm Springs Reservation were very different from one another, with the Wascoes traditionally living along the banks of Wimahl (the Columbia River) where they were primarily fisherpeople who spoke a Chinookan language, the Warm Springs bands lived part of the time along the tributaries of Wimahl where they fished but also traveled for part of the year into the prairies where they hunted game and gathered roots while speaking Sahaptin, and the Paiutes lived in the high plains where they mostly ate game and food plants while speaking a Shoshonean dialect. The Paiutes were the most nomadic of the bunch as they had to follow the game.

As with all the areas we have discussed, these tribes have traditionally and still do maintain and care for the landscape and the various foods and medicinal plants that live upon them. Medicine Mountain is such a marvel for an herbalist because the whole place is just full of a wide variety of medicinal and edible plants, many of them in really thick and healthy patches. These marvelous patches are, clearly, gardens. I have never run into an obviously indigenous person up on this mountain or in the surrounding mountains that I have explored, mostly it is local white folks with guns who are up there hunting for Deer during root season, so I am not sure if tribal peoples are still working with and tending patches but I act as though they are. These places are really special, and it is important to act very intentionally and with great integrity in these places, especially if you are the descendant of colonizers (not that I am assuming that everyone who will read this will be that) who is interested in working with the medicines of these places. Act as though you are in someone's garden that their family has been tending for millennia. Be very careful to help the plants living there to be more prolific rather than depopulating them. Also, learn to keep some places a secret, which is what I am trying to do here by being somewhat vague about where I am talking about. It is better to introduce new people to places like this in person, and with promises from those people that they will keep the secrets and be very careful and respectful in their interactions with the place.

THE ROOTS

The main plants that I work with in this area have medicinal roots, although there are a number of species growing here whose medicine is in their flowers, leaves, or bark. The medicinal roots that live in this high desert environment are really special beings. All the plants are perennial, and many of them are very long-lived organisms. They need to do all of their photosynthesizing, blooming, pollinating, *and* set seed during the brief period in which the snows are melted, so between about Beltane/Solstice to about Equinox/Samhain. Then they put their energies down into their often huge and substantial roots where they sleep during the long snowy winter. All these root medicines have a certain wisdom to them and a resilience, which they can impart to the human who works with them.

While many of these roots can be harvested in a way that does not kill the plant as a whole, that is not true for all of the species I will discuss, and even if the harvest does not kill them it is certainly causing a large injury to them, therefore it is extra important to learn best practices around harvest, to be doing a lot of propagation, and to only take what you need. Some of these plants have analogues that can be grown in the garden, and these are worth looking into, although the deep wisdom of these old desert dwellers is hard to replicate in the garden. For some reason that I have not been able to figure out, many of the roots out in the desert are beautifully fragrant and full of resins. I suspect that this has to do with handling temperature extremes, especially the cold, as I know that often resins and essential oils can function as a sort of "anti-freeze" in plant tissues such as the oils in coniferous needles. The smells of these desert plants are medicine for the spirit, with the smell of Juniper filling the air on warm days.

The first plant that I would like to discuss of these root medicines is the most abundant of them all, growing in huge patches all over the inter-mountain West, which is Balsam Root (*Balsamorhiza sagittata*). This is a beautiful perennial herb in the Asteraceae family, often called the Sunflower family. Like the sunflower, Balsam Root has a large bright yellow flower. They stand two to three feet tall and have large leaves that are mildly fuzzy which could be said to be heart shaped or arrow shaped, hence the common name for this specific species which is Arrow Leaf Balsam Root. The Latin species name *sagittata* also relates to the arrow shaped leaf, being derived from Sagittarius, the archer. All parts of this plant are workable as a medicine, and also as a food. The flowers are fragrant and resinous, and can be worked with externally as a vulnerary and antiseptic in much the same way that Calendula (*Calendula officinalis*) flowers are. After the flowers have passed, the plant produces an abundance of large nutritious seeds similar to sunflower seeds which are good for eating. The leaves and stem of the plant can be either infused into oil or powdered and worked with in that form similarly to the flowers, although I have heard that the leaf is especially helpful for external fungal infections and tineas. The main part of this plant that is worked with as a medicine, however, is the root. These long lived perennials have huge fleshy taproots that are full of a sweet, fragrant, sticky resin, hence the name Balsam Root. One of the first things that you learn when learning to harvest Balsam Root is that most of the plants are actually too big to harvest. You can tell by looking at the root crown of the plant how big and old it is, with younger plants having a root crown only the size of a fifty cent piece and one or maybe two flowering stalks coming off of them. This size plant will have a root maybe six inches long (although sometimes much longer) which will not weigh very much, and I like to leave those ones to grow. Balsam Root is not a plant that will re-grow if you replant the root crown after harvesting the root, so the plant is going to die if you harvest their root for medicine. I like to get the medicine/individual lives ratio skewed towards more medicine per individual life. Some of the Balsam Roots are clearly very old, I have no idea how old but I am sure they are much older than me. These plants can have a root crown that is almost a foot in diameter, and the roots of these plants can be three feet or (maybe much) more in length. It is rude to harvest the old plants, which we often call the Grandmothers of the stand, for a variety of reasons that I will go into later when discussing Kishwoof/ Oshá. Also from a practical standpoint it is extremely hard to physically dig these roots out of the ground. They usually grow in very dry and rocky soil, and the roots like to wrap themselves around rocks, or worm their way between two huge underground rocks and keep growing beneath them for a couple of feet. It can take hours of hard physical labor to get one of these roots out of the ground, and they are sometimes the size of a small baby. I leave these ones in the ground so they can produce seeds and keep getting wiser, and to save my back. The best to harvest, I think, are in between these two sizes. A root crown of four to six inches, let's say, with six to a dozen flowering tops coming off of them, is usually a big enough root that you will only need to harvest one or maybe two individuals (and that is if you are making enough medicine for a large community like I do) to get plenty of medicine, and you can do it in a reasonable amount of time without hurting your back or hands too much.

Balsam Root has one huge taproot, which sometimes splits closer to the end, especially to wind around rocks and make you struggle to get them out. The roots are very beautiful and have a strong presence to them, and they are very fragrant and often ooze sap. The top of the roots, the root crown, has the fuzzy bear toes look that is a distinguishing mark of a bear medicine, which I will discuss more in the section on Kishwoof/Oshá. The roots very often have the shape of a human body to them, which reminds me of a Mandrake (*Mandragora autumnalis*) and seems to speak to a special affinity to the humans. I like to tincture the root fresh, hopefully in the field immediately after digging and washing the dirt off, but these roots are very tough and stable and will stay fresh without rotting for a long time. The roots can also be extracted into honey, which is a very nice preparation.

The medicine of Balsam Root has a lot to do with those sweet and fragrant resins. Like many resinous plants, the resins in Balsam Root after being ingested by a human circulate through the body and are excreted in a variety of ways, including through the lungs via respiration. As these resins raise up through the lungs they work as an expectorant and as an antiseptic, loosening up stuck mucus and helping it to get out of the lungs while also helping with any infections that might be present. The resins are also soothing and coating to the mouth and throat, which is nice when a person has a cough or sore throat. The medicine as a whole is rather warming and moving, acting primarily on the lungs and also on the digestion, where the medicine acts as a carminative and can be nice for gassy burpy bellies. There also seems to be an immune stimulating aspect to this plant. The taste of the tincture is complex, warming, spicy, and sweet. It is really nice to mix the tincture with a little bit of honey that has been infused with the root to thicken and accentuate the sweetness, especially for sore throats and coughs. The honey also helps to balance out the little bit of heat and dryness that the tincture has. Balsam Root brings you into your body, warms you up and helps you to take a nice deep breath. My teacher taught me about taking Balsam Root during the wintertime to help with the Winter blues, i.e., Seasonal Affective Disorder (SAD) since the plant opens up those bright yellow flowers all Summer and soaks in that sunshine which they then store down in the root in the form of the resin so you can take a little in the Winter when you miss the sun. Balsam Root has this deep wisdom, and they hold the warmth in the dark places. They dream during hibernation.

A good friend of Balsam Root that is also a bear medicine and often grows in the same general area is Kishwoof/Oshá (*Ligusticum grayi*). Oshá is the name broadly given to many species of this genus, and is most commonly associated with *Ligusticum porteri*, a species that lives among the Rocky Mountains and the continental divide. Kishwoof is apparently an indigenous name for this specific species, although I am trying to track down more information on this, and is the name I will stick with when referring to this plant for the rest of this chapter. Another common name that people have given this plant is Oshála. Kishwoof grows in moist meadows in the upper elevations of the Cascade, Coastal, and Sierra mountains. *Ligusticum porteri*, Oshá, grows more in the middle of the continent, and their range extends down into Mexico. Both of these species have a long history of being worked with as a medicine by the indigenous peoples of Turtle

Island in a variety of ways including as an herb that is strewn on the coals during sweat lodge and chewed for singers to keep singing. Oshá is a very popular herb that has really entered the global marketplace. All the species of *Ligusticum* are notoriously difficult to cultivate in a garden, although some people are starting to work it out and have some success. I know that Richo Cech of Strictly Medicinals seeds has Oshá that he has grown from seed (or maybe the workers at the company are the ones that grew them from seed, hard to tell). There are species of *Ligusticum* all across the Northern part of the globe, over 60 species in all, and I know that some of them have been successfully brought into gardens such as *Ligusticum striatum* which is worked with in Chinese herbalism. A dear accomplice of mine has successfully germinated out local lowland *Ligusticum* in her garden here in Chehalis territory. For a long time the story was that Oshá was impossible to grow in a garden and had to be wild harvested to be worked with, which was part of their charm. Unfortunately for the plant they are such a great medicine that they have come to be pretty badly overharvested in much of their range, at least in places that are more easily accessible. This is due to a few large herb companies incorporating this herb into some generic formulas that were sold in huge amounts, and also due to the pressures of individual herbalists. I have heard more than once that the first Oshá patches to go were the ones near herb schools, and that is a good reminder to be careful with how we interact with the wild plants in general in terms of herbal education. It is really easy to show your favorite Oshá patch to a group of students and maybe dig just a little, but then your students come back without you and they bring their friends, and maybe one of them starts an herb school and brings their students there, etc., until the patch is gone. Many herbalists have declared a moratorium on working with *Ligusticum porteri* due to over harvest. Kishwoof is still relatively abundant in the places where they grow, but we should look at what happened to the Oshá stands as a cautionary tale of what could happen to Kishwoof. A perennial plant that is very easy to grow in the garden and shares many of the medicinal aspects of the various *Ligusticum* species is Lovage (*Levisticum officinale*), which I would encourage people to grow and work with.

Kishwoof, just like Oshá, is in many ways the quintessential bear medicine. The name Oshá itself means "bear," like the Spanish word for bear which is *la osa* or *el oso*. Many traditions credit the bears with teaching the humans about the *Ligusticums* since the bears love this plants and will apparently roll around on the plants and dig up the roots to eat them like a cat playing with catnip. I have heard that bears will dig up and eat Kishwoof in the Spring after they have come out of hibernation, which serves to wake them up and get their metabolisms going, sometimes to the point of inducing vomiting or pooping. This is an anecdote, and I have never met someone who has seen this or otherwise can provide a strong reference that it happens, but I love the image and it speaks to the ways that humans like to work with this herb. Bear medicines in general tend to be warming and

stimulating and invigorating to the organism. They are usually roots that have fuzzy root crowns, and they are plants that
stimulate the breath and digestion. In many cultures the bears
are the ancestors to the humans and taught us a lot of the
tricks that we currently know, including herbalism. The bears
are familiar with the dream world and the spirit world because they spend the entirety of the winter buried under the
ground, hibernating and dreaming. Kishwoof is certainly a
bear medicine. They are in the Apiaceae family, also called the
Carrot family, and have the characteristic umbel of flowers of
many in that family. The flowers are white, and the leaves are
lacy and deeply serrated. They grow in moist meadows and
along streams, growing to be three feet tall or so. The entirety
of the plant has a very distinct odor that is characteristic of
many plants in the Apiaceae family, but the smell of Kishwoof
or Oshá is distinctive from other members of that family. It
is very important to be 100% sure of your ID before ingesting
any plant, but this is especially true of the Apiaceae family
which contains several deadly poisonous plants including Poison Hemlock (*Conium maculatum*). The **roots of Kishwoof**
have fuzzy root crowns, and are usually composed of many
individual tap roots which are all entwined with one another.
They can be up to a couple of feet deep even though they are
much more slender than the baby sized roots of Balsam Root.
The odor of the roots is very strong and one of my favorite
smells. I will often choose which of the Kishwoof to dig in
a similar way to Balsam Root, not the smallest ones and not
the biggest ones. Kishwoof is another plant where it is very

important to leave the grandmothers of the patches, which are the biggest plants. You will very often find Kishwoof growing on slopes, with the smallest plants near the bottom of the slope and the grandmothers up at the top.

The grandmother plants are the largest plants and they produce the most seed. All the plants on the lower parts of the slope are the children or grandchildren of the grandmothers at the top. It will take many years for those children to get to the maturity level that the grandmothers are at where they will really be able to start to drop a whole lot of seed every growing season, so if you harvest the younger plants they can be easily replaced by the grandmothers as they produce so much seed every year, but there is no replacing the grandmothers once they have been dug. One nice thing about Kishwoof is that you do not have to kill the entire plant in order to harvest root for medicine from them. If you dig up a

middle sized Kishwoof plant that has several flowering stalks coming off of them, the root will likewise have several distinct root crowns, each of which will have a taproot or several coming off of them, as well as a number of smaller roots coming directly off of the root crown itself. You can cut off the longer taproots and re plant the root crown with those smaller roots and the plant will keep on growing. You can also dig up a largish plant, harvest the taproots, and break the cluster of root crowns up into several smaller clusters, then weed out an area and plant those individual clusters in that spot with some space between them. This way you can harvest some medicine while also creating several smaller plants out of one larger plant, and given some time each of those smaller plants will grow to be the size of the original plant. I no longer harvest the entirety of any Kishwoof plant that I harvest medicine from. It is worth the extra time and effort to break up and replant the root crowns in order to maintain the health of the wild gardens. During the time of root harvest, the Kishwoof also have ripe seeds on them. It is a nice practice to snip off the seed heads from the plant that you want to harvest roots from, set them aside while you do root harvest, and then place the seed heads upside down on the soil that you loosened up and then replaced from digging up the root and replant the crowns. That nice loose soil will be easy for the seeds to get down into and germinate in. I like to clear some surrounding spots of other plants that I am not as interested in and sow some Kishwoof seeds in those places. I must admit that I have not yet done a careful study to check in a way that I feel totally confident about that the replanted root crowns are in fact surviving, but I am pretty sure and am devising some methods to flag or otherwise mark the replants in order to be able to tell how effective that process is. I strongly encourage you to carefully check that the propagation efforts that you are undertaking in the field are actually working! I have found through research that many of the methods that people will throw out there as a way to harmlessly harvest a plant do not work as well as they are presented.

The medicine of Kishwoof is similar to Balsam Root but hotter, sharper, and more lively. The roots have a long history of use as a medicine by the indigenous peoples of this area, and they function basically interchangeably with Oshá, *Ligusticum porteri*. Chewing on the root or taking an extract of the same has an immediate numbing effect of the mouth and anywhere that the root infused saliva touches including the throat when you swallow. This is part of the reason that Kishwoof is so popular with singers, as they numb and soothe a throat that may be getting irritated from singing all night. This is also a really nice aspect of Kishwoof for people who are sick with a sore throat, or who have an irritated throat from smoke exposure or allergens. The root is also warming to hot in flavor, with a bitterness underneath. Like Balsam Root, Kishwoof opens up the lungs and makes it easier to take a deep breath, and also helps to encourage expectoration while clearing out unwanted microbes in the lungs. Kishwoof is generally expulsive, as we can see with the anecdote about the bears eating the root until they vomit and poo. Kishwoof taken in large doses can cause nausea and vomiting. I have not seen them cause someone to poop in an obvious way. The expulsive effect does include the uterus, and for this reason pregnant people should not work with Kishwoof or Oshá internally as they can induce uterine contractions. I know of practitioners that will work with Oshá to help expel the afterbirth or any tissues that may be left behind after an abortion. The heat in Kishwoof will get the blood moving and get people sweating, and is nice to help someone to break a fever in the same way that many other diaphoretics can be. This is especially useful for someone with a lung infection and fever as the Kishwoof acts as an antimicrobial, will loosen up and help to expel the mucus in the lungs, and will help to sweat out the fever. The plant is generally enlivening, warming the body while helping to take deeper breaths and getting the digestion going. Kishwoof is really nice for a person who is depressed or exhausted, or who has been denying their body what it wants in order to function in capitalism, to kind of wake them up and bring them back into their body. It is nice to combine Kishwoof with honey, or to incorporate them into a formula with moistening and soothing herbs if you are giving them to someone who is sick with a cough. The Kishwoof will help get the mucus up and out and hasten the death of the microbes that are causing the problems, yes, but they can also be irritating or too hot for some people so it is nice to temper them with some other herbs. If a person has a dry, non productive cough, Kishwoof is not the best herb to reach for since it will exacerbate the situation. I would think of an antispasmodic in that situation like Cherry bark (*Prunus serotina*). Finally, Kishwoof is a great herb to work with if you are suffering from being in high elevation. They help to take deep breaths, often slow and strengthen the pulse, and generally help a person to feel comfortable and at home up on the mountains.

Perhaps my truest love of a plant grows up on the flat tabletop parts of these mountains, and that is Western Peony (*Paeonia brownii*). This plant is in the same genus as the

Garden Peony, which maybe your grandmother grew in her garden. They are in the Paeoniaceae family, which makes much more sense to me than their previous designation in the Ranunculaceae, or Buttercup, family. The genus *Paeonia* has species all across the Northern hemisphere from China to Greece, to here on Turtle Island where there are only two endemic species, namely *Paeonia brownii* and *Paeonia californica*. *Paeonia brownii* grows in the more Northern part of the continent, East of the Cascades in "Washington" and "Oregon" mostly, while *Paeonia californica*, as the name suggests, grows mostly East of the Sierras in "California." *P brownii* is the less abundant of the two species, often growing in a pretty scattered way even in those places where they are abundant, while *P californica* can form large stands. Many species in this genus have been worked with as a medicine in a number of different cultures and places.

The Latin name for the genus comes from Paeon, who was a student of Asclepius, the Greek god of the healing arts. All the species in the genus have beautiful and showy flowers, and *P brownii* is no exception. They seem really out of place in their natural habitat, which is usually high elevation in the desert or at least in arid pine forests, often growing in very dry and rocky soil surrounded by sagebrush. I once was shown a patch of them that was growing in an area that was pretty thickly wooded, and in that situation they were growing in loose and duffy soil (which made digging the tubers so much easier), but usually they live in very harsh environments. The plants themselves are a beautiful glaucous color, fleshy, almost like a succulent, with deeply lobed leaves and pinkish stems. The flowers are usually a deep maroon with yellow margins, although when I went to visit a flowering stand in "Idaho" several of the plants had green flowers. The flowers are drooping and always are looking at the ground so that you have to lie on your back in order to see them. They are fertilized mainly by wasps and yellow jackets who eat the abundant nectar that the flowers produce. They flower early in the Summer, often around Mother's Day, and die back during the heat of the Summer as a protection from the intense drought of that time. As the seeds, which are very large and heavy with a thick seed coat, become mature the flower head bows all the way down to the ground and gently releases them there. There is a huge fluctuation in how many seeds the plants in a patch will produce from one year to the next, at least in my experience observing this one patch for the past seven years. Some years they barely produce any seed at all while some years each plant will have a ring of seeds on the ground all the way around them. It is on the seed abundant years that I feel most comfortable harvesting tubers from the plants, so that I can sow seeds in the loosened soil after digging alongside the plant. I do wonder if this is not the best choice since the plants have clearly put a lot of their energies into producing seeds so maybe that is not the a great to also remove some of their nutrient and water storage by digging tubers, but I am not sure. One really sweet thing about working with Peony as a medicine is that you can harvest their tubers without killing the plant or even disturbing them very much at all. Each individual plant has a central root and also six to a dozen long dense tubers that grow off of the central root. These tubers are where the plant stores nutrients and water that they live off during the long droughty Summer months when they go dormant. The tubers are the part of the plant that is worked with for medicine, and you can harvest some of them from the main plant by digging a little trench alongside the plant and then carefully digging with your fingers or a hori hori towards the center of the plant until you run into some tubers. You can tell immediately that you have hit a tuber and not one of the many, many rocks that are often in the ground because the slight injury to the tuber will emit a strange, sweet fragrance which is the smell of Peony. Once you have found one tuber you can just work around it until it is free of the soil all the way from where it connects to the main plant to the very tip, and then give it a little pull in an upwards direction and it will cleanly break off from the main part of the plant. Maybe take one more from that hole and then fill it back in and plant the seeds in the loosened soil and you have harvested roots from a plant without ever needing to pull them out of the ground, which is a very nice feeling.

I learned one year that the very best way to harvest Peony is at night during a full moon. I learned this because that year during root camp there were a group of campers in a spot pretty close to where I was camping, hunters, and they had a pretty different idea about how to have a fun time in the forest than I did. They really liked to fire up a generator as the Sun went down to power their very loud sound system

(Lynyrd Skynyrd was on constant rotation) and also the wide screen TV that they had hauled up the mountain, and proceed to get shit-faced drunk and do a lot of yelling until pretty late at night, then wake up early and walk around with guns, hungover looking for deer. This resulted in me having a very hard time sleeping at night, and I had been struggling to dig the Peony during the day because it was so very hot and there was very little cover up there, so one night I just got out of bed and hiked all the way up to the Peony fields and did my harvest by moonlight. I tinctured some of the roots under the light of the moon, fresh in the field, then wrapped the jar in a cloth for the ride home so that they were never exposed to the Sun at all, which was a very fine batch of tincture. Peony tincture can be made either fresh or dry, and I was taught to make it dry to avoid the potential for nausea with fresh preparations but I have since switched to preferring a fresh tincture which seems much stronger to me and does not seem to cause nausea in me or anyone else that I have given it to. The taste of Peony tincture is very much like the smell of the roots, sweet with a strange and lovely medicinal tinge to it that many people love and some people really do not like. The fresh preparation especially has a distinctly wintergreen taste which I assume must be methyl salicylate, or, oil of wintergreen. I have not yet been able to find a constituent analysis of this species, so I do not know for sure, but it seems like it could not be anything else.

Methyl salicylate would make sense as a constituent for Peony since the plant is very good for pain and inflammation, both of which respond well to salicylates in general, such as the salicylates in Willow *(Salix spp.)* bark or the very well known acetyl salicylic acid (Aspirin). Underneath the complex of sweet flavors there is a pleasing bitterness. Along with the simple anti-inflammatory, pain relief properties of this plant, they also are nicely antispasmodic and deeply calming, soothing, and grounding. I like to work with this plant with people who are prone to panic states and/or depression. I have been told by several different people, and certainly noticed in my own self, that Peony seems to help with mental health issues that result from trauma that happened in childhood. A dear friend of mine thinks of this plant as a specific for people who have gone through sexual trauma, and many of the people that I know who really have a deep love and affinity for this plant have a history of childhood/adolescent sexual trauma, including myself. They seem to be able to get way deep down in there and give some comfort and love to the hurt child who still lives inside the person.

The first time that I harvested this plant, under guidance from my teacher and mentor, I was having trouble finding the tubers and then a cut into one of them when I finally found it, while I was trying to be very gentle and intentional in this process, and I got super triggered out in my all too familiar "I am no good at this; I can't do anything right; such a fuck up, etc., etc., etc.," shame/despair spiral that I am prone to, which I think stems from early traumas. The sweet smell of the root immediately brought me back to present and calmed me down, and I thanked the plant and asked them if they would show me more about what their medicine was all about. They promptly got way down inside of me and found my infant self. I was born very prematurely, while I was at the very end of the second trimester, and was very close to death, needed to be on a ventilator and live in a warm plastic box on a morphine drip for the first few days or maybe even weeks of my life, and that is my baseline trauma that all the other ones have built upon. Peony found that little scared teeny tiny baby Sean who was so confused and not getting the snugs and human companionship that they needed, and just sent them so much love and compassion, then gave the baby to me and I snugged my own baby self with so much love, and that very simple and brief vision/somatic experience was so helpful and continues to be. So I think they can help with deep baby trauma and birth trauma, for the child and the mother. My teacher says that Peony is like a mother who is totally capable of giving unconditional love to all parts of us, even our most wretched and damaged parts.

Peony can be worked with in situations where the menses are not flowing well and are painful, to increase flow and relieve pain while also being helpful to calm a too heavy flow. They are generally a very nice plant for pain in the pelvic region for people with all kinds of genitals. I have seen a nice reduction in pain for people living with ovarian cysts a couple of different times, and I have found them helpful in reducing bladder pain. Michael Moore says that the European species has been worked with as an abortive and an oxytocic,* which I am curious about mainly in the way that the plant feels, that

* See Moore, 194.

lovey feeling, and wondering if that could be tied in to an oxytocic action. Peony is also known to be rich in antioxidants, which is visible in the rich deep purple color of the tincture, although there is clearly some kind of oxidation reaction happening to create that color, since the freshly sliced root is white on the inside and then slowly turns purple as it dries, and the fresh tincture likewise starts off almost clear and then slowly turns purple over the course of several weeks. Within Chinese medicine the most commonly worked with of the Peonies is White Peony, *Paeonia lactiflora*, which is worked with as a blood builder, to harmonize menstruation, and as an antispasmodic and painkiller, especially of the smooth muscles, which relates to the use of this plant to relieve some lung complaints such as asthmatic wheezing which is caused by tightened smooth muscles around the lungs. The European species, *Paeonia officinalis,* was worked with by practitioners in the 1800s as a treatment for epilepsy and seizures, although William Cooke in his *The Physiomedical Dispensatory* says that this was a fanciful idea, and the plant is not strong enough to deal with such intense conditions, but can be worked with as an antispasmodic in "the spasms and colics of children."† Reading some of these ideas got me to dig up some tubers from a flowering Peony that I was growing as an ornamental, and the tubers had that familiar smell and taste to them. The tincture that I made from the garden Peony was not quite as strong as that of the wild species, but did work just fine. I would encourage people to do more research into working with the garden Peonies, which are very abundant in many established gardens.

† See Cooke, 399.

I really like incorporating Peony into herbal formulations as a harmonizing herb. I got this idea from one of Michael Tierra's books, although I cannot find the reference now, which said that Peony is a nice herb to include in a formula because they calm and relax the organism, allowing the other herbs to move through the body freely and better do their respective workings. The plant also adds a nice taste to a formula, much like adding Licorice (*Glycyrrhiza glabra*), which is also a harmonizing herb, does. I also think that a little bit of Peony in a formula allows them to work on a person's underlying traumas, whatever they may be, and getting some relief for those deeply buried things can help to clear up present-day illness.

The plant that is probably most abundant on Medicine Mountain, at least of the non-tree medicinal plants, is Baneberry (*Actaea rubra*). If you go to the mountain early in root season the Baneberry are still lush as they grow in the shadows of the forested parts of the trails. They are a deep vibrant green with their shocking red or white berries on full display. They really stand out and draw attention. Baneberry is an interesting plant to work with because they have such a bad reputation among many herbalists, especially the herbalists that attend herb conferences in West coast cities with an affinity for naturopaths. The berries are known to be toxic, and the name Baneberry seems to point to this idea, *bane* meaning "A cause of ruin, harm, or death" according to the *American Heritage Dictionary of the English Language*. Luckily the berries taste bad, and it is rare for anyone to eat enough of them to become poisoned, especially children. I cannot find any recorded deaths from this species in any of the literature that I have dug through, although most sources when discussing this plant say that the berries and all other parts of the plant are poisonous, and when most sources mention medicinal use of the root they usually emphasize that is is very strong and perhaps dangerous.

It is interesting to watch Michael Moore's views of this plant change from his earliest books to his later ones. In the first edition of *Medicinal Plants of the Mountain West*, which came out in 1979, he says of the plant: "It is an acrid irritant and moderately poisonous internally, depressing vagus function, with cardiac arrest possible from large doses" (45). While in *Medicinal Plants of the Pacific West*, which came out in 1993, he says, "Internally, the root has the same uses as listed under Black Cohosh, with the exception of estrogenic" (60), and in the second edition of *Medicinal Plants of the Mountain West*, which came out in 2003, he says, "I now use it as an across-the-board substitute for its very close relative, black cohosh (*Cimicifuga racemosa*)" (45). When I vend medicines at herb conferences, people often see that I have tincture of Baneberry root for sale and give me a little talking to because it is such a strong and toxic herb that only advanced practitioners should use it, except one time I had a man come up to me who was a tribal member who was so pleased that I was carrying the plant and bought some from me. He said that in his tribe (I forget which tribe, I'm sorry) the plant was called "sweet medicine" and was most often given to Mothers who had just given birth to help them regain their strength, which is probably not what you would do with a super toxic plant.

I find Baneberry to be very much like Black Cohosh (which used to be *Cimicifuga racemosa* but has since been switched into the genus *Actaea* right along with Baneberry which is *Actaea rubra*) in their effects. The only real difference I can find between the two herbs is that Baneberry has this deliciously sweet taste to the fresh herb tincture that Black Cohosh does not at all, which to me makes Baneberry seem like more of a tonic and building herb than Black Cohosh, and in some ways I think of them as gentler than Black Cohosh. Like Black Cohosh, Baneberry is a nice antispasmodic for cold and dry pains, and like Black Cohosh, they help to bring moisture to dried out and atrophied tissues.

I think of Baneberry as being especially helpful for a melancholic constitution in the model of the four temperaments, so, cold and dry. These people are often hard workers but kind of up in their heads all the time, and they may neglect their bodies, tending to be thin and tense. This kind of chronic pain, that responds well to warmth to loosen and relieve it, will be well helped by Baneberry. I also like to work with them as a general smooth muscle antispasmodic, so they can be helpful for uterine cramping, asthmatic symptoms, and tension or cramping in the urinary or digestive tract. I have not yet worked with Baneberry in this way but I hear they can be useful for those people who are going through menopause to relieve some of the hot flashes and other estrogen based symptoms. Baneberry can also be really helpful for depression, also much like Black Cohosh. The type of depression that Baneberry is good for is more of a deep and chronic type. Whereas I would reach for St. John/Joan's Wort (*Hypericum perforatum*) for someone who is having a mild and transient depression, like the Winter glooms or situational depression, I would think about Baneberry or Black Cohosh for a person (who, again, may have a melancholic temperament) who is chronically depressed especially if there is a corresponding tension and pain in the musculature. It was once described to me by a teacher as relieving depression by bringing moisture to the nervous system, which is of course made out of fats and oils and, in the case of the brain and spinal column, bathed in cerebrospinal fluid. If the fluids become too dried out, then the nervous system becomes brittle and irritated and cannot work properly, but Baneberry can bring moisture and relax the body so that the now once again supple nervous system can work freely. I have found Baneberry, as well as Black Cohosh, to be really helpful in my own chronic (although not as chronic as it used to be) depression. I think that the antispasmodic nature of the plant is a big part of the help, because there is this constant tension and tightness in the body that really amplifies the negative thought patterns, and if you can calm and soothe the body, the mind goes along with it.

I think of Baneberry as being a building and strengthening tonic that can be worked with over an extended period of time because of their sweet taste. This is not often how I hear this plant or Black Cohosh as being worked with, but looking through Cook's *Dispensatory* again provides this thought of his about Black Cohosh: "One advantage to this agent, is the fact that it leaves behind a gently toned impression, rather than a relaxed one. While it soothes, it also gently strengthens" (165), which seems to agree with me. It is interesting to me how many herbs had so much of their complexity stripped away from them during the 1980s and 1990s, when American herbalists were looking for herbs to act as "little drugs" that were for one specific ailment based upon constituent research. It was at that time that Black Cohosh became reduced to an herb that was primarily good as an estrogenic to deal with menopausal symptoms. One thing to look out for with both Baneberry and Black Cohosh is a frontal headache if you take too large of a dose, which is caused I believe by vasodilation through relaxation.

In many cases I would encourage people to work with cultivated Black Cohosh over Baneberry primarily because Black Cohosh is grown on farms and gardens all over the place, while Baneberry is rarely cultivated and in most wild places is very scattered. In the woods around me I rarely run into more than one Baneberry plant at a time, never a patch. However, on Medicine Mountain (and maybe in other places East of the mountains I am not sure), some of the wooded slopes are literally carpeted with Baneberry; there is no other under story vegetation. So I have harvested Baneberry from this mountain twice now, about seven years apart. Baneberry grows in much the same way as Black Cohosh, spreading by rhizomes to form a dense carpet of roots over an expansive space, and I have been propagating Baneberry out in the woods in the same way that I propagate Black Cohosh in my garden: by harvesting the majority of the root structure of a plant while leaving behind one or two of the root crowns and enough root to support them, then replanting those. If I dig up a bigger plant I will cut out three or four such root crown/ root pieces and plant them all back in the space where the original plant was. When I visit the patch the next year there is no longer a visible gap in the Baneberry carpet, so I think that it is working. I also scatter the berries around and lightly cover them with the duffy soil, although I kind of suspect that those berries need to go through somebody's digestive tract before they will germinate. I keep meaning to transplant some Baneberry from the mountain to my garden, in which Black Cohosh does very well, to see if they can be domesticated as easily which would encourage me to really work on propagating out the Baneberry intensively in my garden and work on getting other herbalist gardeners to grow them as well. Black Cohosh, of course, is a good reminder to be careful about wildcrafting, since the wild stands of this plant in the Appalachian Mountains have been severely depleted.

The final root medicine that I want to describe in this chapter is another very fragrant one, which is appropriately known as Sweet Root (*Osmorhiza occidentalis*). This is another Apiaceae, or Carrot, family plant and has the characteristic umbel of flowers much like Kishwoof, except Sweet Root's flowers are yellow. They grow in the same sort of environments in which you would find Kishwoof, Balsam Root, or Lomatium, and they grow rather abundantly in the intermountain West from as far North as "Canada" to as far South as Southern "California." The individual plants can grow to be quite old, with older individuals often having dozens of flowering stalks coming out of the root mass, which is itself much more substantial and more fragrant than the roots of younger plants. Sweet Root is impossible to misidentify once you have dug the shallow laying roots out of the ground. They have a spicy, sweet, rich safrole like smell to them that is just divine. Much like Kishwoof, which is often growing right next to them in the field, Sweet Root can be very easily propagated by breaking up the larger root masses into several smaller pieces, clearing some space for them, and replanting. I also do quite a lot of seed planting while I am out there, as Sweet Root produces seed very abundantly every year. The roots of this species are much easier to dig than most of the other desert roots because they grow more as laterally expanding masses of roots, with no tap roots to speak of. I will usually go up the hill with a digging fork and dig up one plant from a massive stand, replant a bunch of it, then walk a ways to another massive stand and dig one plant, replant a bunch of it, etc., until I have my desired harvest.

Sweet Root is worked with primarily as a gut herb. They are a nice and strong carminative as a simple. The spicy sweet taste gets saliva moving right away and helps to clear up any gas or nausea especially after eating a very rich meal or maybe something that was a little bit rotten. They are also helpful in cases of acute food poisoning with vomiting, cramps, and diarrhea, in which case they reduce the cramps and gas, often help with the nausea, and cover the taste and smell of the vomit. People who have food allergies that cause stomach upset seem to respond well to this plant to reduce symptoms, and if someone is so sensitive that they can tell if someone has served them food that was chopped up on a cutting board upon which someone cut bread earlier in the day, getting some of the tincture or tea into them right away when they are very first noticing symptoms can often seem to keep the more acute reactions from taking place. Sweet Root has some anti fungal properties and can be worked with both internally and externally to reduce yeast overgrowth. Sweet Root is also just a nice tasting plant and is nice to add to formulas for its sweet and spicy taste. They go really well into digestive bitters and provide some warming oils to balance out the cold nature of the bitter plants. This year we planted some of the Sweet Root that I brought home from the desert into pots in the garden, and they are already starting to put out fresh growth!

One plant that I want to briefly touch on as a warning is known by many names including False Hellebore and Corn Lily (*Veratrum viride*). This plant has been worked with as a medicine to lower blood pressure and slow the heart rate, but that is rarely done anymore because the alkaloids in this plant can very easily slow the heart rate to the point where you die. *Veratrum* is one of the few acutely poisonous plants that grows in this part of the world, and they very often are growing in the same fields as the Kishwoof and Sweet Root. I strongly encourage people to learn to identify this plant both by their above ground portions and by the appearance of their roots, which look like spooky squid monsters and are very easy to identify. The main reason for this is that sometimes the above ground parts of this plant will have entirely died back and the roots will be entwined with the roots of a medicinal species. I once dug up a clump of Kishwoof and upon breaking it up and shaking off the dirt I found a small *Veratrum* root in the very center of the clump. If I had not noticed it and had tinctured all of those roots together I think it is possible that I could have killed people with that tincture. Please do a little research on this plant, and dig one up to get a good look at the roots. The above ground parts are striking and beautiful and do not look like any other plant that grows in the region.

The high elevation deserts are sacred places full of so many medicinal plants. While I want to express how wonderful these plants are I once again want to urge people to be very slow and careful when and if they decide that they want to interact with these root medicines. In many cases it might make sense to just buy a small amount of a finished tincture from someone who you know works with them in a good way rather than going out to the field yourself, where it can be easy to harvest much more of a plant than you will ever use. I encourage people to learn the skill of keeping some things quiet and secret (says the person who is writing all this stuff down, I know...). In the age of oversharing everything, destructive things can happen when certain plants suddenly become Instagram famous, and it is an act of defiance to the dominant culture to keep some things secret and only tell the people you trust. Working with the roots should be like that. I would encourage people to acquire the medicines from a trusted source, maybe go and sit with the plants without harvesting them, work with analogues that can be easily grown in the garden, and actively propagate the wild species for a time *before* you ever harvest them. Also think about how these plants are going to fare as the planet continues to warm and dry, and try to figure out how you can best be of service to them through that process.

8

THE EQUINOX AT LAST, RAINFOREST ROOTS & MEDICINAL MUSHROOMS

EQUINOX TRADITIONS

The Equinoxes happen two times of the year, in the Spring and in the Fall. The Equinox is the moment in time when the plane of the Earth's equator lines up with the very center of the Sun. At this time the length of the day and the length of the night are just about equal all over the world, hence the name Equinox which is derived from the Latin *aequinoctium* which is a combination of *aequus,* meaning "equal," and *nox* meaning "night." This chapter focuses on the Fall or Autumnal Equinox, which is a beautiful time of year. In the Northern hemisphere the Autumnal Equinox takes place around September 23rd, which corresponds to the High Holy Day of Rosh Hashanah in Judaism. Rosh Hashanah marks the beginning of the civil year and is considered to be the anniversary of the creation of Adam and Eve, the first two humans created by God according to many religious systems. This Holy Day marks the traditional period of agricultural harvest in the ancient Near East and is considered a day of judgment during which the fates of people are recorded. The month leading up to Rosh Hashanah and the day itself is a period of self reflection and repentance. On the day itself there is a traditional ritual action known as *tashlikh* which involves saying prayers by flowing water and casting one's sins into the waters in the form of pebbles or bread. Symbolic foods are eaten to bring in a good new year, such as apples dipped in honey for a sweet year, which is an Ashkenazi tradition, or the eating of pomegranates to have a fruitful and abundant year like the many seeds of that fruit.

On the Pagan wheel of the year, the Autumnal Equinox is the middle point between Lughnassa and Samhain and is called Mabon. It is a time to celebrate the harvests of the year, which are coming in abundantly at this time, and to prepare for the upcoming dark time. The main tradition is feasting. It is considered the first day of Fall and is a harvest festival in most cultures across the Northern hemisphere, including the Chinese who celebrate the full moon closest to the Equinox as the Harvest Moon at which time the good rice and grain harvests are praised and people stay out to watch the Moon. During the French Revolution, the new French government implemented a new yearly calendar which was to be devoid of religious or royalist influence, and in this calendar the new year began at the stroke of midnight on the Autumnal Equinox. This calendar lasted from 1793 to 1805, at which time Napoleon Bonaparte banished it, but it was briefly resurrected during the Paris Commune in 1871. Each month of this calendar was named after the prevailing weather and seasonal progressions around Paris such as *brume* or "frost" which was late October–November and *prairial* or "meadow" which was late May to June. In terms of astrology, the Sun moves from Virgo the Virgin which is an earth sign, to Libra the Balance Scales which is an air sign. This period is considered a time of great balance and is ruled by *Iustitia* or Lady Justice who is a Roman deity who is in turn based upon the ancient Egyptian deities Maat and Isis. All these figures serve as sources of balance and order, and are involved in the souls of humans being judged or otherwise entering into the underworld. This is appropriate as the Equinox is the step before Samhain when the dead and the living are closest to one another.

The Equinox is a balance point in which yin and yang are in equal ascendance, to use a Chinese metaphor, and the veil is not exactly thin, but kind of feels thick and supportive, which makes this a potent time of year in which to do some heavy magical work without being thrown about too much. Aleister Crowley named the publication that he put out regularly, with information about the workings of his magickal order, *The Equinox*. During this time of year the plants are preparing to go to sleep or die and are having some of their most abundant times in terms of creating fruits and berries. The leaves on the trees are starting to change colors and fall off, the roots are becoming plump and lively, and the rains return at last. Often the rains of the Equinox are what finally put out the fires of the summer. The rains also bring on the fruitings of the mighty and beautiful mushrooms which are so abundant in my specific corner of the world, and you can find families out in the woods on the nicer days beginning to pick some of the many edible and medicinal species that are available. At this time of year I am mostly going out into the woods to harvest medicinal roots and mushrooms.

RAINFOREST ROOTS

The medicinal roots of the Rainforest are much different to work with than the medicinal roots of the Desert. The two landscapes are unlike one another and so the plants exist upon them in different ways. Whereas the Desert on the East side of the mountains is a place of cold, frigid, snowy Winters and hot, dry Summers with a lot of Sun, the Rainforests on the West side of the mountains is a very temperate environment, with relatively mild Winters that are mostly very wet and rainy without many freezes or snowy times. The Summers are dry, but the temperatures do not climb nearly as high, there are more cloudy and rainy days, and the forests themselves provide a cooling and shady refuge for the hottest parts of the year. So unlike the Desert roots that often form deep, fat taproots full of resins to protect themselves from the extreme temperatures and in which to store moisture and nutrients to get through both the arid hot Summers and the snowy frozen Winters, the Rainforest roots are more often close to the surface and take the form of dense mats of rhizomatous growth. A rhizome is basically an underground stem that often grows horizontally and sends out true roots into the earth to anchor themselves along with upright shoots into the air for leaves and fruits. These types of roots do very well in the rainforest which is full of lots of moving water and often light and duffy soils composed of centuries of dropped leaves and needles because they can form thick mats and therefore cling to the soil in order to keep from being washed away or uprooted. These rhizomes also are often quite good at vegetative propagation, as in they can very easily root themselves into the earth even if they have been broken off from the main body of the plant. This is also nice in a landscape where the Water is often moving things around since a chunk of the plant can be broken off and washed away by the waters and will simply take root wherever it ends up. This type of vegetative growth is also nice for the rivers since it helps to hold together the banks of the rivers by filling them up with root masses so they do not get washed out too easily.

All these things make working with and harvesting the roots in the Rainforest much easier and more forgiving than harvesting roots in the Desert, also many of the root medicines are so abundant in the landscape as to be considered weedy in some situations. The ease of propagation via rhizome fragments is also very nice and means that it is pretty easy to help the wild patches to become more abundant or to transplant them into the garden. The Equinox is a good time of year for such propagation since the rains are just beginning and the plant's energies are starting to move down into their roots. This means that root cuttings are vibrant, and they will get plenty of water while they are putting out rootlets and getting used to being transplanted. This is also a good time of year to propagate some of the rainforest species by upright cuttings, especially *Oplopanax horridum*, i.e., Devil's Club, whom I like to propagate with friends this time of year, every year. This is also a nice time to harvest and often plant fruits and seeds from some of the trees, bushes, and herbaceous plants.

I like to pick the beautiful red fruits of Dogwood (*Cornus nuttalii*) at this time of year and get them into the ground,

THE PLANTS

The first of the Rainforest plants that I would like to discuss is a very common member of the understory of the temperate forest who is called Oregon Grape (*Mahonia nervosa*). The genus *Mahonia* consists of over 70 species of evergreen bushes and some small trees. They are very similar to members of the genus *Berberis* and some species of both genus can interbreed with one another which leads some botanists to argue that the two genera should actually be one. Members of this genus are found in Asia, the Himalayas, and North and Central America. They all have glossy green pinnate leaves, yellow or rarely red flowers that bloom very early in the growing season, produce blue or black fruits, and create the alkaloid known as berberine which we will discuss more later. The genus is named after Bernard Mc-Mahon (M'Mahon), an Irish immigrant and nursery worker who was one of the primary stewards of the plant collections from the Lewis and Clark expedition and wrote *The American Gardener's Calendar: Adapted to the Climates and Seasons of the United States* which was one of the most comprehensive gardening books published in the "USA" at that time.

Two species grow abundantly around me in this area, namely *Mahonia nervosa* or Low Oregon Grape and *Mahonia aquifolium* or Tall Oregon Grape. *Mahonia nervosa* is by far the more common of the two, at least in the forests around me, and does very well in low light conditions. They spread by rhizome, grow at most three feet off the ground, and have matte leaves. *Mahonia aquifolium* is much less common, tends to like to grow in places with more sun, can grow to be over six feet tall, has glossy leaves, and often grows in smaller stands. I work with *Mahonia nervosa* primarily since they are much more abundant, but the two species are interchangeable in their medicinal qualities and in some ways it seems nicer to harvest *Mahonia aquifolium* since the tall upright stems work very well as a source of medicine which can be harvested with a light pruning whereas it is the rhizomes of *Mahonia nervosa* that are worked with which is a bit pushier on the plants. I will from now on be referring to *Mahonia nervosa* when I am discussing harvest and propagation and when using the term Oregon Grape.

Oregon Grape grows abundantly in the forests around me. They almost look like a small Holly (*Ilex aquifolium*) tree, except for when their beautiful racemes or bright yellow flow-

ers are out, or when those flowers have ripened into the blue/black berries that look like little clusters of grapes, from which the common name is derived. Like actual Grapes (*Vitis vinifera*), the fruits of Oregon Grape are covered in a layer of wild yeast that give them a white and dusty appearance, and which can be used to inoculate sourdough starter or to wild ferment wines. These berries are edible when ripe, but very sour and bitter, although you can find a sweetish one

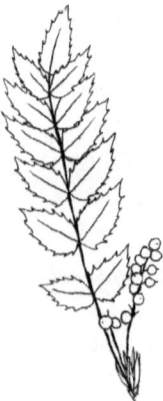

here and there when they are truly and fully ripe. The early Spring leaves can also be eaten while they are still soft and pliable, they have a really nice lemony flavor and are a great trailside snack. Once they harden up and turn dark green they lose their flavor and become much too woody and spiny to eat. My young daughter loves to eat the young leaves which can make walking on trails in early Spring take a long time. All parts of the plant contain a family of medicinal benzylisoquinoline alkaloids known as the protoberberines, the most well-studied of which is called berberine. This alkaloid has one of the cutest molecular structures that I know of, looking like a caterpillar with a methylenedioxy group for a face. This alkaloid is bright yellow in color and is common in many medicinal plants including Goldenseal (*Hydrastis canadensis*), Goldthread (*Coptis chinensis*), and Barberry (*Berberis vulgaris*). It is really easy to see the alkaloid in all of these species by peeling back the bark of the stems or roots which reveals a bright yellow color, which is the berberine type compounds. Peeling back the stem or root bark of Oregon Grape should reveal a golden color, and once you see that you know that you have found the medicine, which will also taste very bitter. These alkaloids are the main drivers of the medicinal actions of the plant, of which there are many.

The bitter taste of the plant functions as a digestive stimulant, as all bitter flavors do. Taking a bit of Oregon Grape tincture or tea will immediately cause your mouth to salivate, and often you can feel your stomach start to gurgle and release digestive juices. This action makes the plant a nice one to incorporate into bitter blends to be taken before or during meals in order to aid in digestion, although I would not utilize Oregon Grape in a bitters formula that is going to be taken regularly for a very long time due to some of the other actions of this plant. Oregon Grape also works as a liver stimulant, which also helps with the metabolism of proteins and is nice when a person is flooded with any unwanted chemicals either self generated (such as stress hormones) or not (such as industrial pollutants) to help and flush them out. This plant, and especially berberine, is well known as an antimicrobial and can be really helpful both internally and externally to help and kill off any undesired microbial life, whether that be bacteria, fungi/yeasts, or even amoebas. *Mahonia* can be really helpful for lingering gastrointestinal infections due to tainted water or food and has even been worked with successfully to clear up *Giardia* infections, at least so says Ryan Drum. The isolated alkaloid berberine is worked with as a supplement to lower both blood sugar levels and blood pressure, and while this has not been studied to the point that there is universal agreement as to the safety and efficacy of this, there is some good research out of China and a lot of anecdotal evidence that it works. There is concern about the alkaloid interacting with other medications, and the dosages at which people are taking the alkaloid (a gram a day or sometimes more) is much more than you would get by ingesting even a huge amount of Oregon Grape, but I do think that it can be a nice plant to work with for people living with these conditions and the liver stimulant qualities will help the body to process sugars.

Oregon Grape is very easy both to harvest and to propagate, although propagation is a little harder than how I was initially taught to do it. When you find an abundant patch of Oregon Grape it can often encompass hundreds of square feet on the forest floor, and this whole patch may be one clonal colony as in each "inidividual" plant is connected to all of the others via rhizomes. The rhizomes are usually buried very shallowly, like a few inches down, and they often grow in duffy soil. The nicest way to pick from a stand like this is to feel around in the soil between two plants until you find the rhizome that connects them, then cut out the middle part of this rhizome between two nodes without ever disturbing the two upright plants on either side. This technique leaves enough root and rhizome behind that the plants will be just fine. You can also grab an upright plant and pull on it until the long rhizome comes up out of the ground, sometimes for six to ten feet or more, and just pull until it breaks (which will usually be at a node). You can take most of that rhizome for medicine and replant the upright part of the plant with about a foot of the horizontal rhizome left on it and the plant will survive. This technique seems to work very well. I was originally taught that you could harvest all of the rhizome and just replant the upright stem which would root and continue growing, but when I flagged a bunch of plants that I replanted in this way they all died over the course of a year. When I have left behind a large portion of the rhizome and some true roots, at least 2/3rds of them survive. In some schools of Chinese medicine the color yellow is associated with the liver and the emotion of anger, and I like to work with Oregon Grape for people who have the liver-deficient grumpies. The plant themselves has a kind of grumpy or angry or strong boundaries kind of feel to them, with the sharp pointy leaves and the bitter taste. They told me once that they need to live in the cool soils of the Rainforests in order to cool and soothe some of that strong and hot energy of theirs.

The next plant I would like to discuss is one that I actually rarely find in great abundance in the forest and therefore have taken to growing them in garden settings and harvesting root from there. This plant is called False Solomon's Seal, Solomon's Plume, or Dragon Root depending on who you are talking to. The Latin binomial is *Maianthemum racemosum*, which used to be *Smilacina racemosum*. This plant is only found on Turtle Island, where they grow all across the continent from "Canada" down into "Mexico." They thrive in deep, moist, dark woodland settings and can be abundant in some areas, although around me I rarely find them in very thick patches, often just running into a single plant every once and awhile. *Maianthemum* is very similar in appearance to Solomon's Seal (*Polygonatum biflorum*), hence the somewhat rude name of "False Solomon's Seal," however *Maianthemum* blooms and fruits in a cluster at the end of the upright growth, while *Polygonatum* has a series of flowers and fruits that dangle down from nodes on the bottom of the upright growth. The flowers of *Maianthemum* smell and look quite a bit like the flowers of Elder trees (*Sambucus spp.*), except they grow in a panicle. The rhizomes of this plant are white, cylindrical and fleshy, growing in a jointed fashion that looks much like vertebrae in a spinal column. This appearance points towards some of the medicinal qualities of this herb, which are similar to those of the "True" Solomon's Seal (*Polygonatum biflorum*). Both of these root medicines are primarily moistening agents, much like Marshmallow (*Althea officinalis*) or Slippery Elm (*Ulmus rubra*). Like those herbs, the roots of *Maianthemum* are nice to work with for people who have dry, hot, inflamed pulmonary or gastrointestinal systems. The polysaccharide rich extracts of this plant will moisten, soothe, and promote healing of these tissues. This plant, along with *Polygonatum*, however, also has an affinity for the musculoskeletal system, in which they work to moisten and lubricate joints as well as ligaments and connective tissues. This action can be really helpful for people with achy joints as well as dried out and atrophied connective tissues which are tight, sore, and hard to loosen up. Recently there has been a lot of research and attention paid to the fascia, which is a layer of connective tissue made up primarily of collagen that attaches, encloses, and stabilizes the organs and muscles of the body. Fascia, a crucial part of the anatomy that has been largely overlooked, is now thought to play a role in a lot of chronic pain type conditions, and can be thought of as an extension of the nervous system which collects and stores information in the body. Chronic tensions in the body can cause the fascia to become stiff and to hold these tensions in place. Practices that cause the fascia to release and loosen up can be really helpful in chronic pain as well as chronic mental health challenges such as anxiety and depression. *Maiainthemum* and *Polygonatum* have both been looked at as medicines to bring moisture and suppleness to this crucial and often overlooked part of the body, and I have seen nice changes in chronic tensions in the bodies of people who have worked with these plants over a longish time, especially if they are paired with nervines, nervous system trophorestoratives, and antispasmodics. Both of these plants are considered to be yin tonics in Chinese medicine systems and are worked with as tonics for the urinary tract, the digestion, the lungs, and the cardiovascular system.

As I said at the beginning of this section, since I do not find *Maianthemum* in huge patches in the woods around me, I have taken to transplanting them to a garden setting. You can often find them already growing in people's ornamental gardens since they are a nice shade tolerant ornamental, and while the roots of the wild plants grow very slowly and rarely get to a very large size, roots that are grown in loose, rich garden soil that are tended to will grow relatively rapidly and can get really large. This is also true of the "True" Solomon's Seal, which is moving towards being overharvested in the wild in many locations but can easily become somewhat weedy and abundant in a garden setting. I would recommend to anyone who is looking to work with these plants to purchase propagation material in the form of root fragments from an herb farm or ornamental plant nursery and grow them out in the garden rather than harvesting the roots from the wild.

The final root that I like to harvest in the Rainforest this time of year that I will mention in this section is that of the

Stinging Nettle, *Urtica dioica*. I have already discussed this plant in detail in the Spring Equinox chapter about the Black Hills, but I would like to briefly discuss working with the root of this plant in the Fall. At this time of year the Nettles have gone to seed and are starting to die back, turning from green to yellow to brown and tumbling over. The sting of the leaves is still present but is much attenuated and less painful. It is very easy to find the roots of the plants, which are rhizomes, by digging around with your fingers in the soil between two upright stalks. The rhizome is often only an inch or two beneath the soil line, and is about a pencil-width thick, segmented, and tan in color. A Nettle patch is often thick with these rhizomes. Sometimes they are interlaced or laying on top of one another, so once you get in there it is easy to harvest quite a bit of material in a short time. These rhizomes transplant very well at this time of year, and I strongly encourage you to establish a new patch either elsewhere in the forest or in your garden at home. Nettle root is one of the best herbs for people who are living with prostate issues to work with. Several studies, both *in vitro* and *in vivo*, have shown that extracts of Nettle root shrink the prostate and reduce inflammation. It is hypothesized by some that the main way that the plant works in the body is by inhibiting the aromatase enzyme which converts testosterone into estrogen. There is a clear connection to prostate enlargement and both androgens and estrogen, so this theory makes sense to me. In practice, they help to reduce swelling of the prostate and help with the discomfort and the feeling of needing to pee all the time. The root is also rich in nutrients and minerals much like the herbaceous part of the plant. The mineral content especially provides some nervous system support to the person in question which can help with some of the emotional distress of living with prostrate problems. The root is also somewhat diuretic which gets things moving in the urinary tract in general and lessens the stagnancy that can occur there during prostate enlargement.

MEDICINAL MUSHROOMS

Along with the roots, at this time of year there are an abundance of mushrooms of all sorts fruiting in the forests of this region. The organisms that we place into the Fungal Queendom are some of the most interesting and mysterious of the many organisms that we work with in herbalism. In many ways, they straddle the line between plants and animals, and are more like animals than plants in that they are heterotrophic (need to eat other organisms rather than being able to create their own food from sunlight and CO_2 such as plants), and they take up oxygen and produce carbon dioxide much like humans and other animals do. A good example of how closely fungi are related to humans can be seen in the great difficulty that humans have in killing off infections that are fungal in nature within their own bodies. It is estimated that humans share some 80–85% of their ribosomal DNA with fungi, so anything that would effectively kill off a fungal infection would cause major problems for the human host. Much like our DNA is deeply intertwined with the fungi, the history of humans include working with fungi as food, medicine, and as a means of starting or carrying around fire for just about as far back as we can see.

HISTORY

Two ancient humans provide archaeological evidence of the relationship between humans and fungi. First, the "Red Lady of el Mirón," a person who lived some 18,700 years ago and seems to have been held in high regard within her community due to the way she was buried. She was a part of the Magdalenian culture, which also produced many of the iconic cave drawings that are offered as examples of very early human art. The Red Lady got her name because her bones and the surrounding area were decorated with red ocher, a material that is treasured in many cultures. There were also engravings on a stone that appeared to serve as a marker for her burial. Scientists managed to remove some of the hardened plaque from her teeth and discovered spores embedded there from at least two types of fungi, namely those of a gilled mushroom of the order *Agaricales* and a member of the *Boletaecea* family, which includes many choice edible mushrooms. Second, and much later in history, around 3,100–3,400 BCE, another mycophile ended up buried in the ice up in the Italian Alps. This guy is known today as Ötzi as he was discovered in the Ötztal Alps and he is Europe's oldest known natural human mummy. The story of Ötzi is very long and interesting, but for our purposes the most important relics that were found with him were two species of polypore mushrooms with leather strings run through them, one was *Piptoporus betulinus*, the birch bolete, which is known to be antimicrobial and antihelmetic and is thought to have been used medicinally by Ötzi who had parasitic worms living in his guts at the time of his death. The other species was *Fomes fomentarius*, the tinder conk, which works very well as a fire starter.

Many of the medicinal mushrooms, but not all, that I talk about in this chapter, are polypores like the ones found with Ötzi. They are also known as shelf mushrooms or conks and grow circumglobally, especially in old growth forests where they are a key feature of these places in that they break down the lignin in dead trees thus serving as the first step in food chains that feed on decomposed plant material. Some of them are pretty common when considered as a genus, such as *Ganoderma*, a genus that has species growing from tropical locations where they fruit out of cacao and coffee trees (*Ganoderma philippii*) all the way to the colder arboreal forests where species such as *Ganoderma applanatum* and *Ganoderma tsugae* fruit out of the coniferous trees. These shelf mushrooms may grow annually or perennially and can get to be huge. They are striking out in the forest and lend themselves to being processed into teas since they are so interesting looking but often too hard or woody to eat. In one of the earliest of the known Chinese materia medicas, known as the *Shennong Ben Cao Jing* or *The Classic of Herbal Medicine*, written about 200 or 250 CE, six species of fungi are listed, with there being six listings on different types of *Ganoderma* alone. The *Ganodermas* are placed within the system of this author to be superior medicines, meaning they can be used for a long period of time with no detrimental effects, and that along with helping to correct disharmony in the body they also went so far as to encourage the evolution of the person to a greater state of health than they had been in before. They cultivate virtues. For example, the author says of *Qing Zhi* (*Ganoderma viridis*):

> Is sour and balanced. It mainly brightens the eyes, supplements the liver qi, quiets the essence and the ethereal soul, and cultivates humanity and compassion. Protracted taking may make the body light, prevent senility, and prolong life so as to make one an immortal. Its other name is *Long Zhi* (Dragon Ganoderma). It grows in mountains and valleys.

Which is really a nice recommendation for working with these mushrooms. All the descriptions for the various *Ganodermas* end with the statement about making the body light, preventing senility, and possible immortality. This work is believed to be a compilation of oral traditions, which are said to be passed on all the way from Shennong, the "Divine Farmer," who is a deity that is venerated as an ancient sage ruler of China, the first Emperor. Shennong is said to have taught the practices of both agriculture and herbalism to the ancient Chinese. He invented such crucial tools as the hoe and plow while also significantly improving such methods of working on people's health as moxibustion and pulse taking. Clearly he really loved the genus *Ganoderma*. At the time in which these lessons were passed down orally and written down, methods of cultivating Reishi (*Ganoderma*) had not yet been worked out, although people were already cultivating some edible mushroom species such as Shiitake (*Lentinula eloides*). Since the only available Reishi at this time had to be wildcrafted, and the mushrooms only fruit at certain seasons and are not terribly abundant, this medicine was restricted to the upper echelons of Chinese society. Often it is said that the Reishi was all reserved for the emperor, although of course as always the wildcrafters and herbalists who lived out in the woods and on the mountains where the Reishi grew had ready access to them and could choose whether to give them over to the Emperor or whether to hold on to them for their own health. Reishi was and is widely regarded in Taoism to lengthen life and also to promote spiritual development, so you know that the Taoist herbalists where keeping the finest of the antler form Reishis for their own spiritual work.

Since then, the Chinese first and now many cultures have developed very efficient methods for cultivating *Ganoderma lucidum*, the classic Reishi, in bulk, so these days it is much less of a precious commodity and is utilized by people all over the world. I have recently seen both coffee and skin lotions that have Reishi on the ingredient list so clearly they are pretty easy to get a hold of. Reishi holds a prominent place of esteem in classical Chinese medicine and has been likewise incorporated into Traditional Chinese Medicine (TCM) which is a form of Chinese medicine that is based upon ancient techniques and principals but was codified by the state during the reign of Mao Zedong in the 1950s. During this process the methods of this medicinal system were subjected to great scrutiny and analyses through more "modern" and "scientific" methods, and so Reishi has been thoroughly studied in scientific journals as to how and why it works upon the human body. Reishi has been largely accepted to be beneficial for cancer, high blood pressure, allergies, high cholesterol, insomnia, autoimmune diseases, inflammation, suppressed immunity, and infections of all kinds. Extracts of the mushroom have been found to be cytotoxic, hepatoprotective, beneficial to the parasympathetic nervous system, anti oxidative, and to be beneficial to the heart and cardiovascular system in a number of ways. Much of the modern research on the medicinal effects of the mushroom have been focused on working with them to reduce the progression of various cancers, or to help mitigate some of the side effects that are often brought on by chemotherapy and radiation that people undergo in their quest to heal their cancer.

CONSTITUENTS/CHEMISTRY

It was largely through scientific research into the medicine of Reishi that we came to understand the physiological effects of the various constituents that are found in Reishi and also in many other of our beloved medicinal mushrooms. The main constituents that have been studied and shown to play a key role in the medicinal effects of these mushrooms are a group of complex polysaccharides, or sugars, that exist within the cell walls of the mushrooms often referred to as the $(1,3)$ Beta-D-Glucans. These are a class of beautiful and intricate molecules, much larger than the simple sugars that we often run into and different in their structural nature than even the heavier and more complex sugars found in plants such as cellulose, a polysaccharide that provides much of the structural strength in plants. Cellulose is a long chain polysaccharide that is bonded together in a straight chain, while the mushroom polysaccharides are bonded at their first and third carbon atoms in their D-glucose rings, which results in the chains being in the form of a triple helix that are reminiscent of the shape of DNA. These polysaccharide chains are also similar in their appearance and shape to the bacterial capsular polysaccharides that are side chains that exist in the cell walls of bacteria that can form biofilms that the bacteria live in to hide themselves while they are existing within other organisms. The human immune system, especially T cells via the major histocompatability complex (MHC) proteins, can recognize these polysaccharides as an aspect of bacteria and thereby become primed. I used to think that this communication was more like an antagonistic one, in that the immune system would read these sugars and therefore muster up the army of immune cells to begin the attack, thereby encouraging the body to wipe out any damaging organisms that might be living in it. When I began doing some research for this chapter, however, I found that more recent research on these bacterial polysaccharides shows that they may be a large part of the ways that our gut flora can help the body to be healthy by keeping the immune system primed in a certain way, thereby preventing it from attacking the normal cells in the body (autoimmune diseases). This may explain why we consider the mushrooms to be *immunomudolatory*, meaning that they can be beneficial in situations where a person is needing a boost of the immune system, such as in cases of infections or cancers, but can also be helpful in cases where the immune system is overactive such as autoimmune conditions. Technically, both immune stimulating substances and immunosuppressive substances are considered immunomudulating since the definition of that word means simply "a substance that affects the functioning of the immune system" (Merriam Webster), so it might be more specific to say of the mushrooms that they are *amphoteric* in their action on the immune system. This may explain how so many people turn to Reishi for seasonal allergies, as one line of thought about the current increase in the number of people who have allergies is that the immune systems of so many humans were not exposed to as many bacteria and other microorganisms as they used to be due to the emphasis on sterility within western cultures especially which results in an increase in certain immune and atopic disorders. By bringing in the polysaccharides that mimic those of commensal bacteria, we can encourage the growth and intelligence of the immune system so that it does not get all worked up for no reason as often.

Along with the polysaccharides, the majority of the medicinal shelf mushrooms contain a class of molecules known broadly as terpenoids that are thought to play a major role on the benefits of ingesting the mushrooms. Terpenoids are a class of compounds, often broadly just called terpenes, that are hydrocarbons made up of five carbon units called iso-prenes in a variety of combination. Terpenes that are made up of one to three isoprene units are very light molecules and therefore are very volatile. We interact with these types of molecules most often as essential oils, and many of the shelf mushrooms do produce small yields of essential oils. The heavier terpenes such as diterpenes (four isoprene units) and triterpenes (six isoprene units) are not aromatic but do serve as antiinflammatories and antimicrobials. All the ter-penes are hydrocarbons and are not soluble in water, therefore they need to be extracted into ethanol. Some really interesting diterpenoids are the erinacines found in *Hericium erinaceum*, a medicinal mushroom that we will discuss more shortly. These diterpenoids are known to enhance the production of nerve growth factor *in vitro* and are kappa opiod receptor agonists.

THE GENUS GANODERMA (REISHI)

Around me in the forests along the Salish Sea (mostly Skokomish territory is where I go hunting for medicinal mushrooms), there are several wonderful medicinal species. We have two (or more) species of the genus *Ganoderma* that I love very much and have worked with as medicines and friends for many years now. Ganoderma *applanatum*, also known as Artist's Conk or White Reishi, is by far the most common of the *Ganodermas* that grow in my area. They are a very abundant species in general, growing circumboreally in all of the northern forests of the world, basically wherever there are old coniferous forests. These mushrooms are also nice to work with as medicines because, unlike many of the other *Ganodermas* that we work with for medicine, Artist's Conk has perennial fruiting bodies that will keep growing year after year and can therefore get to be huge. I have seen fruiting bodies of this species so big that my arms cannot stretch from one side to the other, so more than three feet wide. A mushroom of this size would produce enough medicine for many people for years, and often when you find a log with fruiting bodies that are this well established, the whole log will be loaded down with them. Around me, these mushrooms love to grow on old downed Big Leaf Maple (*Acer macrophyllum*) in the deeper forests, especially over rivers or creeks. Artist's Conk has a similar constituent make up to the better-studied Reishi, and has been studied on its own as a medicine both in more modern times in the laboratory and for hundreds of years in a variety of herbalism traditions. Artist's Conk are brown on the tops of the fruiting bodies, unlike most of the other *Ganoderma* species which are a deep red color. This species is also unusual in that the underside of the fruiting body, from which the spores are released, is bright white and will bruise brown very easily upon contact leaving a permanent mark, so people love to draw on them which is the source of the common name.

I have worked with this mushroom more than any of the other species that I discuss in this section, and they remain my favorite of the medicinal mushrooms. There is something about the long lasting and very strong, woody nature of the fruiting bodies that seems to offer assistance at a deep and basic level, like bringing in Saturn or your ancestors. I like to give Artist's Conk as a general tonic, especially to people who are all wound up, not sleeping enough, and maybe have some physical pain or joint difficulties. I find that the medicine helps to calm and ground people, and also brings wisdom and clarity. Artist's Conk is more of a worker, and more about the structural essence of the body. I don't pretend to really understand the intricacies of Chinese medicine and I am certainly not born into that lineage but Artist's Conk seems to be more about the *jing,* or the kidney essence which we come into this world with and is a link to the ancestors. There is something about how common and abundant this mushroom is that also makes me really like it as a medicine and as a greater-than-human person. Like I said, if you can find a good log, you can produce so much medicine from not that much of the total biomass of the organism that lives inside the maple. The fruits are just the sex organs, after all. The majority of the mushroom is in the mycelial body, which in the case of the shelf mushrooms lives inside of the tree or downed log. These organisms can be extremely long lasting, decades at least, and I would imagine more in some cases. They are friends that you return to year after year and they become wiser over time. They have a lot of time to observe the forest and figure out what is going on while they slowly digest the log in which they are living. This year when I went to one of the forested areas that I first began learning the plants in, the entire place had been recently clear cut. It was entirely heartbreaking for me of course, and mostly the trip was one of great grief, but I did notice that one of the logs that I used to harvest Artist's Conk from many years ago but had given up on since it had stopped producing, was having an enormous flush of fruits upon being exposed to more sunlight and presumably from the knowledge that their time there was becoming short and it was time to get the medicines out. They knew that there had been big devastation and trauma and were coming out to see how they could help. They know life, and they know death, and they like to share the things that they have learned.

Although the fruits of this specific species are perennial and can live for a very long time, they don't always live that long, especially when they are starting to use up the nutrients available to them in the log that they are living inside of and also eating. Keep an eye on them and if the fruiting bodies on a log start to rot and fall off, that log is a good candidate to harvest medicine from, since the larger organism is probably starting to die. Of course, maybe it makes more sense to not harvest off of that individual, so that all of the spores that they produce can go towards making babies, but then again you may be moving the spores to whole new locations when you pick the fruiting bodies and carry them away with you.

Often growing in the same areas where I find the Artist's Conk are the Lacquered Conks, also called the Oregon Reishis, or simply Reishi, or *Ganoderma tsugae* or even *Ganoderma oregonense* if they are not growing on Hemlock trees (*Tsuga heterophylla*). These mushrooms look much more like the classic Reishi (*Ganoderma lucidum*) in that they are a beautiful deep red, and they are annual mushrooms which are softer than *G applanatum.* They are less common than *G applanantum* but are still pretty widespread throughout the region, anywhere where there are still tracts of deep forest. Of course, all of the shelf mushrooms are declining overall because the amount of undisturbed forests in the world continue to decrease every year but hopefully we will live to see the reversal of that trend within our lifetimes. In the meantime please try to plant trees and ideally harvest your medicines from areas that are going to be clear cut anyways, of course if you can figure out a way to stop the clear cut I applaud you. I mostly find these mushrooms in the deeper and wetter parts of the forest, often slightly higher in elevation. They love to grow in the downed bodies of ancient conifers along mountain streams where it is misty and quiet. They are so beautiful to see out in the forest, the deep red of their fruiting bodies is like no other color and both stands out and perfectly blends in to the other colors of the forest. More often than not, I run into this species on snags, or still standing but dead and partially decomposed trees. This makes it easy to be judicious in your harvest of the fruiting bodies since there will often be quite a lot of them all up and down the side of the tree, so you just pick the couple that you can reach from the ground and all the ones that are way up high can just spread their spores far and wide.

Again, *Ganoderma oregonense/tsugae* seem to have similar physiological effects as the other members of the genus. I take this mushroom quite a lot, and like to work with them as the basis to a lot of the formulas that I give to myself and also to clients. The extract tastes really nice and can mellow the taste of some stronger herbs. It still has the bitter of course, that is part of the medicine, but especially when prepared from the fresh fruiting body this species makes a very nutritious and earthy tasting extract. It is a nice adaptogenic type herb that is not stimulating, which can be helpful for a lot of people living in these times where everything is already moving so fast that giving stimulating adaptogens can spin folks out and encourage them to use the herbs in ways that cause further damage to their health. This species is also very wise, but I think that it is more heart centered than *G. applanatum*. The fruiting bodies are a deep red color, and they grow fast, are softer, and decompose readily. They are much yangier than *G applanatum* fruiting bodies, and I feel like this mushroom interacts more on the *shen* to stick with the Three Treasures metaphor for the differing actions of the various *Ganoderma*. While the *jing* is considered the most dense physical matter in the body and is therefore very yin, the *shen* is very volatile and therefore yang. The *shen* can be thought of as the spirit or the mind, and is said to live in the heart. When the *shen* gets disturbed it can lead to insomnia, and a classic sign of healthy and happy *shen* is bright and shining eyes. These mushrooms can help in cases of insomnia, not in a knock-out kind of way but increasing the strength and length of sleep over time, and of course the brightening of the eyes is a classic symptom of long term Reishi use.

I first noticed the strong connection of this mushroom and the heart when I was out in the forest doing a pretty big pick of them for a client. I had made a sling out of my jacket and filled it with a number of huge fruiting bodies and was hiking them back out the several miles to the car when I began to notice that I was in a very good, light, and lovey mood. I could feel the expansive nature of the mushrooms expanding my own heart, settling the anxieties so that it could open up. It felt warm and good, loosening. When I got to the truck and unwrapped the fruiting bodies I was amazed because they were HOT. They give off quite a lot of body heat so it is important to cool them down quick if you are planning to store them fresh for any amount of time because they will begin to compost/rot pretty quickly since they are relatively fragile and warm one another up in a collecting bag. This makes them feel more like animals when you interact with their body heat, and is also a good indicator of their yangier nature.

There is a well established connection between working with *G lucidum* and general improved cardiovascular health including lowered blood pressure, and it sure seems to be true of this species as well. I am more speaking of how working with this mushroom leads to the opposite feeling of heartbreak, or how helpful it can be to help you to work with your broken heart. Overall they help the organism to feel safe yet also aware of what is self and what is other, lowering the blood pressure while simultaneously getting the immune system working harmoniously. I think a lot about the name *Lingzhi*, which translates literally to "spirit mushroom," and how the various forms of Reishi do lead to this calm and centered place from which it is easier to see the spirits, or the life in everything. Not in a pushy way like members of the genus *Psilocybe,* but slowly and gently, and the change in vision is much more long lasting and less potentially confusing than the changes brought on by *Psilocybe.* I'm not sure that I want to be immortal, in reference to the name "The Mushroom of Immortality" that is also granted to this genus, but I think this means something more like gaining access to the spirit realm.

THE GENUS HERICIUM (LION'S MANE)

Another genus of medicinal mushroom that I have run into in the woods around where I live, although I think they are much more common further South, is *Hericium,* often called Lion's Mane mushrooms. This genus of mushroom is also circumboreal, growing in the northern forest of the globe. They are worked with as a food and a medicine in many of the cultures that do and have traditionally lived within the ares where they grow. Members of this genus have a very distinctive physical appearance, often compared to coral, brains, or the fur/hair/mane of various animals. They are bright white and fuzzy looking, basically. They are very delicious and safe to eat, and this is how I was first introduced to this genus, as a choice edible. They have a nutty and neutral flavor, also single fruiting bodies found in the wild can weigh several pounds and therefore feed a whole camp's worth of people at once. Along with being a great food source, Lion's Manes have been worked with in many cultures as medicines for centuries, of course. Most of the information that I have been able to find on traditional usage comes from the well-documented

Chinese herbal tradition, in which the genus is worked with mostly for digestive reasons, to strengthen the stomach and improve digestion, while also calming the spirit and strengthening brain activity. The effects on the digestive system can go so far as to be corrective to long term digestive illnesses with severe symptoms, indeed they have been worked with in the treatment of *H. pylori* infections with some success, mostly due to immunomodulatory effects. Like most of the medicinal mushrooms, there seems to be anti-tumor compounds in this genus, but modern science and herbalists have been really excited about the benefits that certain compounds found within members of this genus can have upon the physical structures of the nervous system itself. The two classes of compounds that I have found the most research on are the hericenones and the erinacines. These families of molecules have been shown *in vitro* to stimulate the biosynthesis of nerve growth factor, a protein that is utilized within the human organism to promote the growth of new neural tissues and to help to repair existing structures. In the clinic, ingestion of these molecules has been shown to decrease the severity of cognitive impairment in people with dementia. Extracts of these mushrooms have also been shown in the lab to promote the repair of injured nerve tissue in rats. I have experienced some enhancement of my own memory and cognitive abilities upon working with this mushroom, and have seen this genus be helpful for people with nerve pain from old injuries and for folks living with degenerative nerve disorders such as Multiple Sclerosis in that they felt like their mobility was better and pain was lessened. Lion's Mane mushrooms are also being explored for people who are living with long term depression since it seems that encouraging neuroplasticity and the creation of new neural networks can be beneficial to the depressed person to help them to move out of the ingrained thought patterns inherent to that state.

While I do not have a lot of experience interacting with this genus out in the forests, a dear friend of mine lives in the Redwood forests along the coasts down south and he lives in an area where both *Hericium erinaceus* and *H coralloides* grow in great abundance, mostly fruiting off of dying or downed Tan Oaks *(Lithocarpus densiflora)*. He tells me that simply interacting with the mushrooms out in habitat brings a great feeling of ease, and that he is deeply enmeshed with the genus after working with them for some time, he sounds like me when I talk about *Ganoderma*. Paul Stamets, founder of the well known and respected mushroom company Fungi Perfecti, has given several talks lately, the most famous was on the Joe Rogan podcast, in which he describes combining the genus *Psilocybe* with the genus *Hericium* as a potent combination for neurogenesis. This combination has a pleasing intuitive feel to it and those who I know that have worked with it have reported very interesting preliminary results in terms of enhanced cognition and help with mental health overall.

THE GENUS PSILOCYBE (MAGIC MUSHROOMS)

Speaking of Paul Stamets brings me to the final genus of mushrooms that I would like to discuss in this chapter, since Paul literally wrote the book on identifying members of this genus (entitled *Psilocybin Mushrooms of the World*) and named a few species himself. I am speaking of the genus *Psilocybe*, which I have alluded to several times already. Probably the best known species of this genus to most people across the world is *Psilocybe cubensis*, which are the most widely cultivated, sold, and traded "magic mushrooms" of the black market across most of the world where the genus is illegal. It is worth pointing out here that if you are interested in exploring this genus of mushroom, the entire genus is considered Schedule 1 under the US Psychotropic Substances Act here in the United States, and there are similar laws in many other parts of the world. We are starting to see the laws shift towards decriminalization in some states in the US, and in several countries *Psilocybe* mushrooms are either totally legal or at least sold openly, and the laws against them are largely ignored by the police. If you live in the "United States" or the majority of the countries in the world, be aware that working with these simply beautiful organisms, especially if you should choose to cultivate them, could easily result in booted thugs from the government kicking in your door, shooting your dog, locking you in a cell, and claiming your home and all of your assets for the state. All these things and more have occurred to people who have ended up on the wrong side of the war on drugs.

Beyond legal repercussions, there remains a culture of stigma around people who choose to use drugs no matter what their origin, or how useful they may have proven to be in the realm of mental health and spirituality. I am always a little bit hesitant to talk about this genus of mushroom since I imagine that somebody is rolling their eyes right now, but please forgive me. This genus of mushroom in many ways was the first one that helped me to see the fungal queendom as a special thing, not to mention really inspired my lifelong devotion to ethnobotany and herbal medicines.

Anyway, the genus *Psilocybe*, although believed by most Westerners less than a hundred years ago to only grow in remote parts of Mexico, is now known to have more than a hundred species that are active psychedelics, and they grow all over the world. Famous for growing on fecal matter, the majority of the species actually grow in grassy areas that are often supplemented with decomposing wood. The most common species worldwide seems to be *Psilocybe semilanceata*, or the Liberty Cap, which grows in cow fields throughout the northern part of the globe. *Psilocybe cubensis* is now cultivated all over the world since it is very simple to grow indoors under controlled conditions. *P cubensis* also has a very wide natural range, spanning several continents in the subtropical and tropical zones where they are found growing on dung.

The medicinal uses of these mushrooms have been most thoroughly studied by the *Curanderas* of Meso-America. The best known, at least in the Western academic world, is María Sabina Magdalena García (1894–1985). María Sabina lived in the outskirts of Huautla de Jiménez in the Sierra Mazateca and worked with the mushrooms in her healing practice, which she inherited from her grandfather and great grandfather, who had also been healers in this lineage. María was also a skilled ceremonialist and poet. María first took the mushrooms when she was a little girl and became a well respected healer over the course of her life. She would take the mushrooms at the same time as her patients in all night rituals called *veladas*, which were syncretic rituals that were heavily flavored by Catholicism. María was a devout Catholic all of her life. The mushrooms would help her to see what the problem was with the person, and hopefully would allow the person to vomit out the sickness. If they could not get it, then María would vomit for them. In 1955 R. Gordon Wasson, then Vice President of JP Morgan, came to Huautla de Jiménez to learn about the sacred mushrooms, being a devoted mycologist with financial ties to the CIA who were interested in the mushrooms as mind control agents. He talked the mayor into introducing him to Sabina so that he could participate in a *velada*. She was hesitant, and he basically scammed her by claiming to be concerned about his son's whereabouts, when in fact, what he actually wanted was to have the experience as part of his personal spiritual journey, which was not how María worked with the mushrooms. Wasson got his experience and went on to write a sensationalized article for *LIFE Magazine* which made the mushrooms an international sensation and basically introduced them to the West. Huautla de Jiménez was soon flooded with gringos picking the mushrooms and seeking out María or anyone else to provide them with the experience, which was all good for those people but the unwanted attention to the mushrooms caused the government to treat María as a drug dealer, and she was ostracized by her community. She regretted ever allowing Wasson to come to her ritual and said that after the outsiders came the mushrooms were spoiled and could not perform healings as well anymore.

So from this tragic cooptation of a culture's medicine comes all of the remarkable healings that have been "discovered" in the Western world since the identification of the mushrooms and especially of the main alkaloids that cause the psychedelic effects: psilocin and psilocybin. Synthetic psilocybin has been the main psychedelic utilized in a lot of the studies done by psychiatrists and psychologists in the "United States" both in the early 1960s before the compounds were made illegal, and since about the late 1990s when researchers started to do some work with these molecules legally again. Johns Hopkins University School of Medicine, for example, has had promising results using psilocybin to help people with addictions and with end-of-life depression and anxiety for cancer patients. These studies often utilize high doses of the compound, closer to the "heroic" five dried grams of *P cubensis* dosage that Terrence McKenna recommended in his books to access the mushroom realm. There is a lot of anecdotal evidence for people working with the mushrooms every once and a while at a higher dose to improve mental health in a number of ways.

Microdosing of *Psilocybes*, which means taking a sub-perceptual dose of the mushroom on a specific schedule such as every four days for a month, has also been found by many people to be helpful for a variety of complaints such as depression, cluster headaches, and addictions. People also like to microdose as a kind of nootropic to help them to be more creative in their problem solving, in life or work or their art. There have been some remarkable improvements to people's mental health when working with the microdose regimen without the weirdness that can sometimes go along with the occasional high dose regimen, although I have heard that people with a tendency towards mania can go in that sort of direction from microdosing. It can bring a sensitivity that can be pretty unpleasant depending on the person's life circumstances. Of all the medicinal mushrooms, these ones should be worked with cautiously, if at all. I would try *Ganoderma* first, but in the right circumstances and especially with a supportive community the *Psilocybes* can bring about strong and good changes for people.

All these medicinal mushrooms grow wild across the globe, where they help to pass communications and nutrients from other members of the forest communities or the habitats in which they live. In many ways the mycelial networks function as the neural pathways of the forest, or some like to make the comparison between the mycelial networks and the internet. When we learn to work with the fungi and allow them to shape and change us we also gain access to all of the learnings, wisdoms, and feelings of the forest as a whole.

9

THE DEAD ARE NEAR AS
WE MOVE INTO WINTER (SAMHAIN)

THE GOLDEN LIGHT of sunny Fall days lasts often pretty deep into October. It is one of the secrets that people who live in this area like to keep to themselves; that the early Fall has some of the most beautiful days out of the entire year. Many people say that the Summer in the Pacific Northwest is so beautiful but that they cannot handle the rest of the seasons. Those of us who really know this place smile and nod our heads, looking forward to late September and most of October when outdoor spaces are far less crowded by tourists, all the mushrooms are flushing all around, the air is crisp and clean, and the majority of the days are still pleasantly warm and sunny with patches of delicious rain, along with our beloved protective blanket of clouds overhead. It is often in late October that the season really starts to shift, and many years I have noticed that it is either right on Samhain or right around then that we get the first cold and soaking rain, and just after that the first frosts usually come. The plants in the gardens and in the forests have been moving towards senescence for a while by the time these big weather moments arrive, and this usually pushes them over the edge, with the majority of the herbaceous plants finally browning and dying back all the way after the first frost, and the deciduous trees finally losing all of the leaves that have been tenaciously clinging to their branches although yellow and brown for weeks due to the strong wind and rain. The return of the big rains changes the feel of the landscape, in both good ways and overwhelming ways, depending who you are and what you like to do with your time. In many ways this period is a period of new life, at least for the many organisms that depend on having ample water to live their lives in full abundance; the mosses, lichens, tardigrades, and mushrooms are singing and dancing, while the rest of us put on thicker jackets and hunker down around the wood stove. The Rivers regain their strength and vigor at this time. Right behind my house the Black River, who is my primary teacher and accomplice, undergoes a great transformation, going from a languid, thin and warm trickle during the droughty time of year to a fat, swollen, rushing river during the Winter. This is the time that the Salmon (*Onchorhyncus spp.*) have been waiting for, of course. They begin to travel up the Rivers in order to dig into the gravelly beds to create their nests (known as redds), battle one another for prime spots, mate, spawn, and die. The sides of the Rivers become covered in rotting Salmon corpses which is a boon for many animals, but the smell is pretty intense. If you are the type of human who lives with Dogs as companions, then you need to look out for them because they love to both roll in the rotting Salmon, which makes them truly disgusting to share a home with, or even worse, they will eat the rotting fish which at this specific latitude contain a fluke known as *Nanophyetus salmincola* which can then transfer from the rotting fish to the intestines of the Dog, where they attach to the intestinal walls and begin feeding on the Dog's blood. This in itself is not pleasant for the Dog, and can lead to intestinal distress, but if the fluke happens to also be infected with a rickettsial organism known as *Neorickettsia helminthoeca* this bacteria can then enter the bloodstream of the Dog and lead to an intense disease state that is commonly known as Salmon poisoning. The poor Dog will begin to have uncontrollable diarrhea and vomiting, often accompanied by swollen lymph nodes and neurological symptoms which can include seizures. Left untreated this condition can and often does kill. If the Dog is taken to the vet and given IV fluids and antibiotics they usually make it through just fine, dehydration being one of the main ways that the condition kills them. This specific situation for me is an interesting parallel to the process that is occurring around Samhain: so much life is wrapped in death, abundance and decay at the same time. The Salmon make their epic quests home from the great Ocean to their home Rivers, begin to rot away while they struggle with all their strength to make it back to the spot where they were born, where they put the last of themselves into producing the next generation before they die. Their dead bodies go on to feed so many animals (including humans who catch them at the mouths of the rivers before they have started to rot) and to feed the forests and plants also. The dead Salmon are a crucial aspect in the fecundity and abundance of the Rainforests, yet they also carry this tiny germ that can cause an agonizing death for some specific animals.

SAMHAIN TRADITIONS

All throughout the Northern hemisphere, this transition from Fall to Winter is known and honored as a time in which the veil between the worlds is thin and the dead can walk the earth and make their presence felt to those of us who are still alive. In my own early life this was marked by the holiday called Halloween, which like so many "American" holidays has been largely stripped of its sacred meaning and its connection to the land and the spirit world. In my own suburban childhood, which I cherish by the way, Halloween was a time in which people decorated their houses in spooky things made out of plastic, often with various motors and lights to make them move, startle, and amaze children. The other main part of Halloween was and is, of course, candy. The tradition of "trick or treat"ing involves the children getting dressed up as various spooky or fantastical creatures and roaming the neighborhoods, stopping at each door that has a light on to demand of the inhabitants: "Trick or treat!" It is implied that if you do not give the kids candy then they will play some kind of a prank on you, and sometimes this does happen in the form of covering someone's house in toilet paper or throwing raw eggs at them. The kids (especially the older ones) often just do the tricking part on one another, and part of the spooky nature of this holiday for youngish children who no longer go out with their parents is that the big kids might get them in some way or another. I have noticed that just within my own lifetime trick-or-treating seems to have become less common or widespread due to fears that people will give out tainted candy, or other concerns about how the neighborhoods "are not safe anymore," with the result that it is often only the wealthier neighborhoods that have thriving trick-or-treating, while many kids go to malls, downtown businesses, or to the parking lots of churches or hospitals where they can go "trunk-or-treating" which involves walking from parked car to parked car. This year, the Plague Year, trick-or-treating basically did not happen at all to prevent the spread of COVID, although many of us made it work for the kids in any way that we could. Games associated with Halloween that are still pretty common include bobbing for apples, carving pumpkins into Jack O'Lanterns (these were originally turnips in Ireland), and watching horror films.

Halloween is derived from several traditions, most immediately from the Christian tradition of Allhallowtide, which is a triduum composed of three days being All Saint's Eve (Halloween, October 31st), All Saint's Day (November 1st), and All Soul's Day (November 2nd). In the Western Christian tradition this is a time of year to remember the dead, especially the saints, the martyrs, and all the dead faithful Christians. In Mexico there is the related tradition of *El Dìa de Muertos*, i.e., the Day of the Dead. This Catholic tradition may be a syncretic one, influenced by indigenous Aztec traditions as well as the Catholic traditions that were brought over during the European invasion of that place, although there is some debate in current Mexican academia as to how much of these traditions actually have an indigenous source. During this time, which is a time of celebration, people honor their ancestors and their beloved dead through the creation of altars, both at home and often in cemeteries, upon which they will place marigolds and other beautiful flowers, good food and drink including alcoholic drinks, and other treats that their dead loved when they were alive, such as cigarettes and candies. People will then feast and drink, often all night, while inviting the dead to come and join them, telling stories and singing songs.

The tradition of Samhain itself is of Celtic pagan origins, and is clearly an ancient festival, with some of the earliest surviving Irish literature dating back to the ninth century referring to these festivities. Samhain is the cross quarter between the Autumnal Equinox and the Winter Solstice, and is the beginning of the dark times of the year. Samhain lies at the opposite side of the yearly circle as Beltane, and like that time of year Samhain is a time during which it is said that the veils are thin, the doorways to the Otherworld are open, and people can travel back and forth between the worlds. This is also a time when the beloved dead are close and can be communicated with. This festival is celebrated with bonfires, divination, and feasting. Traditions that continue today in modern Halloween celebrations have their origins in Celtic customs such as bobbing for apples, as apples are believed to have a close relationship to the Otherworld, the Jack O'Lantern which was originally a carved turnip, and even trick or treating. Traditionally people would be wary and careful when they would travel around the time of Samhain because the people of the Otherworld, called the *Aos sì*, were out and about and could cause trouble for the living. People would dress up to either imitate the Aos sì or to scare them, either way, to ward off trouble. People would travel from door to door gathering supplies for the ritual bonfires and foods for offerings, and it was a quick step from this custom to going about dressed as ghosts causing mischief of their own.

Working with these various traditions can be helpful for those of us who are practicing animists living in this strange world which is late stage capitalism in "America." The dead and the denizens of the Otherworld are still here of course, and the more that we can honor and feed them, the more that they will honor and feed us. For many people this time of year can be a hard and sad one, many grieve the end of Summer, but getting the ancestors on your side is a deep well of strength and inspiration from which we can draw as we continue to do our work, especially with the plants and as healers.

END OF HARVEST TIME

HAWTHORNE

Samhain basically marks the end of the wildcrafting season, and is right around the time of the final medicine harvest from the garden. You can theoretically keep picking roots all Winter, but I think that they are so deep in their slumber once we get very much past Samhain that it is best to just wait for early Spring when they start to wake up and get plump again. Often the final wild harvest that I do at this time of year is to go out and gather the berries of the Hawthornes

(*Crataegus monogyna*). This is an especially potent time to do this harvest since I gather the leaves and flowers of this plant around the time of Beltane in the Spring. One of my teachers likes to remind me that when the Hawthornes are rich in fruit and dropping their leaves to slumber in this world, they are just opening their flowers and unfurling their leaves in the Otherworld, which is an inverted mirror of this one. The two holidays of Beltane and Samhain are in many ways polar opposites of one another, which of course they literally are in terms of the wheel of the year. They also have a lot in common with one another and in many ways they can bleed into one another and they both are portals to the Otherworld and to the infinite space beyond that in which the polarities become one.

Working with Hawthorne at both of these times of year is a grounding and a celebration that leads to a beautiful and useful medicine. I like to pick the berries as close to Samhain itself as I can get, and I try to leave offerings such as honey and whiskey for the people of the Otherworld at this time (and also at Beltane). If it looks like the frosts are going to come early, however, then I will pick the berries ear-

lier in the season because I think that the **Hawthorne berries** lose something after they go through a frost, they become softer and fall apart more easily, and the medicines I make from them do not taste as good to me. The Hawthornes produce berries in great abundance, and berry harvest is a good time to double check that you are indeed picking the European Hawthorne if that is your goal, as that specie is identifiable by the presence of only a single seed within the fruit, hence the Latin name of *monogyna* meaning "one seed." The berries, which are also known as *haws*, are bright red and often grow in thick clusters.

It is tempting to harvest them by sliding your hand down the branches of the trees so that they all fall off quickly and easily, and this technique is an easy way to harvest many pounds of the haws in a short period of time, however this method of harvest will often strip the small twigs at the ends of the branches of the trees which are loaded with the buds that will be next year's new growth. It is a better practice to carefully pick each cluster of haws individually, although this is certainly slower and more tedious. This careful process will also help you to avoid getting too torn up by the thorns on the branches. While picking haws it is a nice practice to also look around the Hawthorne patch to see if the trees have produced very many seedlings, which they will often have done in great abundance. So far, I have had very little luck propagating Hawthorne by either seeds or cuttings, however they do a very good job of propagating themselves via seed, I assume with the help of the gastrointestinal tracts of the birds who live upon them and feast on the haws all Winter. You can often find dozens of seedlings from very tiny to several feet tall all around older Hawthorne trees. Samhain time is a great time to dig these little trees up and transplant them to new places, such as your garden or some other public place where you think they would do well, since the rains have begun and the little trees are starting to go dormant so they will not get too shocky from transplant and will be more than adequately watered in throughout the long and wet winter so that they will most likely be well established by the next warm season and will need little to no care from you.

It is good to remember that in many places in "America" this specific species of Hawthorne (*Crataegus monogyna*) is on the Noxious Weeds list and you may get into trouble with the state or with nosy and/or anti-"invasive species" conservationist types, so look out for that. I have a long and strong critique of the whole "invasive species" narrative and its colonialist/eugenicist/racist roots, but I will not get into that now. Suffice it to say that I would encourage anyone to plant the Hawthornes, especially in places that are already disturbed by human activity, as they thrive in these places and will provide ample shelter for animals and birds (and the denizens of the Otherworld), food for the birds, and medicine for the humans. Even small seedlings often have a very deep taproot and it is important to damage this root as little as possible in the digging and transplanting of the baby trees, but even if you do they are often very tough and tenacious.

The haws can be worked with either fresh or dried. My favorite thing to do with them is to tincture them fresh immediately after harvesting and removing any leaves and twigs that are clinging to them. I tincture them at a 1:2 weight:volume ratio in a 65% ethanol solution without grinding or crushing them at all, just drop them into the jar and pour in your menstruum. Over time the red of the haws leaches out into the menstruum which takes on a deep, blood red color while the haws bleach out and begin to look like little skulls, which is a very Samhain or even Scorpio-type process.

One thing to look out for with a tincture like this is that sometimes the tannins in the berries will precipitate out over time. This can happen with the leaf and flower tincture also or the final blend of the two. It will look like a sludgy layer settled at the bottom of the extract. Many people add 10% glycerin to the menstruum to avoid this, which works. I prefer to not work with glycerin myself for reasons that are hard to explain, so if the precipitate occurs I just filter it out of the tincture. It does not seem to me that a tincture that have precipitated and then been filtered loses any of the medicinal qualities and might even taste better. I have not had the precipitation re-occur after an initial filtering, and I go through Hawthorn tincture so fast that I usually get it all out to other people and drink it myself before the precipitation has time to happen. Once the haw tincture is all done and pressed out I like to mix it 50/50 with the leaf and flower tincture that I make at Beltane. This is a very well balanced medicine that is great for cardiovascular health, as a calming nervine and trauma reliever, to strengthen the spiritual heart and help with heartbreak, and to touch upon the Otherworld as needed. Hawthorn once revealed themselves to me as a maybe German old man living in a very cozy cabin. They had a wood stove that was perfectly banked, not running too hot or too clod, so that it produced a nice even heat that was comfortable but not overwhelming while also not consuming the fuel too quickly. He explained to me that this is how the plant works with the heart and the heart's fire, and also that I could come back to this place anytime I wanted, which I have taken him up on a few times.

WRAPPING UP THE MEDICINES

The end of the harvest season is also the time to finish up all of the medicines that we have been creating and accumulating over the course of the warm times. Ideally I would love to have my tinctures macerate for only one moon cycle and press them out 28 days after putting them into the menstruum, but in practice I make tinctures all harvest season long, and the jars just accumulate on my shelf until around Samhain, at which time I start to have the time and space to get them pressed and bottled. These days I have a hydraulic tincture press that I love very much which does an amazing job of squeezing every last drop of tincture out of the marc, leaving it a dry flat cake. I would recommend getting some kind of a mechanical press if you are going to be making tinctures in any quantity since it improves your yield and the mechanical squeeze pushes out this deep layer of the medicine that is hard to get at with just your hands and a cheesecloth, although squeezing them out in this manner does work just fine.

After pressing out the tinctures I allow them to sit overnight or longer which causes any fine particulates in the tincture to settle out to the bottom of the jar. You can then decant off the majority of this clarified tincture, until the sludge on the bottoms starts to get stirred up from the pouring action at which time I like to pour that part of the tincture through a paper coffee filter in a funnel to filter out any of the sludge while also getting all of the clarified tincture. I will often actually just filter the whole thing, even the clear tincture at the top, since this part of it filters very quickly and it feels thorough and good to me. Once you get to the sludgy part at the bottom it can sometimes take a long time to gravity filter, and it can be helpful to change out the filter a couple of times as they get clogged up to speed up the process. Theoretically clarifying the tincture will give it a longer shelf life, but I mostly just do this as a final act of devotion and because I think it improves the taste a little bit. Once the tinctures are clarified they are ready to be stored in amber glass bottles, ideally in a cool, dry, and dark place. In these conditions most tinctures will stay good for at least a decade, although some of them will go off in only a couple of years, and some seem to stay good indefinitely.

This is also a good time to garble and store any dried herbs that you hung up over the course of the warm season. Some dried herbs such as sliced roots need very little processing after they dry and can just be put in a glass jar or plastic bag and stored away from moisture, heat, and sunlight, while some herbs such as the aerial parts of herbaceous plants are nice to garble, which means to separate the desired plant parts such as the leaves and flowers from the less desired plant parts such as the stems. It can be nice to shred these at this time also so that they take up less space in storage and so that you can just scoop them out and use them directly for tea later one with out needing to crumble them up. Infused oils can also be pressed out, and it is good to either store them cold like in the refrigerator or if you are intending to make them into a salve to do that quickly since the bee's wax will help to preserve the oil and keep it from going rancid.

There is a deep satisfaction and a feeling of preparedness for the upcoming cold months that goes along with finishing up all the medicines and getting them stored away. This is a good ritual activity and adds to the sense of abundance that goes along with the deaths and endings of Samhain, especially since in many cases the plants had to die or at least lose a part of themselves in order to provide you with all of this medicine, it is a great sacrifice on their part. I would recommend that you not forget that the plants are also your ancestors when you are honoring your beloved dead.

PRACTICING AND DREAMING

Once all of the medicines are finished and put away it is time to get them moving around. I have found that it can be really easy, and really problematic, to get obsessed with making medicines from all of the plants that are easily accessible to a person and just end up with a shelf full of tinctures that then gather dust until they are discarded years later. This is an insult to the plants and is a reflection of the hoarding/ compulsive acquisition that so many of us have been indoctrinated into via the dominant culture. I strongly suggest *not* harvesting plants, especially plants from the wilds, that you do not have a plan for working with as medicines either in your own body or in the community around you. While I realize that harvesting and making medicine can be done with great honor and respect, and is a process that feels good to the human who is doing it, it is disrespectful to the plants to just claim them and hoard them. If you want to meet and interact with all the plants that I have mentioned in this book, for instance, I would suggest first of all simply finding them and sitting with them, talk to them, leave them offerings. Ask them if they want to work with you and how they want to work with you. Learn how to propagate them and do that work for a couple of years, ideally you would make your "own" baby plants or clones from the plants that you initially meet, and then harvest *those* plants to make your medicine, that would be beautiful, and you would be sure to have a good and strong relationship with the plant at that point. If you want to make social media posts about how you are learning about herbalism, take pictures of the *Salix* cuttings that you have planted along a river, or of the *Dicentra* plants that you dug up from an area that had been clear cut and moved to your garden, rather than just taking pictures of the macerating tinctures. I am really concerned about humans getting in to making plant medicines because it is cool or will up their social capital as I think that this mindset can easily lead to pushy and exploitative relationships. Also, it is easy to think about all the *money* you could make by picking these plants, making medicines, and selling them. I acknowledge that I pick plants and sell medicines for a living, and that I have had to slow myself down and check myself after doing some harvests that I later realized were not sustainable or respectful. The relationships to the plants is *muy delicado* as they say down South, and we should always be checking in with ourselves and with elders in the community about how we are doing this work.

Learning to practice herbalism, as in learning how to work with the herbs with people to help those people with their health, is a whole other world that is beyond learning about the plants, although the more you know the plants the better practitioner you will be. Don't forget about the Dunning-Kruger curve, which shows that people who are just starting to learn about something often overemphasize how much they know about a subject, and also try not to just start giving herbal advice to everyone that you know without them asking for it, it is important to get consent before giving out health advice. On the other hand, so many people never make the move into practicing because they never feel that they have learned enough to be a good and safe practitioner. In some ways it is good to be cautious like this, but it is also important to move forward with helping people even if you are just starting to learn how to do so. It is good to start off treating yourself, then your friends and family. It is very simple to just tell people that you are still learning about this, and if you don't know how to help someone *tell them that*, and seek guidance from an elder. You can, however, help people quite a bit with simple and safe tonic herbs or by focusing on simple goals such as increasing a person's digestion, helping them to get enough sleep, lowering their inflammation and pain levels, and helping them to calm down and reduce stress. These simple things can have a profound impact on even acute and complicated health problems.

The beginning of Winter is when I personally begin to reach out to my community and offer herbs and consultations to people. This is a time of year when a lot of people start to get sick, especially with respiratory conditions here in the Rainforest. People also often have some mental health stuff come up around this time, as many people have some iteration of Seasonal Affective Disorder. When I used to practice in the Olympia Free Herbal Clinic we would be super busy and overwhelmed with clients in the Winter while the Summer would often be slow since people are feeling good at that time of year and are focused on other things, so these days I do most of my practicing in the Winter months when I have the time and when people most need it. It is important to reach out to communities of humans who are disadvantaged in any number of ways, and try to be of service to those people. I would strongly suggest working for free or at least having a sliding scale that goes down pretty low, if you can manage to do that and if you have some financial or other forms of privilege yourself. People that live outside especially are having a hard time in the cold Winter months, and often do not have the best access to health care, so reaching out to these communities and trying to help people out is important and helpful. So many people have not been served well by the current dominant model of health care in this time and place, often feeling that their doctors do not listen to them or respect them, and it is a great service to perform to just sit with someone and listen with great care to what is going on with their health, and then give them some advice and some empowerment. Tapping into various mutual aid networks that already exist and offering your abilities as an herbalist, or even just offering herbs can be helpful. I have started to make formulas that are very non-toxic and that are energetically pretty neutral so that I can just get them to various people and groups where they can be dispensed by people other than me and still be helpful and safe.

This year (2020), my main focus has been on working with people around the COVID-19 pandemic while also providing support to various groups that are working to resist the oppressive forces of society such as BLM protesters and tribal members who are resisting the construction of the border wall down in "California." In most of these situations it has been much easier to make simple, safe, and effective formulas that I just get out to people while trusting them to work with them in a good and safe way. At the time of this writing, November 20th 2020, we have gotten past the election which is a relief, but the "third wave" which is actually the third crest of a single wave of infections across the "United States" is starting to ramp up in a big way, and I am preparing to get a lot of herbs out to people both to strengthen people so that they do not get the virus and to help people get through the virus safely if they do catch it. I am also thinking a lot about mental health, as we are all exhausted be being in quarantine, all the deaths, the economic repercussions, and etc., so I made a lot of tinctures that are helpful for anxiety, depression, and exhaustion. I am just starting to reach out to the wider community and start shipping out medicines.

The Winter is also a time for dreaming. It is a time of rest when the nights are long, and it is often harder to spend time outside. I like to focus on listening to my dreams at this time of year by keeping a dream journal, and in general to focus on that inward life that can be neglected during the busy and hot times of year. This is also a great time of year to go deep with the plants in a more spiritual kind of way. Pick a plant that you want to work with and take a bit of their medicine every day for a moon cycle, go and sit with them in the woods often, place a sprig of the herb under your pillow and invite them into your dreams. Record any results or lack thereof in a dedicated journal. You will be surprised with how much you can learn with these kinds of practices. This is also a time to dream of who we want to be, and what kind of a world we want to live in. How do we make our lives more beautiful and helpful to those around us? How can we work to transform the culture in which we are enmeshed to make it more healthy and beneficial to all beings? The Winter, and the falling waters, helps to provide some clarity and stillness to explore these deeper questions without so many distractions. Another world is always possible, and in many ways it already exists, if we can just find our way into it.

As the Winter deepens it is good to continue to get outside into the woods, and just walk around without being focused on working, harvesting, or anything like this. Of course there are plenty of opportunities to do some propagation by, say, gathering the downed Alder (*Alnus rubra*) cones and drying them out at home, at which point you can knock out hundreds of tiny seeds to be planted. This is also a great time to take cuttings of Willow (*Salix spp*) or Cottonwood (*Populus tricho-carpa*) and plant them to bring about future trees, but it is also good to just get out and feel the forest. There is a certain life and abundance even in the darkest and coldest times. Even around Samhain there are already tiny buds on the Cotton-woods that will be swollen with resins in just a few months, and the Alder catkins are visible, yet tiny, and they too will be ready to pick in just a few months. Spring is actually just around the corner, and then it is time to do it all over again.

SELECTED REFERENCES

Avrich, Paul. *The Haymarket Tragedy*. Princeton: Princeton UP, 1984.

Bartlett, Robert Allen. *Real Alchemy*. Ibis, 2009.

Bhrolcháin, Muireann. *An Introduction to Early Irish Literature*. Dublin: Four Courts, 2009.

Boeckner, L. S. *et al*. "Inulin: A Review of Nutritional and Health Implications." *Advances in Food and Nutrition Research* 43 (2001): 1–63. doi:10.1016/s1043-4526(01)43002-6

Bowcutt, Frederica and Hamman, Sarah. *Vascular Plants of the South Sound Prairies*. Olympia, WA: The Evergreen State College Press, 2016.

Buhner, Stephen Harrod. *The Secret Teachings of Plants*. Rochester, VT: Bear and Co., 2004.

Cook, William. *The Physiomedical Dispensatory: A Treatise on Therapeutics, Materia Medica, and Pharmacy, in Accordance of the Principles of Physiological Medication*. Cook, 1869, accessed through medherb.com

Culpeper, Nicholas. *Culpeper's Complete Herbal*. London: W. Foulsham, 1978. Also, Avon: The Bath Press.

The Divine Farmer's Materia Medica: A Translation of the Shen Nong Ben Cao Jing Translation by Yang Shou-zhong. Boulder, CO: Blue Poppy Press, 1998.

Felt, Margaret Elley. *Capitol Forest: The Forest that Came Back*. Olympia, WA: The Washington State Department of Natural Resources, 1975. Accessed as a PDF at: http://www.capitolforest.com/files/capitol_forest.pdf

Francolini I, Norris P, Piozzi A, *et al*. "Usnic acid, a natural antimicrobial agent able to inhibit bacterial biofilm formation on polymer surfaces." *Antimicrob Agents Chemother* 48.11 (2004): 4360–65.

Ganora, Lisa. *Herbal Constituents: Foundations of Phytochemistry*. Herbalchem Press, 2009.

Geniusz, Mary Siisip. *Plants Have So Much to Give Us, All We Have to Do is Ask: Anishinaabe Botanical Teachings*. Minneapolis: University of Minnesota Press, 2015.

Holmes, Peter. *The Energetics of Western Herbs*. Contati, CA: Snow Lotus Press, 2007.

Ingólfsdóttir, K. "Usnic acid." *Phytochemistry* 61.7 (2002): 729–36. doi:10.1016/s0031-9422(02)00383-7

Junius, Manfred M. *The Practical Handbook of Plant Alchemy.* Rochester, VT: Healing Arts Press, 1990.

Kloos, Scott. *Pacific Northwest Medicinal Plants.* Portland, OR: Timber Press, 2017.

Kluger, Richard. *The Bitter Waters of Medicine Creek: A Tragic Clash Between White and Native America.* New York: Vintage Books, 2012.

Ma, Bing-Ji, *et al.* "Hericenones and erinacines: stimulators of nerve growth factor (NGF) biosynthesis in *Hericium erinaceus.*" *Mycology* 1.2 (2010): 92–98, DOI: 10.1080/21501201003735556

Maciocia, Giovanni. *The Foundations of Chinese Medicine.* Elsevier, 2015.

Manske, Richard H. F. "The Alkaloids of Fumariaceous Plants: IX. Dicentra Formosa, Walp." *Canadian Journal of Research* 10.5 (1934): 521–26. https://doi.org/10.1139/cjr34-047

Markowitz, John S et al. "Effect of St John's wort on drug metabolism by induction of cytochrome P450 3A4 enzyme." *JAMA* 290.11 (2003): 1500–4. doi:10.1001/jama.290.11.1500

Mazmanian, Sarkis K, and Dennis L Kasper. "The love-hate relationship between bacterial polysaccharides and the host immune system." *Nature reviews. Immunology* 6.11 (2006): 849–58. doi:10.1038/nri1956

McCoy, Peter. *Radical Mycology: A Treatise on Seeing and Working with Fungi.* Portland, OR: Chthaeus Press, 2016.

Miettinen, A., *et al.* "The palaeoenvironment of the Antrea Net Find," pp. 71–87. In *Karelian Isthmus.* Finnish Antiquarian Society, 2008.

Mizuno, Takashi. "Bioactive Substances in *Hericium erinaceus* (Bull.: Fr.) Pers. (Yamabushitake), and its Medicinal Utilization." *International Journal of Medicinal Mushrooms* 1.2 (1999): 105–19. DOI: 10.1615/IntJMedMushrooms.v1.i2.10

Moore, Michael. *Medicinal Plants of the Pacific West.* Santa Fe, NM: Red Crane Books, 1993.

———. *Medicinal Plants of the Pacific West.* Santa Fe, NM: Red Crane Books, 2001.

———. *Medicinal Plants of the Mountain West.* Santa Fe, MN: Museum of New Mexico Press, 2003.

Mori, Koichiro, *et al.* "Improving effects of the mushroom Yamabushitake

(Hericium erinaceus) on mild cognitive impairment: a double-blind placebo-controlled clinical trial." *Phytotherapy research: PTR* 23.3 (2009): 367–72. doi:10.1002/ptr.2634

"*Oregon Lung Lichen—Lobaria Oregana.*" *Encyclopedia of Life*: eol.org/pages/2860165/

Pendell, Dale. *Pharmakognosis.* San Francisco: Mercury House, 2005.

Rogers, Robert. *The Fungal Pharmacy: The Complete Guide to Medicinal Mushrooms and Lichens of North America. Berkeley, CA: North Atlantic, 2011.*

Shulgin, Alexander T. *The Simple Plant Isoquinolines.* Berkeley, CA: Transform Press, 2002.

Stavish, Mark. *The Path of Alchemy.* Woodbury: Llewellyn, 2006.

Storl, Wolf D. *Culture and Horticulture: A Philosophy of Gardening.* San Francisco: Bio-Dynamic Farming & Gardening, 1979.

Tizon, Alex (February 7, 1999). "The Boldt Decision/25 Years — The Fish Tale That Changed History". *The Seattle Times.* https://archive.seattletimes.com/archive/?date=19990207&slug=2943039

Trout, K. Hericium coralloides (https://troutsnotes.com/hericium-coralloides/) Published 2015

Turner, Nancy & Deur, Douglas. *Keeping It Living: Traditions of Plant Use and Cultivation on the Northwest Coast of North America.* University of Wasington Press, 2005. Seattle.

Turner, Nancy J. & Deur, Doug. *Keeping it Living: Traditions of Plant Use and Cultivation on the Northwest Coast of North America,* University of Washington Press, Seattle, WA. 2005.

Wasson, R. G. "Seeking the Magic Mushroom." *LIFE* 49.19 (1957): 100–2, 109–20.

Wood, Matthew. *The Book of Herbal Wisdom: Using Plants as Medicines.* Berkeley, CA: North Atlantic, 1997.

Wong K.H., et al. "Functional recovery enhancement following injury to rodent peroneal nerve by Lion's Mane mushroom, *Hericium erinaceus* (Bull.: Fr.) Pers. (Aphyllophoromycetideae)." International Journal of Medicinal Mushrooms 11.3 (2009): 225–36. doi: 10.1615/IntJMedMushr.v11.i3.20.

Wray, Jacilee, ed. *Native Peoples of the Olympic Peninsula: Who We Are.* Norma, OK: University of Oklahoma Press, 2002.

PERSONAL NOTES AND REFLECTIONS

ACKNOWLEDGMENTS

I have had so much support from so many people who have supported me over the course of writing this book and learning the plants, it would be impossible to thank everybody, so here is an abbreviated list: ¶ Thanks to my immediate family, Thea, Juniper, and Willow. To my parents, Joyce and Larry. To my extended blood relatives who are many. An especial thanks to my grandmother Ruth for being my first garden inspiration. ¶ Thanks to the community of people that I live with at Ursa Major, especially Joanna who is part of my family as well, and her parents Lydia and Joe. Also to Murphy, Jo, and Acacia. ¶ Thanks to Jenn at Revelore for helping this book be born. ¶ Thanks to my teachers and comrades in working with plants, including Taryn, Rylee, Joyce, Marcus, Scott, Sean, GaChing, Thea, Jean, Lauren, Katie/James, Renee, Peter, Erin, Megan, Willow, Whitney, Sarah, and River. ¶ Thanks to my teachers who are also plants, including Oplopanax, Ganoderma, Trichocereus, Urtica, Mimosa, Paeonia, Alnus, Banisteriopsis, Leonorus, Tabernanthe, Dicentra, Cornus, Psilocybe, and Anadenanthera. ¶ Thanks to Rick at the Bog and Jeanne and Eric at the 2323 house for providing safe spaces for me to live, study, and work. ¶ Thanks to everyone who has ever studied with me via the Hawthorn School. ¶ Thanks to my many familiars including Emily, Curtis, Cloud, Rue, Georgia, Buddy, Angel, Ruby, Noodles, Buttercup, and Daffodil. ¶ And finally, thanks to the various bioregions and landscapes that I have lived within and upon, who have taught and guided me so much, especially the Black River/Black Hills and the greater Cascadian bioregion as a whole.

ABOUT THE AUTHOR

SEAN CROKE is a wildcrafter, medicine maker, clinician, and gardener who has been working with the plants of the Pacific Northwest for more than a decade. He is the founder of the Hawthorn School, and the primary teacher for most classes. He is a co-founder of Understory Apothecary which produces small batch tinctures of local herbs, is the founder of the Hawthorn School of Plant Medicine, and is also involved in Cascadia Terroir, which produces small batches of essential oils from garden grown and sustainably harvestable native plants. Sean is a graduate of The Evergreen State College with a BA/BS where he focused on Ethnobotany and Organic Chemistry.

Sean has studied wildcrafting and plant spirit medicine primarily with the plants as his teachers, and has also studied with GaChing Kong and Scott Kloos. Through his botanical medicine business Understory Apothecary, he makes ethically harvested herbal products for the community. Sean was the main medicine maker as well as a clinician for the Olympia Free Herbal Clinic, and has been teaching about Pacific Northwest healing plants since 2012. He still sees clients on a sliding scale down to free in the continued spirit of the free clinic. Sean lives on Chehalis land in the prairies along the Black River just outside of Olympia with his partner, their kids, several dear friends, a sweet goofy dog, and too many houseplants.

ABOUT THE HAWTHORN SCHOOL OF HERBAL MEDICINE

THE HAWTHORN SCHOOL OF PLANT MEDICINE offers classes aimed at cultivating healing relationships between people and plants. Through experiential education drawing from a wide array of perspectives, we strive to connect people with the wisdom and generosity of the plants.

Our work is grounded in love for the plants and an ethic of mutuality—in learning how plants can heal and care for human people, we believe that we must also learn how to care for the plant people and their home ecosystems. Our intention is to foster relationships that help plants to flourish and thrive—in our gardens as well as within wild spaces.

Our programs take place in and around Olympia, WA, with field trips throughout the greater bioregion.

Learn more at:
https://blackriverbotanicals.com/hawthorn-school